W9-AAP-778

SMILE AT STRANGERS

SMILE AT STRANGERS

And Other Lessons in the Art of Living Fearlessly

SUSAN SCHORN

HOUGHTON MIFFLIN HARCOURT
BOSTON • NEW YORK
2013

www.hmhbooks.com

Library of Congress Cataloging-in-Publication Data
Schorn, Susan.
Smile at strangers : and other lessons in the art of living fearlessly / Susan Schorn.
pages cm
ISBN 978-0-547-77433-6
1. Self-esteem. 2. Self-defense. I. Title.
BF697.5.S46S36 2013 158—dc23 2013000390

Book design by Brian Moore
Illustration by Patrick Barry

Printed in the United States of America
DOC 10 9 8 7 6 5 4 3 2 1

The events described in this book have all actually happened in my life, in approximately the order presented here, to the best of my recollection. Readers should bear in mind that I have been hit in the head quite a bit more than the average memoirist. To preserve privacy and confidentiality, I have used composite figures to represent participants in self-defense workshops, students junior to me in rank, and a few innocent bystanders—most notably Anna, Raven, Celia, and Patty—and in a few places I have used pseudonyms ("Stan" is not Crazy Stan's real name). Otherwise, all the characters in this story are quite real, and know where I live.

Readers are also advised that this book contains my personal and somewhat quixotic opinions on self-defense, and that no self-defense system or book will make them invulnerable (especially this one). Do not use this book as a flotation device; close cover before striking. MY PUBLISHER AND I DISCLAIM LIABILITY FOR ANY ADVERSE EFFECTS RESULTING DIRECTLY OR INDIRECTLY FROM INFORMATION CONTAINED HEREIN.

The quotations from Daidoji Yuzan's *Code of the Samurai* contained herein are the author's own translation from the original Japanese, produced by reviewing the Japanese characters in consultation with a native speaker and referring to several contemporary English translations (including those by Thomas Cleary, A. L. Sadler, D. L. Tarver, and William Scott Wilson).

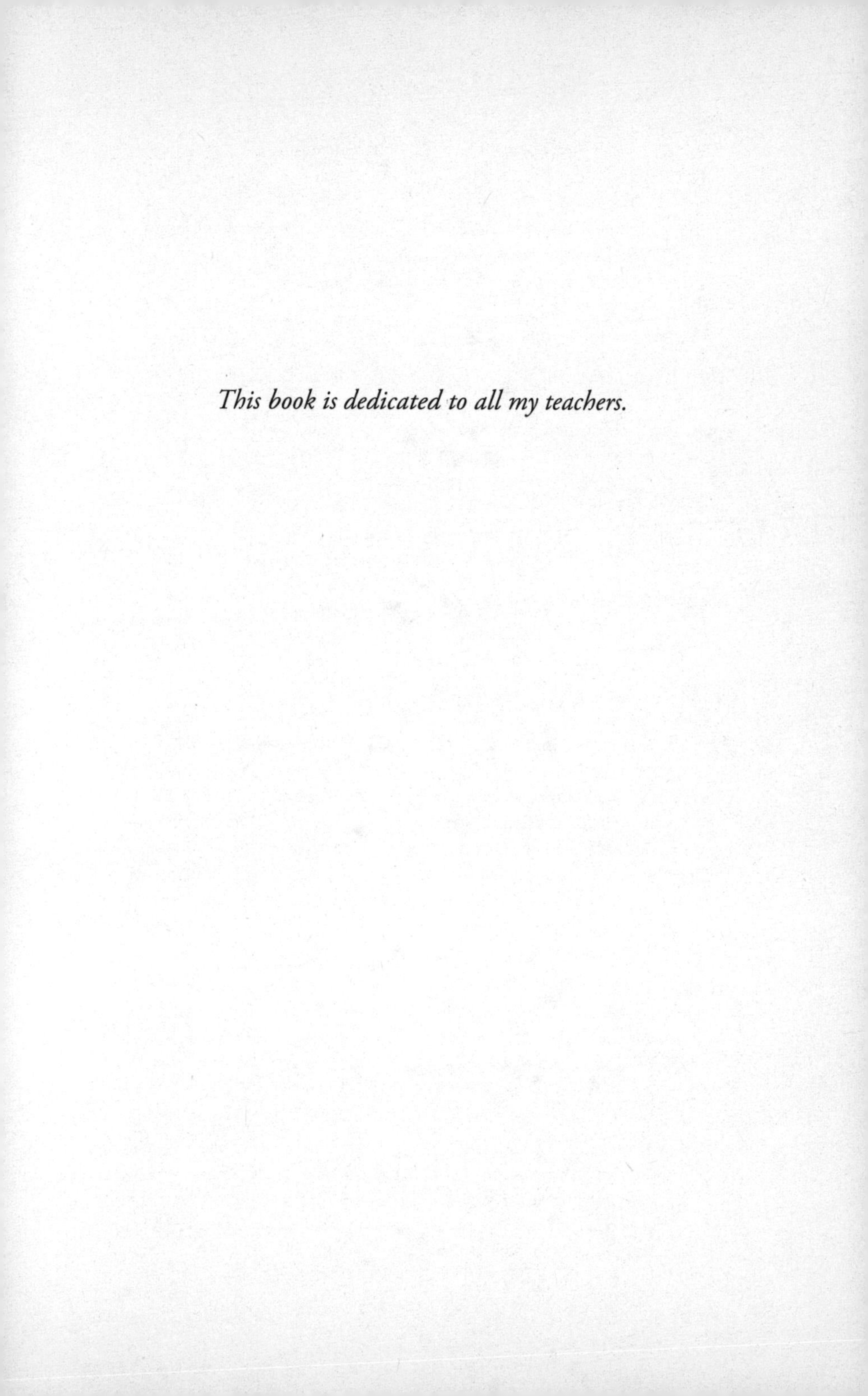

This book is dedicated to all my teachers.

Contents

SMILE AT STRANGERS

Fall down seven times, get up eight.

七転び八起き。

I'M PONDERING THIS phrase, a traditional Japanese proverb—*Fall down seven times, get up eight*—as I kneel, my feet tucked beneath me, on the hard wooden floor of my karate school. I am attempting to meditate.

Meditation class at my dojo revolves around proverbs like this one (we call them *kowa*). They're part of the Zen tradition that infuses our karate practice, and they all impart some wisdom, advice, or warning: *After the rain, the earth hardens,* or *A wise man hears one and understands ten.* They give you something to think about as your legs go numb and the muscles between your shoulder blades curl themselves into intricate knots.

In Japanese, *kowa* can mean either "voice" or "tone." I like the idea of tone, of the *kowa* as a keynote, meant to reverberate in your mind like the bell the instructor rings at the beginning and end of each meditation session. Ideally, you allow a *kowa* to rest lightly on your consciousness as you meditate. You don't interrogate it or try to solve it. You just let it register at whatever level of awareness you've achieved.

I'm sitting in a row with all the other students, in the position we call *seiza.* All around me I can sense stilled bodies; I can hear quiet breathing and the faint tick of the clock. My hands, clenched into fists, are propped on my hips. My back is straight, my eyes are closed, and my mind is supposed to be calm. Instead, tonight's *kowa* ricochets from one corner of my consciousness to another, making the inside of my head buzz and rattle like a racquetball court: *Fall down seven times, get up eight.*

I'm having trouble with the math.

I know, from long hours spent in this kind of contemplation, that it doesn't pay to overthink anything related to Zen, yet my mind insists on pointing out the obvious discrepancy: if I fall down once, and I stand back up, I've gotten up once. If I fall down again, and get up again, the count is still even: down two times, up two times. Extrapolating on through three, four, five falls, the logic holds. As long as I get up the same number of times I fall, I should end up on my feet. So isn't the eighth time superfluous?

For some reason, I cannot move past this.

Crap. Meditation class must be halfway over and not only have I not calmed my mind, I'm still bogged down in basic arithmetic. I feel a distinct sense of envy toward my fellow students, whose calm immobility surrounds me. Our instructor, Sensei Joy, is to my left, and has not stirred since we closed our eyes. On my right, my friend Doris Ann exudes an almost palpable air of serenity. She is, like me, the mother of two children, and I feel her tranquility as a silent rebuke to the spasmodic workings of my own mind. I dig my fists into my thighs and take a deep breath.

Calm down, I tell myself. Start over. This proverb is hundreds of years old. You need to *listen* to it, not proofread it.

Fall down seven times, get up eight. If I can forget about the numbers, it's not that complicated; the *kowa* merely stresses the value of perseverance. The importance of getting back up. Once, twice, eight times, or eight hundred—it doesn't matter. The lesson is, Always get back up. Simple enough.

It's a nice, tidy slogan, like "Never say die" or "Keep on truckin'!" It would fit inside a fortune cookie or look good on a bumper sticker. But the reason I'm sitting here in a sweat-soaked, malodorous white uniform, torturing myself with Japanese syntax, is not that I need slogans or reminders. I don't need someone to *tell me* to get back up every time I fall down. I'm here because I want to *be* the kind of person who always gets back up, whether anyone tells me to or not.

I don't take naturally to meditation, or reflection, or sitting still. Being quiet is foreign to my nature and causes me actual physical discomfort. But here I am anyway, banging my consciousness against the brick wall of Zen meditation, because I want to make the idea expressed by this *kowa* an integral part of me, my instincts, my approach to life. This desire is the primary motivation for my karate training, which I've been pursuing now for a decade and a half. Over the years I've sweated and yelled, meditated and broken boards and held ice packs to my face, all to convince myself that no matter what happens in my life, no matter what I'm hit with, I will *always* get back up, however many times it takes; even after I've lost count of all the times I've been down; even when—and here I have a sudden burst of insight—even when it's mathematically impossible for me to get up again. I want to be a woman who gets back up, whether she falls, or trips, or is shoved, or knocked down and stepped on, every time she has to—plus once more after that.

The *kowa* says to me, *Fall down seven times, get up eight.* I listen to it, and sit with it, and make it mine. And then, when *I* say the *kowa,* it comes out as this: "Knock me down seven times, and I won't just get up seven times. I'll get up *eight,* because that's the kind of stubborn bastard I am."

It's not a perfect translation, not really a translation at all; it's what the *kowa* turns into when it becomes part of me. It sums up why I'm here: because there are many dangers in the world, but the scariest one is the possibility that we might not get back up—that we might give in to our fears.

Whereas if I *know* that I will always get back up—because that's just what I do; it's who I am—then the thought of falling no longer has the power to terrify me.

I've always been a fearful person. I think I was born that way. How else to explain my mother's inscription across the back of my baptism-day photograph, *Susan, October 1967—She just wouldn't smile*? Why did my kindergarten teacher describe me with amusement as a child who acted "like a little old lady"? Why was I the only kid who cared that the school bus didn't have seat belts?

Environment may have played a role, too. Being the youngest and smallest of five children in a loud, often chaotic household did little to soothe my fears or reduce my startle reflex. And I did seem to run into more than my share of snakes, even for someone growing up in Texas. Whatever the cause—whether it was genetics, or competition with my siblings, or something that scared my mother before I was born—I grew up in constant terror of thunder, darkness, strangers, wasps . . . you name it, it made me nervous.

My fears were manageable when I was young, because my safety was ultimately my parents' problem. But as I grew older, the circle of danger widened, and the perimeter of my safety became harder and harder to maintain. And then when I was fourteen years old, the mother of a friend of mine was murdered. It was one of those rare events, a completely random crime. The killer was never caught.

Laura's mother's death was the first real experience my friends and I had with mortal fear, our graduation from the minor perils of childhood to the terrible losses of adult life. The memory of it remained potent through the rest of my adolescence, as I got a job, dated, and then moved away for college. Every time I stayed out late, went somewhere new, met a stranger, I thought about that tragedy. This was different from my earliest fears. It wasn't a hypothetical danger, something that *could* happen. It *had* happened; I had seen the impact on my friend and her family. Now I knew what devastation was.

I had always been afraid, but after Laura's mother died, I understood why. The stakes became very clear. And once the enormity of what could be lost sank in, it almost felt like an obligation, that I owed it to myself—and to the memory of Laura's mother—to be afraid.

And that sense of obligation, the feeling that it was in some way my duty to be afraid, made me angry. I was angry at the way fear constrained my life; angry at the world for failing to obviate my fear. I was angry that society seemed to think women should just get used to seeing themselves as victims. I was angry that a lot of women seemed to agree.

Unfortunately, anger, as I have learned, makes you do stupid things. It leads you to jump out of your car at stoplights, pick up smoldering cigarette butts, and hand them back to the startled strangers who just tossed them out the window. It compels you to tell people exactly what you think of them, at precisely the wrong time. Or anger can tie your tongue, leaving you voiceless and impotent in the midst of your outrage.

It can prompt you to make impetuous hand gestures—gestures of the type that have never, in all of recorded history, brought about greater understanding and goodwill among peoples. Anger, in other words, can get you into the very same kind of trouble you feared in the first place.

I was dogged by fear and hamstrung by the anger that accompanied it until I found karate. It took me thirty years to find. I had dabbled in other martial arts, thinking they might make me a better person somehow, but the magic didn't happen until I connected with a school, and a teacher, who understood my fear and anger. Karate's fusion of physical and meditative practice helped me control the effects of those emotions on my body and mind. Karate taught me how to fight, when to fight, and how to keep fighting even when the fight went badly. It taught me how to handle conflict in all kinds of situations, dramatic or mundane. It taught me how to fall down, get back up, and then deal with whatever knocked me down.

My dojo also gave me a framework for assessing risk and understanding violence systematically, and a spiritual foundation to sustain me when analysis failed. My training made me a member of a community where I came to know others in relation to myself. I learned how to acknowledge others' authority, and how to wield my own. I got better at negotiating differences, communicating respect and appreciation, and showing compassion—all things I was dreadful at before I started training. And through karate, I came to realize that the connections we form with one another do just as much to strengthen and protect us as any physical training ever could.

I spent many years as a fearful person. Karate made me less fearful, and more of a person.

It hasn't made me perfect, by any stretch of the imagination. Even after all this time, I still frequently have moments of doubt, frustration, and even blind panic—the feeling that *I'm never going to get this.* I still try my family's patience and irritate my training partners. I still, once in a while, say rude things with my hands. My attempts to live without fear have been characterized by failure, contradiction, and a lot of low comedy. There's been a lot of falling down. But I keep trying; I keep getting back up. I'm pretty sure now that I always will.

The lessons I've absorbed on this journey don't fit neatly on a bumper sticker. Some of them aren't even appropriate for polite company. Yet I think they have a certain resonance. So I have prefaced each of the following chapters about my journey with my own *kowa,* hoping to condense each messy, inexact lesson into a single note; a precise tone. These *kowa,* skewed though they are, reflect the way I've come to think about the world, and the way I prefer to live in it. I offer them here for everyone who has known fear and anger, as proof that you can face an uncertain world, fight your fears, and come out smiling.

If you want to feel safe, be prepared to feel uncomfortable.

安全や安心感を得たいのなら、
気まずい思いをすることも覚悟しよう。

I DIDN'T GO LOOKING for a karate school, let alone one for women only, which was the policy at Sun Dragon when I enrolled. I had tried martial arts briefly during college, training in a Korean system for about a year, until the novelty wore off. Then, in 1998, when I was finishing my PhD in English literature, my classmate Gina invited me to visit her dojo on the south side of Austin. Gina, curly-haired and perpetually cheerful, was studying literature and computer pedagogy—not fields that would seem to require a lot of fighting prowess. But one afternoon during a seminar on Jane Austen, when I expressed a desire to travel back in time to the eighteenth century for the sole purpose of kicking Jean-Jacques Rousseau in the balls, Gina told me, "You should check out my karate school. You'd fit right in."

Me, fit in somewhere? It seemed unlikely. I was by far the most belligerent Victorianist in our graduate program, and couldn't imagine any other community that would countenance my habitual spleen. But I was intrigued. I was still carrying around an extra ten pounds from the birth of my year-old son, and the idea of losing weight while hitting things and yelling was appealing. I decided to see what Gina's dojo was like.

SUN DRAGON MARTIAL ARTS FOR WOMEN AND CHILDREN, read the sign out front, which at the time just struck me as friendly and welcoming—like the YWCA, but for karate. I assumed it would be a lot like the place where I'd trained years before; a Korean school, or *dojang.* Karate is Japanese, and a karate school is called a *dojo. Dojang, dojo,* I mused. *How different can they be?*

As I discovered, the vocabulary and basic technique were indeed pretty similar, but in more important ways, Gina's school was poles apart from my previous experience with the martial arts. And the difference was entirely the work of the person who had painted the words FOR WOMEN on the sign outside her dojo.

She was introduced to me as "Sensei Suzanne"—*sensei* meaning "teacher." Neither short nor tall, she wore glasses, spoke in a low rasp, and though only in her forties had a lion's mane of prematurely silver hair. Officially, she was Sun Dragon's founder and head instructor. More simply, she was the school.

I had spent time around black belts before, and I was familiar with their deliberate movement and unconscious grace. I had noticed the way a black belt's body seemed to take up precisely the amount of space it needed and no more. I knew that a black belt's presence could be imposing. But Sensei Suzanne was something entirely outside my frame of reference. "Purposeful," you might have said about the way she moved, but that wouldn't explain the alacrity with which people got out of her way. "Stern," you could have remarked about the set of her jaw; you might have called her expression "intense," or "formidable." All of which would have been accurate but still didn't communicate the feeling you had when you were around her, that intense and formidable things were about to start happening, right then and there.

And they did happen, every night at Sun Dragon.

My first class was exhilarating. I had forgotten how much I enjoyed punching, and kicking, and yelling. It was nice to be reminded that I had a natural aptitude for those things. My brain had forgotten, but my body remembered, and responded with a rush of adrenaline. I came home glowing, and wondering if, by some stretch of imagination, budgeting, and scheduling, I might be able to study Jane Austen and karate at the same time.

It was not a convenient time to enter a new discipline. I was thirty years old, with a kid and a lot of student loans, and I felt pretty well locked into the professor-and-mom vocational path, despite constant doubts about my fitness for it. (I didn't hear any of my professors talking about kicking dead authors in the groin; not even the Irish studies crowd.) I was pretty much the same person I'd been after high school, older and supposedly wiser but not really feeling that way; still anxious and bad tempered.

But I wanted to try. Gina was already a green belt, about halfway along the path to black belt, and while she didn't have a spouse or kids to worry about, she was facing the same professional challenges I was. A black belt just might be feasible for me, too.

I gingerly broached the topic of Sun Dragon with my husband, who would be left home alone with the baby while I trained.

"Go," Scott said. "Please. Go. Hit things."

"Are you sure?" I asked him. "I'd be gone at least two nights a week, and classes are an hour and a half long, so I wouldn't be home until nine o'clock."

"Absolutely. Stay as long as you like," he assured me. "Two nights a week, three, four—however many you need."

"Well," I said, feeling a little miffed, "if you're sure you won't miss me . . ."

"Dave and I will be fine," he said. "It'll be good for you—I mean, for all three of us."

This wasn't very flattering, but I was grateful for his honesty and his support. I nervously double-checked the balance in our bankbook, bought a uniform, and enrolled at Sun Dragon.

Sensei Suzanne was on a mission to teach karate to women. And she had definite ideas about *how* to teach karate to women. The assumption underlying Sun Dragon's women-only adult classes (boys were allowed in the children's program) was that the mere presence of men can have a detrimental effect on women's training. It's a provocative idea, and I wasn't sure what I thought of it. I had trained with men before, at the *dojang*. Men always seem to be everywhere—especially places where people go to sweat—and I hadn't thought much about how their presence colored or limited my training. But as I came to know the other students at Sun Dragon, I grew to appreciate Sensei Suzanne's point—that for some women, especially women who don't feel physically confident, the absence of men can make training much less stressful, and more productive.

Sensei Suzanne's methods were likewise radical. At my Korean school, I had learned choreographed forms, and sparred, and practiced self-defense drills. We did all of that in my initial weeks at Sun Dragon, too (in karate, forms are called *kata*), but we also did stuff that initially seemed bizarre. A lot of role-playing. Sleazy guy at the bus stop wants to sit too close to you: what do you do? Overly friendly nightclub patron follows you out to the parking lot: how do you react? Your boss calls you "sweetie." What do you say? We practiced making eye contact, speaking assertively, ignoring verbal insults, not smiling or laughing in awkward situations—the most basic of self-defense skills, the ones that are so basic no one ever thinks about practicing them. It seemed silly. I felt as if I were back in grade school, being forced to watch *Free to Be . . . You and Me* all over again. But I quickly realized these exercises were harder than hitting things. Harder, and more gratifying.

If you stuck with Sensei Suzanne's program, what you received in return was a chance to confront danger one glance, one word at a time. Walking through these scenarios was a way of slowing down fear, observing it dispassionately, and finding a good response. It made us look directly at the little everyday assaults that we normally sense with our peripheral vision but tend to ignore in favor of the big, colorful threats that fill our imaginations and TV screens.

We also learned more traditional skills. And while the art of karate was certainly respected at Sun Dragon, there was an immediacy and urgency to the training there that made my previous martial arts practice look like ballroom dance. At Sun Dragon, we didn't just talk about smashing someone's trachea; we worked on it, repeatedly, with an anatomically correct dummy. We didn't just learn the standard hammerfist technique to the groin; we had very specific discussions about tissue damage, pounds of pressure, and long-term physical effects (take *that,* Rousseau). It was a good thing we didn't train with men in those days. They would have been dreadfully uncomfortable much of the time. (This despite Sensei's constant reminders that an attacker could just as easily be female; that women could and did commit violence, despite what we saw on TV.)

One evening, when I'd been coming to class for a few months, Sensei Suzanne had us take turns punching "the cube"—a big block of foam rubber about four feet high—and yelling continuously. We each did this for one minute. I could punch, and I could yell quite loudly (*kiai,* it's called in karate). I'd never done either for a full minute. Punching something five or six times and yelling is easy. Doing it for ten seconds feels pretty definitive; you become aware that you need a lot less time than that to hurt someone. But there is something transformative about continuing to punch and yell, on and on, much longer than you could ever imagine needing to punch something or make noise, until your throat is raw and your arms feel like they belong to someone on the other side of the room.

And the whole time you were punching and yelling, the women at Sun Dragon surrounded you and told you how great you were doing, that you looked fabulous, that they loved you.

I mean, it was really weird.

It wasn't until several months into my training, though, when I attended a self-defense workshop at Sun Dragon, that I received the full impact of Sensei Suzanne's approach.

I remember feeling like a complete idiot.

I was just doing as instructed: looking at the woman across from me—whom I had never met—listening to her ask me questions, and responding to her with "no."

That's all I was saying. I was not allowed to say anything else. I was also not allowed to smile, laugh, look away, or move from where I was standing.

I was doggedly not doing any of those things because Sensei Suzanne had told me I needed to attend a self-defense workshop in order to be promoted to yellow belt. And when Sensei told you that you needed to do something, it was rather like having a doctor tell you that you need to put your affairs in order. You didn't waste time asking questions. So there I was, on a lovely, sunny June day, in a dark, musty warehouse, saying "no" to a complete stranger.

I had been training at Sun Dragon for about half a year at that point, and I'd found that the physical skills came in handy pretty often outside the dojo, whether I was trying to open a stuck fire door (a front thrust kick near the handle) or exit a crowded elevator (a gentle palm-heel block into the small of the back). I was not convinced that I needed an additional five hours of instruction in how to fend off potential rapists or subway gropers. I could beat up all kinds of people, I figured. Why bother specializing?

The rest of the women in attendance were not karate students. They were college girls and housewives and divorcées who wanted basic training in self-defense. Most of them had filed into the dojo nervously, looking around at the targets and mats, wondering how much punching and kicking would be expected of them. I'm sure they were expecting one of those classes where they dress a guy up in enough padding to make him look like the Michelin Man and then let everyone kick him in the groin for a while.

Instead, we spent the opening hour talking about how to stand, walk, and look at people. I was accustomed to doing peculiar things in Sensei Suzanne's karate classes, but I was just as surprised by this as everyone else. I had assumed the workshop would be a slightly less strenuous version of what we did in karate—a little role-playing, some target striking, probably an extra round of groin work. I hadn't anticipated that it would involve such exquisite discomfort on my part. I wouldn't have minded physical pain. In fact, I would have preferred it.

My partner in this particular exercise was obviously as uncomfortable as I was, but she kept gamely asking questions, following one of the scenarios Sensei Suzanne had suggested: "Do you have change for a dollar? Can I have a quarter to make a phone call? For bus fare? Can you give me a ride? Why not? Don't you like me? What's the matter with you?"

"No," I told her. "No. No. No. No. No. No."

This would have been boring if the embarrassment weren't so agonizing. "I *hate* this," I thought; "I hate it so much I can feel it physically." The sensation of saying "no" to another person's face made me writhe internally, and it took all my energy not to squirm. Since I couldn't say anything but "no," I didn't have a lot of decision making to do, so I could at least think about whatever I pleased. What I thought was: Why in God's name am I doing this? I already know about self-defense. I can break boards with my bare hands, and I'm sure I could break bones, too. And I know how to say "no."

Knowing how to do something is different from actually doing it. It occurred to me, somewhere around my twentieth "no," that I had probably said the word more times in the preceding half-minute than I had in the preceding month. I thought back over all the times I could have said "no" and didn't—to the student who made a Friday-afternoon office appointment to come in and complain about the grade

I'd given her on a paper (and then never showed up); to the woman at the post office who asked if she could cut in line in front of me (leaving everyone behind me seething); to the nice young Mormons outside the library who asked if I could spare a few moments of my time to talk about God. I wanted to say "no" to all of them, and I didn't.

I kept looking at my partner, but I thought about those other people, and saying "no" started to feel a little easier.

"No," I told her when she asked if I knew what time it was; "no," when she asked if I had a spare cigarette. It started to feel like the perfect weapon, this single syllable; or perhaps *shield* is a better way to put it. The questions came at me from all angles, but the same word deflected and defused all of them. *No.* Repeated over and over, without explanation, without placating gestures, without apology, it formed an unassailable verbal wall made of just one brick, one tiny word: *no.*

When sixty seconds had passed (it felt like sixty minutes), and Sensei Suzanne said, "OK, you can stop," I no longer felt like an idiot. I probably still looked like one, but I didn't care anymore.

Then my partner and I switched roles, and I had to ask inane questions for sixty seconds while she said "no" to me. Here again, I wasn't allowed to smile, and I wasn't allowed to look away. (Nor was I allowed to threaten her; we had to wait until the second half of class to do that.) All I could do was ask her for something.

This, I discovered, was even more agonizing than saying "no." Because, as I had just discovered, "no" is quite a powerful word. If we appreciated how powerful it was, we'd use it a lot more often. We're conditioned to respect it. Every time my partner told me "no," it got harder to ask the next question.

It made me feel bad. Not just rude, or aware that she didn't like me. It made me feel like a bad person, like I ought to be ashamed.

And that started me thinking about the mind-set of people who keep asking for things, in normal life, even after people tell them "no."

I always thought of them as annoying—the pushy guys in bars, the aggressive panhandlers, the telemarketers. But if they can keep asking me for something even when they know I don't want them to, well . . .

Wow, those people are assholes. And they deserve to be told "no," and not a single thing more.

"Transformative experience" is a cringe-inducing phrase that I generally try to avoid. But there's no other way to honestly describe Sensei Suzanne's self-defense workshops. Like her karate classes, they were built on what's called the "empowerment approach," a term that makes me roll my eyes a little even now, because "empowerment" is a word I avoid even more assiduously than "transformative."

Now I *teach* self-defense workshops using the empowerment approach, and the highest praise I can receive on an evaluation is for someone to say, "It was a transformative experience!"

The irony here is kind of cringe-inducing, too.

If I try to put the effect of that earliest workshop into less bromidic words, the best I can do is this: it was like having my world turned upside-down, and then realizing that, in fact, the world had always been upside-down, and *I* had just come right-side up. There was a sense of relief in knowing that all those things that had looked so wrong—the injustice of violence against women, the limits placed on us because of our gender, the fear of losing our mothers, our sisters, ourselves—*were,* in fact, wrong. That I was right to be angry about them. Empowerment-based self-defense training left me with a completely new way of looking at self-defense—a perspective diametrically opposed to mainstream approaches to safety.

Let me explain the difference.

Smile at strangers.

見知らぬ人に微笑もう。

IT'S STANDARD PRACTICE, in any book about violence and women, to include a vignette featuring one lone female, innocent, unsuspecting, going about her normal activities and, in so doing, drawing unwittingly and inexorably closer to some ghastly fate.

A lot of horror movies start this way, too, not to mention most television crime shows, and about every third Lady Gaga video. It's a proven formula.

So let's consider, then, a typical American woman as she's preparing to go out for the evening. She's dressed in a modest skirt—not long, but not too short—a camisole with a blazer over it, maybe some nice pumps with creditable heels. Her nails are freshly manicured, and she's put a little extra effort into doing her makeup and hair. She makes sure her cell phone is in her purse. Being safety-conscious, she even carries a small canister of pepper spray on her key chain. And there she is, ready to step out her door and into the wider world: a prepared, confident, self-reliant woman.

Now, what do you suppose is wrong with this picture?

The average woman *wants* to stay safe, obviously; we all do. She may go to some lengths to assure her own safety. She knows it's safer to park in a lighted area, to walk with a friend, and to not accept drinks from strangers. She has taken what appear to be reasonable steps to reduce the odds that she'll become a victim of violent crime. So what is she doing wrong?

Nothing. Absolutely nothing. *She's not doing one single thing wrong.* Why would you or I think, even for a moment, that the risks this woman faces—and those risks are real, and plentiful—are the result of some error on her part? Even though I've been teaching self-defense and martial arts for over a decade now, I'm still flabbergasted at people's willingness to assume that violence happens because women make mistakes. It doesn't work that way.

The only problem here—and it's a *problem,* to be explored and solved, not an *error* to be corrected—is that this woman, like any woman (or man), might be doing things for reasons that don't, upon closer inspection, make much sense. She may be adapting her behavior, her lifestyle, even her thoughts, in ways she presumes increase her security, but actually don't—ways that may even increase her vulnerability. And there are a lot of factors affecting her safety that aren't related to her actions at all. She doesn't control them. She's probably not even aware of them.

That's not her fault.

For example, let's talk about the skirt our typical woman is wearing. Skirts in and of themselves don't make their wearer any more vulnerable. Depending on how they're cut, they can allow a person to move quite freely. The Roman army marched thousands of miles wearing skirts, and they did all right; the Rajputs did, too. A regiment of Scots Highlanders doesn't come across as especially fragile, either. But our typical American woman isn't marching with Germanicus against the Cheruscans; she's climbing onto a bus or out of a Honda, or navigating a subway escalator. Those around her are likely to be looking at her legs, not running away screaming at the sight of her *hasta* (the standard-issue Roman spear, six feet long and tipped with iron). So even if her skirt isn't physically confining, the expectations of the people around her place certain constraints on her movement when she's wearing it.

In short, a modern woman in a skirt has to keep her knees together. True, there's no law to that effect, but have you ever seen a woman in a skirt who, for one reason or another, didn't? It looks *very* peculiar, doesn't it?

If you want to understand why a skirt is a safety-related problem, try this simple self-defense exercise: Stand up and lean most of your weight on one foot. Put the other foot in front of you, or hook it behind your weighted foot, or cross your legs; in other words, stand like a typical teenager. This is an off-balance stance. In it, you're easy to knock over or push around. Next, try putting your feet shoulder-width apart with your weight divided fifty-fifty. Bend your knees just the slightest bit. Straighten your back. This stance is balanced and stable and gives you a lot of options for moving or maintaining your position. It also looks stronger to an observer. It makes you a less inviting target.

Try this exercise in front of a mirror while wearing a skirt. Which stance looks ladylike? Which one makes you look like John Madden in a dress?

There's the paradox. To look "nice," you have to keep your knees together. To feel and be strong, you have to keep your feet apart. It's pretty hard to do both without attracting unwanted attention. A skirt forces you to choose.

Now let's take a look at our average woman's shoes. Of course, high heels make you less stable, and they're very hard to run in. In an emergency, they present a substantial physical handicap. But there's another problem with the designer pumps—a more insidious one.

The next time you're out walking in a public place, try this: Look directly into the eyes of each person you pass. You don't have to stare. Just make brief eye contact. Then look down at the ground as you walk past. Repeat this a few times. Next, try looking at people, then looking *away*—not down, just away. Keep your eyes on the same level and look at something else. I don't care what; use your imagination. There's a lot out there to see.

You've just performed an exercise I learned in Sensei Suzanne's self-defense class when we talked about assertiveness and body positioning. People's responses to this exercise are illuminating: Looking at someone and then looking down, they say, makes them feel "bad," "embarrassed," "weak," "small." Looking away, in contrast, is empowering. It's a very simple thing to do—don't drop your eyes—but it makes you feel strong. It makes you feel confident. And it signals to others that you are confident.

Guess where you end up looking when you wear high heels?

Now, I know perfectly well that women in high heels don't walk around with their eyes glued to the ground. But walking in high heels is tricky. You're more likely to trip and fall in high heels. You have to navigate curbs and cracks and all kinds of minor obstacles that you wouldn't even notice in sneakers but could send you sprawling in heels. You have to take shorter steps and, thus, more of them. No matter how adept you are at wearing high heels, you look down more when you wear them. And when you look down, you feel more vulnerable, and you appear more vulnerable, too. Is this merely a coincidence?

I suspect women are more prone to looking down than men. When men are embarrassed and don't know where to look, they look all around, randomly—sometimes desperately (ask one about his feelings if you want to see what I mean). Women always know where to look: down. We're trained, very subtly, to do so, and I think high heels may be one of the training aids. The Chinese used to deform girls' feet by binding them, making it impossible to walk freely. These permanently hobbled women became ornamental status symbols for the elite men who married them. High heels are much less obvious, but they, too, undermine your balance and stability (and they make your feet look smaller, too). They also make you feel less confident by forcing you to look down. Worst of all, they make you display this visual cue of vulnerability to others. We may describe the body language of downcast eyes as shy, bashful, timid, coy, submissive, modest, demure, or ladylike. Whatever you call it, it's understood to be the opposite of masculine.

Why, exactly, do high heels make women look attractive? Because they make us look taller? Because they accentuate our calf muscles? Because they attest that we can spare three hundred bucks for some slivers of leather and wood?

Or because they make us *look* like we *feel* weak and small?

I know, a lot of women find high heels empowering. I know they can make you feel elegant, and I know they make guys notice you. I know they are fun and frivolous and they come in lots of different colors. I don't think high heels are evil. They do for women what sports cars do for men, at a fraction of the price. But wearing heels has a direct impact on our physical activity, and an indirect one on our poise and bearing.

So the average woman, in choosing what to wear outside her home, is making decisions that affect her power and her safety, even if she doesn't realize it. This particular woman, by choosing a skirt and high heels, has constricted her options for free movement and opted to send messages about her reduced personal power. I'm not saying these are *mistakes*; only that they're choices that matter in self-defense. It's wise to think about them.

I do; when I think about safety, I interrogate everything—my clothes, my belief system, the numbers stored on my cell phone—everything. Admittedly, I'm obsessive, but I'm also just plain curious. I want to know what the risks are. There's a certain amount of danger we all face; that's the nature of our world. But I want to feel that I have some control over my exposure to danger. I'm more than willing to take risks. I just want to choose them consciously for myself.

Other women may make different choices, and whatever choice a woman makes is *fine*. But is it a choice she's aware she has made?

Sensei Suzanne's approach to self-defense made me aware of the choices I was making. She also helped me see that I had more choices than I realized.

Sensei didn't smile much during class (and when she did, we all trembled), but away from the training floor, she smiled often. She made a point of it. "I believe that what you give is what you get back," she told us, "and I want to get positive energy from life. I made a conscious decision years ago to put that belief into practice. So now, as I'm going about my business, at the store or walking around town, when I see somebody, even if I don't know them, I give them a really big smile. I try to connect with that person, just for an instant, and give them some positive energy. It makes me a lot happier to live that way."

From anyone else I would have dismissed this philosophy as hippy-dippy nonsense that would land anyone dumb enough to follow it in deep trouble or a shallow grave. Coming from Sensei Suzanne, though, I had to admit the possibility that it was a valid option. If it was working for her, there must be something to it.

Of course, Sensei Suzanne was a black belt with many years' experience taking care of herself around all manner of people. It's possible that the average woman—say, our hypothetical woman in the skirt and high heels—might not fare so well if she went around smiling at strangers.

But we're not going to follow her around to find out. It would be creepy and voyeuristic. Scrutinizing the average woman seems disrespectful, even if she's not real. So let's bid farewell to our hypothetical woman, and give her back her privacy. Instead, I'll tell you how Sensei's strategy has worked for me. Scrutinizing my own life seems more honest. And I can promise you it will be more entertaining.

I made the choice, a few years ago, on a trip to Chicago, to smile at a homeless man. I was on vacation with my sister and mother, and we were walking along near Michigan Avenue when a man who appeared down on his luck approached me and said, "Hello, ma'am, do you have a minute?" My mother and sister kept walking, saying nothing, looking straight ahead. I looked at him, smiled, and said, "Sure."

I could have said "no." I often do say "no," now that I've

had training. But instead, I smiled and said "sure," for several reasons. For one thing, my on-the-spot read of the situation told me it was probably low risk. It was daytime, we were in a highly populated area with upscale businesses, and there were plenty of people around, including my mother and sister. The man's clothes were that uniform shade of greenish-brown that results from not being washed very often, but they weren't so dirty as to indicate that he'd lost all interest in basic hygiene. He didn't appear drunk or drugged or deranged. I was sober, too (a critical variable in threat assessment), which meant I was probably perceiving the risks accurately.

Secondly, he was holding a stack of newspapers. Back home in Austin, I had occasionally bought copies of a paper written, edited, and sold by homeless people, called the *Austin Advocate.* I knew other cities had similar papers, usually facilitated by social service agencies that help folks back onto their feet. I was always happy to buy the *Advocate* because it provided cash to someone who really needed it. It also acknowledged homeless people's desire to tell their own stories and recognized their ability to produce something of value. So I was interested in finding out if that's what he was selling.

The third reason I smiled was that I knew I didn't have to.

When you know you can say "no," and mean it—because you've done it over and over, at every conceivable point in a conversation—then you can also choose not to say it. Sensei Suzanne wasn't, in that self-defense workshop, training us to always say "no." She was teaching us that we could say "no" if we wanted to, and making us experience firsthand what that choice would feel like. She was showing us how to use a tool most of us had carried for years, but never employed to full effect. Then she left it up to us to decide whether and when to use that tool.

I'm not a risk taker by nature. But the point of learning to assess risk is not to avoid risk entirely. The point is to choose more wisely the risks you do take.

So I chose to smile at the homeless guy and say "sure."

And he was, in fact, selling a paper produced by a homeless advocacy group. He was charging one dollar, and I gave him five, and told him thanks.

My mother and sister were appalled.

My mom, a Chicago native, had spent our entire trip happily demystifying the secrets of the big city for her daughters. "Did you notice the language the cook was speaking at the diner?" she had asked us at lunch. "That was Greek he was speaking." And, "Did you see those men sitting at the table at the café? The clean-cut ones in the white T-shirts? Those were gay men." It was like being on safari: all right, group, everyone mark off *Homosexual Men, Summer Plumage* on your checklist.

Mom took her duties as tour guide seriously, so as we walked on toward the Magnificent Mile, she dispensed some advice about dealing with the local homeless population.

"Don't make eye contact with them," she counseled. "A lot of homeless people are mentally ill, and you don't know how they'll react."

"Actually, I think I'm safer if I *do* make eye contact," I said. I didn't argue about the mental illness. Mom was a nurse; she'd seen plenty of mental illness. But I had plenty of good reasons for choosing not to ignore homeless people, to wit:

1. When you ignore someone, you aren't really setting a boundary. You're pretending there's no need for one.
2. People who feel ignored tend to get louder and more persistent.

3. Any moment of communication, however brief, is an opportunity for assessing behavior and threat potential.
4. Ignoring people denies them their basic human dignity.

Notice I said those are reasons to *choose* to make eye contact. They're not reasons you *always should* make eye contact. I tried to explain this distinction to my mom and sister, to no avail.

"When you looked at him, you gave him an excuse to ask you for money," my sister pointed out. "And then he got five bucks out of you. You see? That's what happens when you make eye contact."

"No," I explained, "that's what happens when someone asks me for money and I decide to give it to him."

"You shouldn't give them the *chance* to ask," Cathy chided. She is older than I am, and has always taken pains to correct my misunderstandings about the way the world works. "You should do what I do: just walk around looking really mean all the time. That way they'll leave you alone."

I'm ashamed to admit that I burst out laughing at this point, which is not the kind of reaction that fosters harmony among relatives on vacation.

What I ought to have said instead was this: I agree, you shouldn't let people bother you—if you don't want to be bothered. But even if "looking mean" does keep you from being harassed (and I doubt it will), do you really want to shut out every stranger? Do you want to build a wall so high and foreboding around yourself? Do you want to be a person who walks around looking really mean all the time? *All the time?* Because I can guarantee that if you walk around *looking* that way, you'll start *feeling* that way, too. And then what's the point of having kept yourself safe? You're still pissed off and angry and miserable. You just don't have anyone to blame.

After I started training in self-defense and learned that I could stop people from bothering me—once I had gained real confidence in my ability to set and maintain my boundaries—then, oddly enough, people started to bother me less. When I didn't have to worry quite so much about being hurt or taken advantage of, I was able to be more generous in my interactions. That ability has paid off in lots of ways, not least of which is that I find, like Sensei Suzanne did, that smiling at strangers—when I choose to—has made me a happier person.

And that, I suppose, is the fourth reason that I smiled at a stranger in Chicago: because I knew Sensei Suzanne would have.

That, ultimately, was why I belonged at Sun Dragon. Not just because of the karate, not just for the self-defense training, but because it gave me the opportunity to change myself into someone better—someone happier, less fearful. Someone who smiles because she wants to smile.

Paradise doesn't count if it's compulsory.

もし無理矢理いさせられるのならば、
パラダイスでさえも不快なものとなる。

SOMETIMES, OF COURSE, we end up in situations we didn't choose. I can tolerate almost anything if I'm able to look for options and choose the ones I think are best. I have a much harder time coping in circumstances where my options are limited. I do not flourish under those conditions.

In 2001, my family and I moved to paradise; an experience I not only didn't deserve, but was wholly incapable of appreciating. We had a house in Hilo, Hawaii, with a view of Mauna Loa Volcano, two orange trees in the front yard, and a chocolate factory (no kidding, a chocolate factory) on the next block. Every day Scott and Dave and I saw rainbows from our porch and whales out in the bay. It was a magical existence, and from my perspective, an absolute disaster from start to finish, possibly the worst experience of my life. All because I couldn't control the situation and—what was worse—couldn't control my anxiety about it, either.

I've always been the kind of person who doesn't like to go

out past waist-deep when I'm swimming at the beach. This is because of sharks. Not that I've ever encountered one; it's the *idea* of sharks that upsets me. And I'll spend my entire day at the beach advising others not to go out too far, because you never know with sharks. If people stay close to the shore, I worry about jellyfish. If I swim in a lake, where I know perfectly well there aren't any sharks or jellyfish, I imagine water snakes, giant catfish, snapping turtles, and U-boats. You may wonder why I bothered learning to swim at all, and the answer, of course, is my fear of drowning.

Having a hyperactive imagination is exhausting, and for a big chunk of my life I spent what little energy I had left over from worrying in search of ways to stop worrying. I had zero success with this project until I dipped a toe into the Korean martial arts and discovered that hitting things—tangible things—was a good way to make intangible threats back off a little bit. This was a revelation to me, that you can change the way your mind works by changing what your body does. Also, I turned out to be pretty good at hitting things.

But while I liked the discipline of training at the *dojang,* and the way it supplied a simple answer to every question (shut up and do whatever the teacher says), and while I certainly enjoyed the virtuous feeling that comes from doing hard and painful things, my early martial arts training didn't make me any less anxious or more pleasant to be around. It just made me a more insufferable perfectionist with better cardiovascular capacity. The martial arts weren't improving me so much as they were bringing all of my most obnoxious character traits into sharper focus. I stopped training after about a year, and didn't really miss it. It wasn't until I stumbled into Sun Dragon that I started to see a glimmer of how martial arts might help me solve . . . well, whatever the hell my problem was.

As I trained at Sun Dragon, learning to speak assertively, set personal boundaries, and crush windpipes, a marvelous thing happened: the more time I spent practicing concrete skills to protect myself—skills I could and did use every day, walking down the street or climbing into my car—the less I heard anxiety's constant, morbid hum in the back of my mind. For once, discipline was making me *less* neurotic. Two years into my training, when I reached green belt (the halfway point on the path to black belt), I had a stable marriage, a PhD, and a son who showed every sign of turning out normal. I was finally getting a grip on my anxieties and my life.

And then we moved to Hawaii and I learned how tenuous that grip was.

When Scott accepted a teaching job in Hilo, everyone told me how lucky I was. They were right, but it was luck that I hadn't asked for and didn't want. It was the *Congratulations! You've won a free lifetime supply of disposable hats!* kind of luck. I didn't know what to do with such luck. There was no way to exchange it for something more my style, and I felt guilty for wanting to.

What had happened, I figured, was that some other woman, somewhere—a nice, deserving woman—had a lifelong dream that her husband would land a job in Hawaii, and somehow (fate is a complicated thing), I got her dream. To this day, I worry that somewhere in rural Vermont or Colorado there is a desperately unhappy woman with a barn full of mustangs and her own karate school who wonders how the hell she got there. If she is reading this: I'm so sorry. Do you need any disposable hats?

Scott and Dave were delighted about the move to Hawaii. I, on the other hand, was horrified. Leaving our old life and jetting off to a tropical wonderland was exactly the kind of new, disorienting situation I detest. I'd have the added pressure of a new job, since the school had graciously rummaged up a couple of classes for me to teach in the English department. We couldn't afford to fly out beforehand and find a place to live, so we'd be arriving homeless and carless in the middle of the rainy season. (Hilo averages 270 inches per year.) I'm also terrified of flying, so the flight itself would be torture, and having survived an earthquake as a child in California, I wasn't thrilled at the thought of living on what one of my friends called "an active, oozing volcano." Not to mention that the town of Hilo has been devastated—twice, in the twentieth century alone—by tsunamis. It was a lot of material for a chronically anxious control freak to work with, and I started in right away.

The omens were bad. A couple of weeks before the move, as I was listlessly trying to pack an entire household into the six suitcases we could take on the plane, Scott received a phone call from his new boss, the chair of the university's sociology department. From several rooms away I heard a long, garbled conversation, with a lot of exclamations, and was just building up a faint hope that perhaps the university had lost all its funding and no longer had jobs for us, when Scott hung up and came to find me. He looked shocked and sick, which are not normal expressions for him.

"Is everything OK?" I asked, with some trepidation.

"They wanted to know if I could teach some extra classes," he said. "As an overload; they'll pay me extra."

"Why?" I said. "Did someone quit?"

"Remember the other professor they just hired in sociology, the one who flew out in September?" Scott asked. "He drowned at the beach this weekend. In front of his family."

We looked at each other for a long moment. It was horrifying, and yet all I could think was *I told you so.* I didn't say it, but Scott knows me pretty well. He stopped talking ecstatically about the move after that. He knows what I'm like at the beach.

Our very first evening in Hilo, we drove our rental car down to the water to watch the sun set. This was not the same beach where the drowning had occurred, so I let Scott and Dave coax me in for a swim. We had a delightful time until a sea turtle, oblivious to our presence, swam past so close we could feel the rush of water as its flippers fanned it along. It was bigger than Dave and completely unafraid of humans—two characteristics that naturally made me think: shark.

You've probably had that dream where something terrible is chasing you and you can't run. Well, standing in waist-deep water, holding your four-year-old son, while what you believe is a shark swims past your leg is exactly like that dream. Only you don't wake up. You just stagger shoreward while wondering if you should use both arms to throw your child into shallower water, or hang on to him with one arm and leave your other hand free to gouge out the shark's eyes.

We laughed about it back at the hotel: *Mom was scared of a turtle!* Scott and Dave laughed, anyway. I did my best to join in the hilarity, but I was still having chest pains.

The next morning, the staff at the hotel warned us to stay indoors as much as possible because the volcano was active that day, and there was a lot of sulfuric acid in the air.

I was completely unmoored by our relocation, to an extent that would have shocked me had I been capable of feeling shock or anything else. I stumbled through Hawaii like a sleepwalker or a Valium addict, indifferent to the miracles of nature all around us. I was likewise dead to the minor horrors of the place, like the gigantic slugs that lived in the rocks in a nearby park, or the overwhelming stench that breadfruits emitted when they fell on the ground and started rotting. I shrugged when I realized that the odd packages in the freezer section of the local grocery store—containing large, round lumps each surrounded by eight smaller lumps—were frozen octopus. The island contained so many and varied threats that I felt suffocated under their combined weight.

I found myself struggling to breathe when I ran a couple of miles on the beach—sea level, for crying out loud! I was normally no bolt of lightning, but I when I left Texas I could manage a 5K without excessive wheezing. In Hawaii, I would plod along the road, gagging every few yards, whenever I passed a frog flattened on the pavement. Many animals in Hawaii are legally protected—geese, seals, and the sea turtle that had swum so blithely past me on our first trip to the beach. But there were literally hundreds of frog corpses on every street during the spring months. People were glad to see them dead, because these particular frogs were an invasive species. Hawaii, I recognized with every fetid step, is not kind to nonindigenous forms of life.

I got by, barely. I taught my classes, did the grocery shopping, paid the bills. On the surface I looked normal, if you didn't know me too well. Scott, however, saw it all, and suffered double what I did.

"What is the *matter* with you?" he asked in exasperation, at least once a week. I would shake my head, throw up my hands, try to put it into words: I don't want to be here. And when I'm not where I want to be, I feel like I've disappeared.

And Scott would throw up *his* hands, and shake *his* head,

and say nothing. It wasn't that he didn't understand. He understood. He sympathized. But having committed the scandalous crime of bringing his wife to Hawaii, he had to watch helplessly as she devolved into a grim, haggard wreck. It was just so unfair.

The only thing that kept me sane in Hawaii—to the extent that I did stay sane—was a ritual I established within a few days of our arrival. Every day at three o'clock, when Scott and I finished teaching, we would pick up Dave from preschool and head out to Richardson Beach, a tiny crescent of sheltered black sand tucked away on the southern cusp of Hilo Bay. The two of them would head into the water to swim with the turtles, and I would walk past the sunbathers and kids with sand buckets, along a thin strip of rocks overgrown with screw pines. When I reached a spot where I could look west across the bay to the summit of Mauna Loa, into the heart of the island, I would take off my shoes, sink my toes in the sand, and settle down on my haunches in *seiza,* just as if I were back at the dojo in Austin, ready to start class.

Then I waited for four o'clock, when five thousand miles away in Austin, it would be nearing eight o'clock at night. At Sun Dragon, a circle of women would be kneeling down on the floor in *seiza,* just like me.

They would have just finished an hour and a half of karate. They would be sweaty and tired and hungry, but before they left the class and the dojo they would bow out, the way they always did: Gina and Jan, the brown belts, newer students like Joy and Doris Ann and, of course, Sensei Suzanne.

"Shinzen ni rei," Sensei would say, and all the students would place their fists on the floor in front of them, and bow

in acknowledgment of the *shinzen,* or spiritual heart of the training space.

"Sensei ni rei," Jan would call out, and everyone would bow to Sensei Suzanne.

"Senpai ni rei," Sensei Suzanne would say, and everyone would bow to the senior students, or *senpai*s.

Finally, at the words *"otogai ni rei,"* all the students and instructors would bow to one another.

On the beach in Hawaii I could hear the Japanese phrases, and see the women uttering them, as clearly as if I were back in Texas. I could see their white uniforms as their shoulders dipped to the floor with each bow. I saw the orange and brown carpet they knelt on. I saw the rafters of the dojo above them, gathering dusk. Sitting alone on my spit of congealed lava, gazing out at the sparkling ocean and the mist-shrouded volcano, I bowed, too. Five thousand miles away, they were leaving the place they had dedicated to physical practice, mental discipline, and spiritual improvement. As they stepped out of that realm, I stepped into something I desperately needed in the midst of my dislocation: a small, quiet space where I understood who I was and what I was doing. I imagined it like the passing of a torch, halfway across the Pacific, from my training partners to me.

It made me feel, briefly, less alone.

The bowing finished, I would stand up, pick a few screwpine needles out of my shins, and start training all by myself. It was no substitute for what I'd had at Sun Dragon, but at least the rituals and the familiar, traditional techniques connected me to something. When I was training, I was able to shrug off, for a brief time, the sense that I was floating unmoored in the middle of the ocean.

With no instructor to guide me, I had to improvise quite a bit. I did all the romantic things that karate masters do when they fulfill the tradition of going off to train in the wilderness. I kicked trees and punched sand (of the two, sand hurts worse). I practiced stances in the surf, trying to make myself rooted and immovable, fighting against the swell, the shifting ground, and the knowledge that moray eels were common in the area.

I can't honestly say I enjoyed training at the beach, though I took an ill-tempered solace in knowing that other people would have. It was the only thing that kept me connected to reality, albeit a reality I had to conjure up in my own mind. It burned off part of the nervous energy that I knew better than to stockpile, and it reassured me that I was still the person I had been before. I remained a dogged, persistent, stubborn student of karate.

Even though I worked out every day, I never slept well in Hawaii, and a few months into our stay, I started to dream about dogs—dogs we had owned years before, and the ones we had left behind when we moved. The week before our flight to Hawaii, Scott and I had driven to my parents' house in rural central Texas and handed our dogs over to them. At the time, Hawaii required a four-month quarantine for pets, and while our dogs would have survived it, the thought was too much for me. (What if we all drowned at the beach? What would become of our dogs, stranded in Hawaii?)

We were sure our dogs would be happy at my parents' house, but that didn't stop me from obsessing about all the disasters that might befall them out in the country: fast cars, carelessly driven; neighbors with shotguns; rabid skunks. I spent the drive out to Mom and Dad's composing a mental list of Things Our Dogs Should Not Be Allowed to Do. (1. Stay outside overnight. 2. Ride unsecured in the backs of pickup trucks. 3. Sleep in the driveway.) I had to remind myself that my parents had raised five children and at least as many dogs in that very same house, without casualties. But it was not a happy parting, and fears about our dogs' well-being stayed in my mind long afterward, nagging me as I slept.

Morning after morning in Hilo, I woke up exhausted and morbidly depressed. By our third month on the island, I had to write down even the simplest tasks for the day, since my memory had ceased to function. I was pretty sure I was losing my mind, but I didn't have enough energy to do anything about it. And around that time, my sister back in Texas e-mailed me with the cryptic question "Did Mom tell you about the alligator?"

My parents built the family home in 1973, when we moved to Texas from California. It sits barely a mile from the Brazos River—a deadly, mud-filled drainage channel that has drowned untold cattle and people. You can't tell you're near a river at my parents' house. It's like the embarrassing uncle no one ever refers to. Moreover, the Brazos River bottom does not encourage rambling. The land harbors, among other surprises, fire ants, chiggers, ticks, briars like razor wire, poison ivy, the odd cactus just to keep you guessing, and all four varieties of poisonous snake native to North America (rattlesnake, cottonmouth, copperhead, and coral).

Throughout our childhood, my friends and I heard legends about alligators coming up the Brazos from the Gulf of Mexico. "The game wardens see them now and then," one of us would say authoritatively, and everyone would nod and shiver just a little. These were fine stories for whiling away a sultry afternoon at the catfish pond, but in the ten or so years during which I traversed every inch of territory around my parents' house, mostly on my hands and knees (the only way through the briars), I never once saw an alligator, an alligator track, tooth, scale, or indeed any evidence of reptiles larger than the six-foot diamondback rattlesnake that my dad killed in the driveway one year. We hardly needed alligators for drama. Between the snakes, the scorpions, the giant centipedes, the wasps, the ants, and our older siblings, life was hazardous enough for us kids. But it was fun to think about: alligators, gliding up the Brazos, invisible in the muddy water, sliding up the banks through the wet clay and dewberry vines, drawn by the scent of livestock and small children.

Despite the snakes and centipedes, despite my fears about fast cars and trigger-happy neighbors, our dogs were blissfully content at my parents' house. They did what they wanted, slept wherever they wished, and ate like some of the more deplorable Roman emperors. They thrived. And then one morning in April when my mother took our dogs out for a walk, Widget started barking at something.

This in itself wasn't strange; Widget barked all the time. She was (from what we could deduce) a mix of Pekingese and dachshund, weighing sixteen pounds in her prime and standing all of twelve inches high. Consequently, she got stepped on a lot and had learned to broadcast her presence loudly, and often. But that morning she was especially persistent, so my mother went to see what the trouble was. She found Widget barking frantically at a large branch lying under an oak tree by the driveway. My mother leaned down for a closer look at the branch, which then moved, and opened its jaws, and hissed at her.

Of all the fears I had conjured when we left our dogs and

moved to Hawaii, an alligator was one that simply never occurred to me. I'm still faintly embarrassed by this failure. I was led astray by what I was sure I knew about danger; alligators were kid stuff. I was a grown-up, and had moved on to grown-up worries, like sharks. Still, an alligator is what I got—or more properly, what my mom got.

My parents were unburdened by any sense of failure for not having imagined an alligator prior to one turning up. They simply called the game warden. He came out, divulged that he had no way to capture an alligator (apparently *he* hadn't taken the rumors seriously, either), and shot it instead. It measured just over four feet long, which probably doesn't seem very big unless it's in your driveway. It was substantially bigger than Widget, who enjoyed a brief moment of fame on the evening news. The whole incident had entered into local lore before I even heard about it out in the middle of the Pacific Ocean.

After my mother relayed the details, I hung up the phone and went into my son's room to look at our driveway in Hilo. Apart from the bed and the few toys we had shipped from Texas, Dave's room was bare. The windowsill held an empty juice box and a bunch of flies that were either dead or just wished they were. The view through the window, like a lot of the less glamorous parts of the island, was unmitigated lava. A single gasping papaya tree stood between the house and the driveway. The ground beneath it was conspicuously alligator-free.

I should have been there, I thought. I felt cheated, somehow. Here I was, in an exotic, hazardous land, living in a constant state of heightened awareness, expecting danger at every turn. And where does danger show up? Back at home. Evidently the same crossed wires that burdened me with someone else's dream home in Hawaii had delivered my personal alligator to the address where I no longer lived.

This, I decided, was stupid. In six months I'd experienced intense dread of flying, drowning, sharks, volcanic eruption, insanity, and alligators, in that order. I was exhausted, and I no longer had any idea what to be afraid of. All my life, I realized, I'd been trying to out-imagine God, and failing miserably. Was there even any point, I wondered, in preparing for danger? In trying to be ready for anything, I'd made myself afraid of everything.

It didn't seem to matter where the danger was—in the water inches from my leg or half a world away in my parents' driveway—the fear was always right there with me.

Six months after we'd left Texas, I sat down with Scott and told him what was already obvious to both of us: I couldn't stay in Hawaii. I needed to be back in Austin, to rejoin the circle of women at Sun Dragon, to be with them while I confronted the fear I carried around with me everywhere.

My training had begun a process of exorcism, of working through the threats in my life step-by-step, night after night. "Learning self-defense" is an inadequate way to express what I'd been doing there, like saying someone "learns religion" by praying the rosary. I had been growing in some subtler way. And our move to Hawaii had short-circuited the process.

Poor Scott, who had a job he loved, in a place he adored, and a wife who had become about as unlovable as anyone can be, nonetheless chose his wife. He resigned his position, said good-bye to the scores of friends he had already made in Hawaii, and started packing.

So when the semester ended, we got on a plane back to Texas. As I buckled Dave into his booster seat, and fastened my own seat belt, I had the most peculiar sensation. I noticed, quite suddenly, that everything around me looked *different*—not brighter or darker, sharper or duller. I couldn't put my finger on what it was, and I kept looking around at the flight attendants, the upholstery pattern on the seat in front of me, the numbers on the overhead bins, trying to figure out what had changed. And it finally occurred to me that I was seeing—had just that moment started seeing—out of my own eyes again. I don't know any other way to describe it. It was as if, up until the instant before, I had been sitting somewhere just to one side of myself, and then when I was in my seat on the airplane and headed home, I had slipped back into my body. I heard an almost audible *click,* like the buckle on my seat belt. Even though I was sitting on a plane, I had the distinct awareness of my legs being underneath me, poised, ready to take me wherever I wanted to go. It was an exhilarating feeling, and I spent most of that overnight flight staring delightedly around me as the other passengers slept and the plane headed east, acutely aware that my mind was once more in control of my body. Wherever I had been, I was back.

You're doing it all wrong. And that's perfect.

あなたのやり方は完全に間違っているが、それでいいのだ。
著者は、劇的な効果を出すため、あえて矛盾した言い方をしている。
要するに間違いを恥じることはないと言いたいのである。

FOR BETTER OR worse, Austin was where I belonged. Hawaii is a gorgeous island full of beautiful and gracious people; I felt like a freak the entire time we were there. Texas, on the other hand, is dry and inhospitable, and Texans are angry, loud, and prone to violence. I didn't necessarily feel safe in a state that issues over a hundred thousand concealed handgun permits annually, but at least I blended in with the general population. These were my people, and I was relieved to be back among them.

I managed, against all odds, to find a job almost as soon as I landed in Texas. I happily put aside my ill-fitting professorial persona and took an administrative position at the same university where I'd earned my PhD. I slipped back into academic life, and after my first day at work, I followed my usual route across town to the dojo.

As I drove south from the university, the great dome of the Texas State Capitol rose up beside me, reminding me of

Texas's long tradition of fiery women. Barbara Jordan's voice had rung out in the Senate chamber. Ma Ferguson and Ann Richards served as governor. Liz Carpenter, Lady Bird Johnson, and Molly Ivins played important roles in the political battles that took place there.

As I turned south at the capitol and headed down Congress Avenue, I passed the statue of nightgown-clad Angelina Eberly firing a cannon. Eberly was an innkeeper's widow who, late one night in 1842, commandeered an army cannon and blew a hole in the nearby General Land Office building. Her fusillade was part of a minor political dustup called the Texas Archive War, a dispute that has been mostly forgotten, except here in Austin.

A mile further south, I crossed the bridge over the Colorado River (home to the northern hemisphere's largest urban bat colony), and turned east on Riverside Drive, making the familiar, abrupt turn into the parking lot of ThunderCloud Subs. ThunderCloud is another Austin tradition, a local sandwich shop that personifies the dusty, funky charm of the city. I coasted past the restaurant's back porch, where the early dinner crowd was drinking Shiner Bock and feeding potato chips to the grackles, and pulled up in front of a long, low shedlike building that had originally been a warehouse, then the ThunderCloud Beer Garden, and finally Sun Dragon Martial Arts for Women and Children.

No city but Austin, I reflected as I climbed out of the car, could have given birth to Sun Dragon.

Sensei Suzanne had founded the dojo as a gift to herself on her fortieth birthday and ran it part-time for years until she had enough students to make it her full-time career. Now Sun Dragon was over a decade old, a respectable age for an American martial arts school. It didn't look very prosperous, however. There was no shelf full of tournament trophies on display in a front window; no gleaming gym equipment; no wall of mirrors along the training floor. It was in many ways a lovely space: whitewashed brick walls, vines growing over the windows—the kind of romantic ruin a disgraced Chinese action hero might hole up in to meditate and practice wushu. The building was spacious and clean, and when the plumbing exploded and soaked the dojo's floor (which happened pretty often), the carpet dried out quickly. There were no frills because frills cost money. Sun Dragon operated on a trifling budget, and as a business it barely kept a roof over Sensei Suzanne's head.

That's probably why, instead of the joyful reunion scene I had pictured in my head, my homecoming to Sun Dragon was marked by little more than a hug from Gina, and Sensei's pointed reminder, "Don't forget to pay your tuition." It felt like I'd never left.

In a traditional martial arts school, our sensei's skin-of-the-teeth existence would have been a shameful state of affairs. Karate students, ideally, show their respect for their teacher by keeping him or her well fed and adequately housed. In today's world of for-profit karate, a successful school might have an extensive payroll of teachers and support staff. At the very least, a martial artist who opens a new dojo hopes to make a decent living. I suspect that's easier when most of your students are men, earning a nice round dollar for every seventy-seven cents a woman makes.

Sun Dragon was *not* a traditional school, and in this one sense that *was* a shame, because if anyone deserved to be supported in style, it was Sensei Suzanne. She believed completely in what she was doing—teaching women and children to protect themselves—and she simply refused to let some idiotic thing like money fuck it up. Even when she had trouble paying the rent on the building, she kept tuition low, lower than any other martial arts school I've come across before or since. When things broke in the dojo, which they did with depressing regularity, she talked people into fixing them for free, or cheap, or if she couldn't afford that, we fixed them ourselves. Those of us who trained at Sun Dragon during those years acquired not only karate skills but a fair working knowledge of plumbing, carpentry, and electrical repair.

There's research showing that women who possess a range of practical skills—knowing how to change a flat tire, or put out a grease fire—are more likely to successfully fight off an attacker during an attempted rape. This has less to do with the skills you learn, and more to do with what acquiring the skill teaches you: there are practical solutions to problems, and you can extract yourself from hazardous situations. Boys learn those lessons early and often; girls often don't learn them at all. So there was a second layer of value to all the rafters we repaired, the valves we replaced, and the carpet we patched.

What we couldn't fix, we did without. The school never had air-conditioning, and there were days at the peak of the Texas summers when the temperature inside topped a hundred degrees at the start of class. In the winter, it was often below freezing, and Sensei would remind us of karate masters who had gone out into the mountains and trained in the snow. We hated the harsh conditions, but we were impressed with ourselves for enduring them.

Somehow, the dojo survived. Unlike the countless strip-mall karate schools that wink in and out of existence like fireflies, Sun Dragon obstinately stayed in business. Even though there were much-better-smelling martial arts schools just blocks away, we preserved a core of students who, like Sensei, simply refused to give up on this peculiar dream. We defied convention and turned a blind eye to the local building codes, and in doing so held together this shabby, homelike place where a bunch of women could sweat and struggle and thrive.

Our classes shared some of the charming eccentricity of our building, and these stood out more plainly than ever when I returned from my Hawaiian exile. Sensei Suzanne's approach to self-defense was, as I've noted, unorthodox. Her karate instruction was, too. Rituals and customs abound in karate, and most of them have evolved from exclusively male military traditions. Sensei Suzanne had little use, and less patience, for these trappings of patriarchy. Like a lot of second-wave feminists, she happily took what she needed from tradition and told the rest to go to hell. So while we had a conventional ranking system at Sun Dragon—with a progression from white belt, to blue, then yellow, green, brown, and black—Sensei departed from tradition after black belt, and determined rank among the advanced students by simple seniority, not by degrees or levels or special titles.

Similarly, we lined up in order by rank, but only at the start of class. After that, everyone was considered equal, and the student who was fastest at returning to the floor after a water break took the first spot in line, regardless of her belt color. We were all simply *karateka*—students. We didn't go in for any of the other ornaments of rank, either. We weren't affiliated with a national organization, we didn't pay testing fees, we didn't wear patches or have fancy embroidery on our plain white canvas *gis*. It was, for a martial arts school, wildly egalitarian, progressive, and politically correct.

Apart from the actual karate we practiced.

• • •

Kyokushin, created in post–World War II Japan by Masutatsu Oyama, is often quaintly described as a "full-contact" form of karate. This means it's the same kind of fighting that got bare-knuckle boxing outlawed, only with kicks and elbow strikes added. Flipping through *Mas Oyama's Essential Karate,* a book he published back in 1975, is like watching a stop-motion film of every street mugging and bar fight throughout recorded history. Everything is on the table, every technique and every target, demonstrated with precision and evident relish by a bunch of tough-looking Japanese black belts who always seem to be beating up the same poor white guy. Mas Oyama's style of karate is renowned, even in the martial arts world, for the brutality of its fighting and training.

I wasn't aware of Kyokushin's bone-crushing reputation when I signed up at Sun Dragon. I assumed most martial arts used some variation of the basic sparring strategy I'd learned at my Korean school: evade, block, and counterattack. With this strategy, your priority is to avoid getting hit. Then, if your opponent's technique creates an opening, you take your shot. This approach appealed to my sense of logic. It's terribly civilized, and predicated on self-control. It also meshes nicely with the legal concerns of your average martial arts school, which has a vested interest in not training its students to go out in public and start fights.

It turns out that evading was not something Mas Oyama did very much. He evidently didn't much care if he got hit, either, because blocking is something of an afterthought in Kyokushin. Hitting the opponent is what it's all about. Oyama was a big man, who spent a lot of time developing his power even further, and he knew how to use what he had. Since his death, in 1994, Kyokushin has splintered into different squabbling factions, but the master's legacy is still evident in all

Kyokushin fighters; you can see it the minute they step into a sparring ring. Kyokushin fighters—Kyokushinkai, they call themselves—do one thing: they fight. They don't circle, they don't work angles, they don't dance around, and they don't do a lot of fancy kicking. They go straight in, and they don't stop. They block solely to clear a path for their own strikes.

Other styles of karate have pronounced strategic preferences—for example, the linearity of Shotokan karate, the circular tactics of Goju-ryu. But the only thing like a Kyokushin sparring strategy that I've ever been able to discern is: hit the other guy first, and hit him so hard he can't hit you back. It is ferocious and brutal and, frankly, not an especially artistic approach to the martial arts. "One punch," Sensei used to tell us, "should be all you need." Or as the samurai used to say, *"Ichigeki hissatsu"*—"One blow, certain death."

That is Kyokushin, a discipline embodying the kind of zeal and fervor that land a lot of people in front of the Hague Tribunal. It's a ruthless approach to karate and to life; it's the way the bad guys fought in *The Karate Kid.* And while it's not an aesthetic that I find inherently appealing, it happens to be an excellent fighting style for women.

Evade, block, and (possibly) counter is what most people would expect a woman to do in a fight, if they expected her to do anything at all besides scream and faint. A cautious response. Negotiation, compromise; the kinds of things you can do in high heels. The last thing people expect a woman to do when threatened is to close the distance while throwing a jab to the face, follow with a reverse hammerfist to the temple, and finish things off by kicking her fallen opponent in the groin.

Of course, if people *did* expect that, women probably wouldn't get threatened as often.

The martial arts were off-limits to women for centuries. Even today, most schools are predominantly male, and the higher up you look in the ranks, the fewer women you'll see. Some styles are better than others at attracting female students. Judo and Aikido have always been popular choices for American women; presumably because they involve throwing and falling rather than hitting and being hit.

While Mas Oyama did eventually accept women as students (perhaps because he himself had three daughters), Kyokushin's übermasculine focus on knockdown fighting attracted far more men than women. Oyama built Kyokushin's reputation through challenge fights, full-contact tournaments, and famously, by killing bulls with his bare hands. Sensei Suzanne (who was a vegetarian) learned Kyokushin, and taught it to women, precisely because of its aggressiveness. She knew firsthand the limits of evasion, blocking, and countering. She had come to believe that causing trouble isn't always a bad idea, and that fighting, ferociously and immediately, brings results. I am utterly charmed by this concept.

Kyokushin training requires students to demonstrate ferocity day in and day out, until it becomes as habitual as brushing your teeth. In retrospect, I couldn't have chosen a more perfect style of karate if I'd done years of research.

I had been away from Sun Dragon for less than a year, but it felt like a lifetime. There were students in class whom I hadn't met before—several white belts, and a young woman named Amy who also worked at the university and was already a blue belt, meaning she must have started training around the time

I left Austin. Gina was a brown belt now, closing in on her black belt. I felt ancient in my green belt. As we lined up to start class, I looked around fondly and recalled how strange all this had seemed just a couple of years ago when I had been a white belt. Back then I had felt daunted by Jan, the black belt who was now leading us through basics. Jan had been a brown belt when I met her, a former military intelligence officer who looked like she could play pro football on the offensive line and, in fact, did so a few years later in the WPFL.

"Sanchin dachi," Jan called out, and the class replied, *"Osu!"* I slid my feet along the now-familiar carpet, remembering how perplexing I initially found this pigeon-toed, bent-knee stance.

And I remembered how, when I originally came to Sun Dragon, I was mystified by *osu.*

"Osu," everybody said at regular intervals throughout each class. I said it, too, even though at first I had no idea what it meant. When we bowed, we said, *"Osu!"* When Sensei called out a technique, we responded, *"Osu!"* She'd ask an obviously rhetorical question, and everyone would say *"osu!"*

Osu doesn't translate well into English; I've been told that it's not even really a word in Japanese, just "something karate people say to each other." Gina, when I pressed her for clarification, explained that it meant something like "I will overcome this obstacle by moving forward." The implication is that you're going *through* the obstacle, not around it—a typical Kyokushin attitude. These days we tell students that *osu* signifies "striving with patience." I've also heard that it may be a contraction of the phrase *oshi shinobu,* which in turn may or may not mean something like "push on and endure." In the dojo, it is pronounced (by Texans, anyway) somewhere between "oos" and "oh-su." When spoken, it is always supposed to be an exclamation: *"osu!"* instead of *"osu."*

Osu is an affirmation, but it doesn't mean "yes." In practical terms, it simply tells the instructor that the students are paying attention. But it remains conveniently open to interpretation by students and instructors alike. I have more than once voiced a loud, enthusiastic *"osu!"* in response to some command that I thought was completely unreasonable, and to me it meant, "I will overcome Sensei's bullheadedness by refusing to feel pissed off."

All in all, it's a handy word to know.

With Gina's help in my first few months, I had adjusted to the idiosyncrasies at Sun Dragon. I had befriended Jan, who would one day do me the honor of knocking me flat on my back in the opening round of my black belt test. I eased my Achilles tendons into *sanchin* stance. I began saying *"osu!"* constantly, even occasionally in my graduate school seminars on Victorian literature, where it was a guaranteed conversation stopper. Like *hegemony,* no one was brave enough to ask what it meant.

Overall, I adapted nicely to Kyokushin, until I started sparring. That was a shock; a series of shocks, actually, the biggest and most frightening of which involved strikes to the head. These, I quickly learned, were not only allowed in Kyokushin-style sparring but expected. "Controlled" strikes, to be sure, but unlike a lot of styles, we could punch—straight punches—directly to the face. If you're not a martial artist you may not appreciate how extreme that is. Trust me, it's not the usual thing. Getting hit in the head is scary as hell, for starters. A lot of damage can happen to noses, teeth, eyes, cheekbones, and the brain, in only a split second. A dojo will lose students quickly if it acquires a reputation for those kinds of injuries.

These dangers are precisely why head injuries are such a common outcome of street fights. Hitting an opponent in the head is relatively easy and gives you very high odds of damaging him or her enough to end the fight. Sensei Suzanne reasoned that because getting hit in the head was very likely in a self-defense situation, and because hitting to the head was a very effective way of stopping an attack, we should learn to fight accordingly. Thus head shots—*controlled* head shots—were part of our practice.

Even with all that explanation, "shots to the head are allowed" is a pretty bland way of describing the sparring at Sun Dragon. The firsthand experience of it is difficult to convey, but basically it boiled down to a sense that everything is happening RIGHT IN YOUR FACE RIGHT NOW.

I was completely unprepared for this. My prior experience with sparring involved people who moved in fast, threw a fast technique, and then retreated fast. This meant all I really had to do was block one shot, and then they would leave me alone and I could regroup. Moreover, I was accustomed to sparring at midrange, with both fighters moving in for punches and out for kicks. Kyokushin fighters stay in close most of the time because, while they do kick, they punch a hell of a lot more. It's quicker. Kyokushinkai like to use their legs for blocking because that leaves their hands free to punch.

And Jesus, how they punch. They stay right there in front of you and hit you, POW POW POW POW POW. Straight punches, uppercuts, hooks, you name it. The first few times I sparred at Sun Dragon, I was baffled from one end of the dojo to the other, completely overwhelmed by the need to guard my head. It was like being trapped in a bag of microwave popcorn. Gina, I discovered, might be an expert on computer-assisted pedagogy at the college level, but she kicked like a diesel-powered pile driver. Worse still, the rare techniques I managed to land had no effect whatsoever. These women could suck up much more force than I was producing with my hands and feet; my stuff wasn't even fazing them. Jan, for example, had an alarming tendency to take full-power kicks to her abdomen, laugh, and then hit me three or four times while I stood there waiting for her eyes to glow red like the Terminator's.

As a beginner, my attempts at Kyokushin-style sparring were pitiful. But I figured out, slowly, that no one was going to injure me during a match (hurt me, probably; injure me, no). I noticed that, crap, I really *did* drop my hands a lot. I awoke to the advantage of having an opponent who always stays within range (you can hit them more). And very slowly, I started to enjoy myself.

After that, my sparring still looked pitiful (even today it isn't much better), but I stopped worrying about it. There is something exhilarating and addictive about hitting people, if you know you won't really injure them—it's like being a kid again, and being able to pound on your obliging older brother. A tremendously liberating feeling. You're free to do all the instinctive things that your body and emotions constantly scream at you to do, and you're also free of the ethical worries that hold you back from doing them. And because you're putting yourself out there, and taking your own damage, you're free to make mistakes without censure.

This is one of the coolest things about learning karate, or anything new, really—the freedom it grants you to make mistakes. It's a given that you're going to do some things wrong in the dojo, especially as a beginner. Karate is difficult. You're going to look foolish as you learn. If you don't, you aren't trying hard enough.

That concept hit me full force when I stepped back into my role as Sensei Suzanne's student. The night of my triumphal return to class after Hawaii, I found myself struggling with the mechanics of a Kyokushin-style roundhouse kick. These kicks were always difficult for me, and I'd lost what little bit of control I'd had over them during my time in paradise. The roundhouse kicks I had learned years before at the Korean *dojang* were always performed while stepping forward: lift the back leg, kick, set it down in front of you. At Sun Dragon, we practiced the kick from a short fighting stance, with our weight balanced fifty-fifty, and didn't step forward. We were supposed to throw the kick, recover the leg, and return to our original stance, every time. This is tough with most kicks, but especially with the roundhouse, because the roundhouse, or *mawashi geri,* is a powerful kick, initiated by the hips, which swing the thigh around at waist level or higher toward the target in front of you. At the moment of impact, the whole leg is a straight unit, like a baseball bat. The foot (or sometimes the shin) slams into the target horizontally, carrying all the energy of the torqued hips; the power of the fully engaged glutes, quadriceps, and hamstrings; and the speed of the whole, massive apparatus being flung centrifugally around your center of balance.

I simply could not recover my leg after this kick the way Sensei Suzanne expected me to. Instead of pulling my leg back, I was spinning past my center line and stumbling forward.

Sensei Suzanne watched me stagger through multiple sets of *mawashi geri* and said sympathetically, "Kyokushin roundhouse kicks are the hardest roundhouse kicks in any style."

I believed her.

"We make you start the kick high and outside to build the hip muscles," she explained, "and we make you resume your stance after the kick so you strengthen your back muscles. Right now, you're generating more power than you can control."

This made sense, even if it didn't make what she was asking any easier. Sensei Suzanne wanted us to execute our kicks the hard way during basics, so we'd improve our strength and our control.

She worked with me one-on-one for a while, standing in front of me with a slap target and making me kick through it, then pull my leg back. Every time, I toppled forward or to the side, spun around by the force of my own kick. Sometimes I ended up with my back to her. Finally, fed up with my repeated failure, I hauled back and blasted out a kick that knocked the target clean out of her hands and halfway across the dojo.

"That was beautiful!" Sensei exclaimed, and then immediately deflated my sense of triumph by adding, "You're still not quite getting it. You have to engage your upper body and your core. But that was a great kick! If we'd been sparring it would have really hurt."

That was better than nothing.

"Don't worry," Sensei went on. "You'll get it eventually. It's hard. If it were easy, everyone would have a black belt, and it wouldn't be cool."

I've done thousands of roundhouse kicks since that evening, and sure enough, I did eventually learn not to fall over when I did them. These days, I fall over when I attempt spinning kicks instead. I also fret over my hook kicks, which because I'm prone to underrotate my supporting foot, regularly threaten to land me on the floor. Glamorous it's not. And I've been training for fifteen years.

But that's the point. Fifteen years of screwing up, and I keep coming back for more. This is an astonishing thing to be able to say about myself, that instead of dreading error, and shrinking from the possibility of committing it, I've discovered that I can just let it happen. I might learn something from it. I might not. Either way it's OK. Simply by putting myself in a place where I make mistakes, I'm doing the right thing.

Because perfect technique doesn't carry over very well into real life, but the courage to make mistakes does. Success in defending yourself doesn't depend on memorizing the proper formula, like evade, block, and counter. Success comes from your willingness to do whatever it takes, to behave outlandishly, to scream and pummel and scare the holy shit out of people who want to hurt you. To find the nearest cannon, and touch off the spark. Or even to open your own karate school.

It's a gift, all right, and perhaps it explains why I feel more at home in a dojo than almost anywhere else, and why I had been so desperate to return there—to the school where it was safe to make mistakes, and the teacher who could explain why mistakes were important. I live most of my life in constant fear of screwing up, so it was liberating to be given permission to do so—to actually be told, *You need to make mistakes. Start now.*

And to answer, *Osu,* Sensei.

To fight fear, you must also fight ignorance. And occasionally, argumentative jerks.

これは日本語に翻訳するにはあまりにも乱暴である。
趣旨は、安心感を醸成するには、知識を他人と分かち合い、
がんこなひねくれ者は避けるべきだということである。

BEING A STUDENT at Sun Dragon didn't just mean that I had the opportunity to make mistakes. In Sensei Suzanne's eyes, it meant I had a formal obligation to do so. Looking back, I can't count the number of times that my involvement with the dojo has forced me, entirely against my will (not to mention my aptitude), to acquire new skills. There were countless ways that Sensei Suzanne expected us to jump in and tackle unfamiliar tasks—partly because she wanted us to develop our abilities, but also because it was the only way to keep the school running.

The choice was always stark: something important, something you really *believed* in, needed to be done. And if you didn't do it, very simply, it wouldn't happen. That's often the way things shake out when you're idealistic and poor. It was also the way Sensei Suzanne preferred to teach us—by putting us in situations where our natural reluctance to take chances was overwhelmed by the need to do *something* about a cause we didn't want to see lost. I suspect this was how she had gained much of her own life experience. Her method wasn't without its risks—exhaustion, martyrdom, and spectacular, flaming failure among them—but it got results.

I had happily re-ensconced myself at the dojo after my detour to Hawaii, taking my place in the circle again, and bowing to Sensei Suzanne instead of a volcano. Now that I had lived without Sun Dragon, I had a better understanding of what it added to my life. My subsequent gratitude inspired me to do more for the school in return. Not long after we'd come back to Austin, I volunteered to help out at a dating-safety workshop for Girl Scouts. And that was how I began my career as a self-defense instructor.

"Help out," as I discovered, could mean different things to different people. Sensei Suzanne was expecting fifty Girl Scouts, which is about forty-seven more than I would care to be in charge of, myself. Any time you have more than three girls in one room, you have a mob. You need adult backup, and crowd control, and someone to check the bathroom periodically. Those were all tasks I felt equal to. I had been an assistant instructor ever since I'd received my green belt the year before, which meant I was qualified to tell people where to stand and when to yell. But the minute I walked through the door that morning, Sensei seized me by the arm far more urgently than was comfortable. "Good, you're here," she said, as she propelled me across the Scout-enswarmed dojo toward the office. "You're a mom. I need your help."

That sounded ominous. "We had twelve mothers, troop leaders, show up with the girls," Sensei explained as we maneuvered around clusters of giggling preteens. Gina, her perpetual smile looking a little strained, was trying to convince all of them to remove their shoes and place them on the shelves by the door. Joy, one of Gina's fellow brown belts, was assisting her.

"And that's great," Sensei went on. "I love to have the moms involved. But here's the problem: If they're out here in the dojo with us the whole time, the girls won't talk to me. They won't ask the questions they want to ask, and we can't have the conversation they need to have."

She opened the office door. "So I need you to keep their mothers busy in here for an hour or so, going over basic self-defense. Come on, we'll clear a space."

She didn't even give me time to squeak out *"me?"* Not that it would have done any good. Panicked though I was, I could tell that none of my standard excuses would work in this situation (not even "I was an art major," which I've found can get you out of almost anything). Sensei Suzanne never lacked confidence in herself, so she tended to steamroll over any hesitation she encountered in others.

Also—and this was the more important consideration—when Sensei said she needed my help, she meant it. She and the two brown belts would have their hands full with fifty Girl Scouts. It might make sense for a more experienced student like Gina or Joy to teach the older women, but the Girl Scouts would be practicing physical skills—hitting the targets, practicing wrist releases with one another—and their safety would be a prime consideration, so the more advanced students needed to work with the girls. And that left me to distract the moms.

Of course, though I didn't see it this way at the time, Sensei Suzanne wasn't exactly asking the impossible. *I* might not have felt qualified to engage twelve moms for an hour on the subject of self-defense, but she was aware that I had plenty of experience teaching college students, and also that I have a God-given ability to talk the hind legs off a donkey. Furthermore, she knew that I was perfectly capable of saying no to her request if I really wanted to, because she had taught me how.

And I knew, deep down, that I needed to do this. Having gained a new perspective on safety and the patterns behind danger, I wanted to do more than just react to fear one threat at a time. I wanted to attack the whole complicated problem of safety. I wanted to teach other people what I knew about it, hear their thoughts, and find some common solutions. It was a daunting project, but one I had to face. This initial foray into teaching self-defense was, in a way, another alligator.

So when Sensei ushered in a dozen shoeless middle-aged ladies, introduced me (with a field promotion to "Assistant Instructor"), and then closed the office door from the outside, I took a deep breath and said (lying through my teeth but trying hard to believe it), "I'm so glad you're all here."

Eleven of my new students were average moms—cheerful, talkative, and eager to learn about personal safety. Even with my limited experience, I'd met plenty of students like them.

I'd never run into anyone quite like Anna before, though.

"I'm Anna," she said perfunctorily, and then demanded, "Are we going to cover weapons?" before my hopeful introductory smile had time to fade. I knew there was no way in hell Sensei would be covering armed attacks in a preteen workshop, and I wasn't even remotely qualified to address them. Yet I hated to disappoint anyone at the very outset of a class.

"If we have time," I said disingenuously.

"Because I wanted to ask about guns versus Mace," Anna went on. For a moment I thought she was describing some kind of contest—like rock, paper, scissors—and I tried to think of a polite way to say, "Ma'am, I'm pretty sure that if you spray someone with Mace while they are shooting you, you will lose," but while I was puzzling through that one, she explained that what she meant was, Which of the two should she carry: a handgun or Mace?

"Why don't we start by talking about the weapons we all have with us right now?" I hedged. "And then we can move on to more advanced things."

Anna looked dubious, but the promise of using weapons of any sort obviously appealed to her.

"OK," I said, seizing on the momentary lull in conversation, "let's all introduce ourselves."

Everyone seemed to expect Anna to go first, even though she already had introduced herself. She explained, with considerable pride and at some length, that she was the council director who had arranged today's onslaught of Girl Scouts. She was a conventional-looking woman, stocky and brown haired, and clearly the kind of stay-at-home mom who has an insufficient outlet for her talents and thus channels her energy into organizing the holy bejeezus out of everyone and everything around her. This woman had, as a weekend jaunt, assembled a small horde of Scouts and registered them all for a three-hour self-defense class, ordered their troop leaders to attend the workshop with them, collected sixty-one signed permission forms and payment, and personally directed the fleet of minivans that ferried everyone to the dojo. The scale of the operation was staggering, and every single person involved followed Anna's orders—not, I suspected, because they loved her, but because she was so completely in charge. They probably would have followed her around in the desert for forty years and eaten locusts if she'd told them to. In fact, it would have been completely in character if Anna *had* told them to eat locusts. "Be sure to chew thoroughly," she would have decreed, her commands booming out over the sound of crunching. "They're full of riboflavin."

There's your alligator, I told myself, as I eyed her nervously.

After Anna's subordinates had introduced themselves, we plunged into the very same exercise Sensei Suzanne made me do at my first self-defense class. I paired the ladies up and asked them to say "no" to each other. I explained that the voice is a weapon with many potential uses in self-defense. We talked about setting boundaries and how it becomes easier if you make it a habit.

Anna, naturally, was the star pupil in this activity. She had an excellent sense of personal boundaries—her own, anyway. She thundered out "no" like a foghorn, and was so good at badgering her partner with questions that I had to step in and remind her that outright verbal abuse wasn't part of the drill.

We progressed to the next exercise from Sensei's curriculum. I had the women form a line and walk past me, looking into my eyes and then down at the ground. On the second pass, I told them to look at me and then look away, without dropping their eyes. This went well, too, though Anna struggled a bit to break the steely gaze she fixed on me as she walked past. We discussed the difference between the two experiences—how dropping your eyes is a submissive gesture and can make you feel less powerful, in addition to telegraphing low confidence to a potential assailant. We talked about body posture and eye contact, how these are tools (or weapons, if you prefer) for projecting strength, and how we don't use them as often as we should. What had been true for me, it seemed, was true for most of my students: it was one thing to hear about these concepts, and something else entirely to experience them bodily. There was a gratifying buzz of conversation when we finished. ("Such a big difference!" "That felt really weird, looking down like that." "I didn't realize how much I do that normally.")

It was going well, I thought. We were already halfway through our allotted hour, so I hurried on to the nuts and bolts: the primary targets on the human body (eyes, nose and mouth, temple, throat, ribs, spine, kidneys, groin, knees, feet, toes) and the potential weapons (fists, fingernails, palm-heel, elbows, teeth, knees, feet, and in a pinch, the forehead and back of the skull). Then we went over three or four basic ways to apply the weapons to the vital points: palm-heel to the chin, fist to the throat, fingernails into the eyes, kick to the knee or groin. The ladies watched closely as I pointed out all the targets on my own body, and then all the weapons.

"All right, let's practice some of these techniques," I suggested. "We'll do five palm-heel strikes to an imaginary attacker's chin, OK? And let's try this, too: I want everyone to use your voice, like we practiced earlier. When you strike, I want you to say 'no!' nice and loud. Just like this." I demonstrated by throwing a palm-heel strike up and inward, as if driving the lower edge of my open hand into the chin of someone standing in front of me. "No!" I shouted, not as loud as I could have (it was a small room), but pretty loud.

Everyone giggled a little. They always giggle, I've learned over the years; even full-grown women. I forged ahead, counting them through a set of strikes. Anna's "no" rang out stentoriously, accompanied by eleven far more anemic ones. Most of their strikes were similarly tepid. This, I said to myself, will never do.

"OK, hang on," I said. "Let's talk about the importance of using your voice. Why do you think I'm asking you to yell?"

"To scare the attacker," Anna immediately answered, and everyone nodded.

"Excellent answer," I agreed. "Yelling can certainly startle or intimidate an attacker. Why else would you want to yell?"

There was a moment of silence.

"Um . . . it makes you feel stronger?" offered a tiny, gray-haired woman wearing a T-shirt that said I (HEART) GIRL SCOUT COOKIES. Beverly, I remembered from the introductions.

"Absolutely," I told them. "Beverly's right: one reason we yell in karate—we call it a *kiai*—is that it makes you feel more powerful, and it can increase the force of your technique. That works for everyone, by the way, not just for karate students. And how *else* can yelling help?"

They appeared to have run out of ideas.

"Well, let me ask you this," I suggested. "Can you tell me why you *didn't* want to yell very loudly when I asked you to just now? What was going through your mind that made you hold back?"

Anna, for once, had nothing to contribute; *she* hadn't been holding back. The others shuffled their feet and looked awkward. Finally, after a few minutes, Beverly murmured apologetically, "I guess . . . because someone might hear us."

"Of course," I reassured her. "We don't want to bother the people around us, right?" I felt a slight twinge of conscience at including myself in that statement, but what the hell, I figured; they don't know me.

Everyone but Anna nodded, relieved that it was OK to not want to bother people.

"But if I'm really being attacked," I went on, "if I feel threatened, I *want* people to hear me, don't I?"

They nodded again, slowly, but more willingly as the concept sank in. And then Anna cleared her throat. I turned to her with a sense of foreboding.

"Yes, but you know," she informed us, politely but firmly, "if you're being attacked, you're supposed to yell 'fire!' You shouldn't yell 'no' or 'stop' or 'rape.' Because if you yell 'rape,' people won't want to get involved."

Anna's fellows murmured in uneasy agreement. They, too, had heard this advice. From whom? I wondered.

"All right, let's think about that," I said carefully. I tried to look thoughtful. "I guess the logic behind that advice is that people don't like to get involved with someone else's problem, right?"

Everyone nodded.

"So if bystanders think they're at risk from a fire, they'll get involved, whereas they won't lift a finger to stop an ongoing sexual assault?"

"There was that woman in New York—" Anna began, but this time I was ready for her.

"Kitty Genovese," I interrupted her. I wasn't about to let Anna lecture all of us on the technical points of the bystander effect. "Yes, that was a horrible crime, although a lot of what people remember about it isn't actually true. For example, some witnesses *did* call the police. They didn't all ignore what was happening. But let me ask you a question about yelling 'fire.'

"Are we trained to run *toward* fire? When you were a kid in school, and the alarm rang for a fire drill, did your teacher line your class up at the door, count heads to make sure everyone was there, and say, 'OK children, let's go find the fire'?"

Everyone but Anna laughed.

"No, of course not," said Beverly, who seemed to be warming to the role of loyal opposition. "And now that I think about it," she went on, "it doesn't make sense to say that no one will pay attention if you yell 'rape.' I mean, you hear about rape all the time on TV, and in movies, and on the news, because people are *drawn* to sex and violence. Sex attracts people. It's disgusting, but that's the way people are."

I could have hugged her, but I contented myself with giving her a huge smile, even though the topic of conversation made it wildly inappropriate.

"That's a really good point. Of course, I don't want any of you to think that yelling 'fire!' would be *wrong,*" I told them, turning my smile on Anna, who plainly didn't appreciate it. "If someone's attacking you, you can yell whatever you want. You can sing show tunes if you like. Whatever works. But there are two ways to use your voice that are important to understand. The first is language directed at an attacker, language that is impossible to misinterpret, like 'No!' and 'Stop!' and 'Go away!' That's what we've been practicing today. The second kind is directive language that will help you turn bystanders into allies. 'Call the police!' or 'Go get help!' and so on. Both kinds of language make it clear that you're not a willing participant in what's going on, that what is happening to you needs to stop.

"It's important to practice both kinds of communication. There are lots of variables in any self-defense situation, so no single response is going to keep you safe every time. But in general, you're more likely to have a good outcome from any conflict if you frame your communication simply and *state what you want.*"

I waited to see if Anna had a problem with stating what she wanted. If she did, she didn't say so.

We did some more palm-heel strikes, some bear-claw attacks, and some groin kicks. The important thing, I explained as we worked through the techniques, was not so much choosing the most devastating target, it was knowing that you always had options available to you. "In the event of a physical attack," I told them, "the last thing you want to do is second-guess yourself. Just *do something.*"

This piece of advice, I felt then and still feel now, cuts to the heart of useful self-defense instruction. A lot of people go into a self-defense class expecting a foolproof plan, a magical set of techniques that will always keep them safe. No such plan exists (though there are plenty of people out there claiming that it does, that they know what it is, and that they will impart it to others for a fee). The best advice for coping with a physical attack, the thing every woman needs to hear, over and over, is simply, *Do something.* And *keep* doing something. Don't stop until something works and allows you to reach safety.

"If one strike doesn't work," I went on, "try a different one. If the best targets are unavailable, go for something more peripheral. You may get a better opportunity later, or you may convince the attacker that you're not worth the trouble."

"Well, you know," Anna broke in at this point, and this time we all turned to look at her. "I've heard some people say that you shouldn't fight back at all, because it just makes them madder."

In the years since I met Anna, I've heard this depressing bit of "advice" pretty often. Usually it's offered up, with real concern, by women who are timid about their own ability to fight (or who have led extremely sheltered lives). But Anna was neither timid nor sheltered; even as inexperienced as I was, I could see exactly what she was up to: she was making trouble. The woman had, not half an hour earlier, told me she was considering carrying a gun. She obviously believed in fighting back. Furthermore, she herself had clearly never given a damn whether or not she made someone madder.

I took a deep breath and counted to ten; then I exhaled and counted to ten again, this time in Japanese. The women all watched me with bright, interested eyes. It was hard to know how to respond. I couldn't, as I had once seen Sensei do, simply say, "If you really think that's true, you should probably leave now, because you're wasting your time and mine." There wasn't anywhere for Anna to go except out in the dojo with the Girl Scouts, which was precisely the place I'd been told to keep her out of.

"Well, that's an interesting theory," I said, stalling for time. "And remaining passive *is* one potential response to an attack. It has worked for some women. But all the research I've seen indicates that, statistically, fighting back is the most likely way for a woman to end a physical assault."

"Statistics can say anything," Anna scoffed.

"They can certainly be manipulated," I conceded. "But are you telling me you've seen evidence that women who let men do whatever they want to them actually end up better off than women who stand up for themselves?"

Anna looked as if she might be belatedly realizing that this wasn't a position she really believed in. But having staked her claim, she would defend it to the bitter end. "It depends on what they want," she maintained stubbornly. "It might keep them from killing you."

"Exactly," I agreed. "It would pretty much depend on my attacker, wouldn't it? And if someone is physically attacking me, he's probably not someone who goes out of his way to honor the social contract, is he?"

Fortunately, Beverly chuckled at that. I wondered if she

and Anna would be riding home in the same minivan, and if so, what the atmosphere was going to be like.

"Look," I went on, turning to address the whole group, "every situation is different and each person has to make her own choices. You're free to refrain from defending yourself if you think that's the best choice for you. For me, it boils down to this: The decision about how much an attacker is going to hurt me? I want that to be *my* decision, not his."

It didn't occur to me until later that I was actually doing a pretty good job here of modeling personal-boundary setting—the same thing I'd been teaching the women to do by saying "no." Anna wanted to challenge me, the teacher, by challenging my approach to self-defense. I was perfectly happy to acknowledge that I wasn't Wonder Woman. But I had my own beliefs about defending myself and my own tolerably well-thought-out reasons for holding them. Those were my boundaries. When I defined them, clearly and unmistakably, Anna backed off.

And when she did, so, too, did my doubts about what I was doing there. My fear of screwing up, of looking stupid in front of an audience, of doing more harm than good, turned and slithered back into whatever river it had crawled out of.

I decided to press my advantage while I still had it. "Let's think for a minute about the bigger picture here, and the impact of advice like 'don't fight back,'" I suggested, and then shamelessly invoked the girls in the next room. "What sort of message does that send to young women like the Girl Scouts you brought here today?

"When we tell girls they should yell 'fire' instead of 'rape,'" I continued, "we're telling them that women have to translate or deny the violence directed at them if they want help with it. We're stating that no one cares if we're being attacked. I worry that if we start to believe that about the world, and convince others to believe it, we're helping to create a world where it's true.

"Often, women who've been raped have a very hard time talking to anyone about it," I went on, "or even admitting to themselves what has happened. When we say, 'Don't yell "rape!"' we're making it even harder for them. We're saying that women shouldn't admit to being raped *even when they are in the process of being raped.*

"Personally, I think if someone is trying to rape you, you shouldn't have to censor yourself."

"I agree with you," said Beverly firmly. "You know, most rapes in this country aren't even reported. I think these kinds of myths might be one reason why." Several of the other women nodded in agreement. *To hell with Anna,* I thought cheerfully. *At least some of them get it.*

Anna appeared to be marshaling her forces for another sally, but before she could say anything, the office door opened. I had never been happier to see Sensei Suzanne than I was at that moment, when she stuck her head in to ask, "How's it going in here? Moms, are you ready to join us?"

With ill-disguised relief I watched Anna herd her troops out the door into the dojo. As she passed Sensei, she paused and remarked, "I hope we're going to cover weapons soon."

"If we have time," Sensei assured her. Had I not known Sensei Suzanne for the extraordinarily self-disciplined martial artist that she was, I could have sworn she winked at me as she left the office.

My experience with those Girl Scout leaders made me appreciate how spoiled I'd been by my self-defense education at

Sun Dragon. Now that I had a more informed perspective on safety, suggestions like yelling "fire" during an assault and being polite to violent attackers struck me as ludicrous. I had been vaguely aware that a few misinformed women might still consider them good advice, just as there are still people who think you can get rid of warts by rubbing them with a potato. But I hadn't realized, until I taught Anna and her friends, how many women actually gave credence to such misguided recommendations. And I wondered where women were hearing these mysterious advisories.

The pieces started to fit together a few weeks after my encounter with Anna, when I received a chain e-mail titled "9 Safety Tips for Women." You've probably seen e-mails like this; they share a state-of-emergency tone, heavily salted with exclamation points!!!!!!! They're also extremely likely to be factually incorrect, misleading, or just plain insulting. One of my favorites, which is still popular today, a decade after its debunking by the urban legends reference site Snopes.com, warns women to avoid wearing overalls, supposedly because rapists find it easy to cut the shoulder straps with scissors.

Now, leaving aside the logistical nonsense (as I recall, overalls can be removed simply by shrugging one's shoulders), is there a single piece of clothing, apart from chain mail or an iron chastity belt, that *can't* be cut up with scissors? Should we therefore conclude that any sliceable item of clothing attracts rapists? Isn't that kind of, I don't know, batshit crazy?

That same e-mail also warns that "The #1 thing men look for in a potential victim is hairstyle," and cautions women not to wear their hair in ponytails, which are easy to grab and therefore attract rapists (no, it's not true; *of course it's not true*).

It's one thing to point out, as I have, that our choice of shoes or skirt can have an impact on our mobility, confidence, and image—all things that affect our safety. But it's something else entirely to reduce that complex interplay of variables to a simple formula: overalls + ponytail = rape. It would be very handy if it were true, but it's not.

The absurdity should be self-evident, I thought. My first try at self-defense instruction, however, showed me I was wrong. Some women not only take the advice offered in these e-mails seriously, they feel compelled to amplify and broadcast it. And most of them don't take self-defense classes, where they might get better information. Instead, they just pass the e-mails along. Pretty soon, everyone with an Internet connection wants to join in the conversation, editing and improving the e-mails, adding their own caveats, warnings, and tips. They send the whole mess on to friends, husbands, sons, and anyone else they can think of. As it's forwarded from one person to another, the document becomes a palimpsest, overwritten and annotated with the worst fears and best intentions of countless people who are truly worried about violence but unfortunately don't know squat about preventing it.

Thus their imaginations tend to run riot on the page, resulting in epic documents like "9 Safety Tips for Women," a classic example of the genre that refuses to die. The Internet's best and brightest have been at work improving it since I initially received it. It showed up again in my e-mail inbox just a few months ago as a veritable rainbow of font colors and styles, retitled "10 Tips Written by a Police Officer."

It's perhaps not surprising, given the infinite number of monkeys crafting this magnum opus, that a few fragments of lucid advice can be descried deep in its depths. There is Tip #5, for example, which advises, "When getting into your car in a parking lot or parking garage, be aware: look around you, look into your car, at the passenger side floor, and in the backseat." That's pretty good advice. Other tips are a more mixed bag. Take #7:

> If the predator has a gun and you are not under his control, ALWAYS RUN! The predator will only hit you (a running target) 4 in 100 times; and even then, it most likely WILL NOT be a vital organ. RUN, preferably in a zigzag pattern!

I'm not sure I'd phrase it quite like this (I try to avoid "always," even in lowercase letters), but it is true that if someone with a gun tries to make you go somewhere else—into a car, inside a building—your odds of survival are much, much better if you run away instead. Still, there are lots of situations where following this rule wouldn't make you safer. Sometimes it might be safer to stall an attacker by talking. Sometimes running might not be an option—if you have kids with you, or you're in a confined space or disabled. Sometimes an attacker might just want your money, which is easy enough to hand over, and cheaper than an emergency room bill for a bullet extraction. (I must say I'm not terribly reassured, either, by the statement that I likely won't be hit in a vital organ. If I'm hit at all it's probably going to at least slow me down.)

And there are other things going on here that make me uneasy. The "4 in 100" odds may well be accurate, but is there a credible source for that statistic? "Run in a zigzag pattern" makes a certain kind of sense, but by this point I think you're starting to ask an awful lot of someone, if only because having a gun pointed at you can make you forget how to breathe, let alone perform fancy footwork. At least, that's been my experience.

Some of the advice immortalized in this e-mail is beyond bad; it's life-threatening. Consider Safety Tip #4a: "If someone is in the car with a gun to your head, DO NOT DRIVE OFF! Instead gun the engine and speed into anything, wrecking the car. Your air bag will save you."

If I accomplish nothing else as a self-defense advocate, I'd at least like to convince people not to rely on their car's air bag to save them from gun-toting outlaws.

I mean, I can imagine a scenario (a very bad one indeed) where crashing my car is the only way to disrupt an armed attack. But I would hardly put it among my top nine or ten options. It belongs way down on the list, past possibilities like driving so slowly I stop traffic, pretending I am insane (I think I'd be good at this), or trying to convince my attacker that I have friends in Hollywood who could score him a movie deal if he just puts the gun away.

The tactical confusion on display in "9 Safety Tips for Women" is bad enough. What truly infuriates me is the way it—and a whole host of books, websites, and television programs that preach the same message—presents fearfulness, suspicion, and obedience to some obscure authority as the keys to safety. Specifically, as the keys to safety *for women.* This perverse framing is combined with an eye-rolling exasperation on the part of the e-mail's authors, a sense that women are feeble-minded children who, honestly, probably deserve to have bad things happen to them if they can't be bothered to *WISE UP.*

It's the same antagonistic tone that Anna brought to our self-defense workshop, and I'm still puzzled and exasperated by it. The other women in Anna's group had echoed her attitude, in their vague recollection that yelling "fire" was the proper response to an assault. They had never really interrogated the concept; they hadn't questioned its logic or thought to examine the motives or qualifications of the people behind it. They just accepted it. It was as if they felt they couldn't be trusted with their own safety, and any other authority at all trumped their own. These women seemed to have internalized the underlying theme of e-mails like "9 Safety Tips for Women"—that women are patsies and easy targets because we're idiots. As Safety Tip #4 explains, women become victims of violence because we don't have the sense to immediately flee the scene of any public activity we've just engaged in:

> Women have a tendency to get into their cars after shopping, eating, working, etc., and just sit (doing their checkbook, or making a list, etc.). DON'T DO THIS! The predator will be watching you, and this is the perfect opportunity for him to get in on the passenger side, put a gun to your head, and tell you where to go.

This single nugget of misguidance encapsulates the very worst elements of popular self-defense advice. In the first place, it frames a deadly attack as inevitable. Secondly, it offers no practical advice for reducing risk, other than generalized fearfulness and a furtive, scurrying exit from every social endeavor. It completely elides the implied corollary that *men* can feel perfectly free to sit in their cars, poring over *their* checkbooks, or making lists (do guys make lists?), or sending nude photos of themselves to their mistresses, or whatever manly things they do, without worrying that they'll suddenly feel the cold barrel of a gun at *their* temples. The bigger question of why women are so much more vulnerable than men is completely ignored. The *problem* is that *women* are *stupid enough to sit in their cars*! Good God in heaven, could a person *be* any stupider?

What astounds me most of all is that these "tips"—these restrictive, neurotic, impractical, unhelpful rules—have been painstakingly constructed by people who crave safety as if it were a drug. They want it so badly they're willing to create and inhabit a dystopian nightmare chockablock with hellish parking garages and armed predators.

The coda at the end of Safety Tip #5c sums up the sentiment behind the safety advice genre as a whole: "IT IS ALWAYS BETTER TO BE SAFE THAN SORRY," it declaims. "And better paranoid than dead."

I'm eternally grateful to Sensei Suzanne for showing me that we don't have to live in a world where those are our only choices.

It mystified me that anyone would settle for the kind of "safety" that denies your agency and rationality. I tried to imagine what living that way would be like, and all I could conjure up was a memory of the helplessness that had overwhelmed and paralyzed me in Hawaii, when I was stuck in a life I couldn't control.

As I thought about how I would respond to the next Anna I ran into (I could tell there were going to be more of them), I asked myself why the disempowering, illogical messages expressed in "safety" e-mails were so popular. Obviously they spoke to people's fears. And I could see, too, the appeal of simple answers, especially in dangerous situations. Fear makes it hard to think and reason; simplicity is a virtue when you're scared. Even bad advice appeals to people's desire for structure, certainty, and rules. I'm fussy about the rules I follow and who gives them to me, but there's no question that I need a significant amount of structure in my life. So I could see the allure in the e-mails' authority, the simplicity of knowing I should *never* wear overalls and *always* yell "fire."

My karate training, however, had exposed me to another, very different, set of rules—one that highlighted all the shortcomings in the "9 Safety Tips" approach to life. In 1938, Gichin Funakoshi, the founder of Shotokan karate, published a book called *The Twenty Guiding Principles of Karate.* Funakoshi's twenty rules, or Niju Kun, instruct students in the proper mind-set for mastering the martial arts. Almost every martial artist will hear something familiar in them, regardless of the style she trains in, whether it's the sober reminder that "to learn karate takes a lifetime," or the more unnerving admonition to "be aware at all times that you have millions of potential opponents." The Niju Kun cover all the bases.

I don't wish to oversimplify Funakoshi's rules (for one thing, I don't want to piss off the Shotokan people; they're pretty badass). But every time I reread the Niju Kun, I'm struck by their simplicity. The principles are short and to the point, and they're grounded in the rich, reliable experience of a master who dedicated his life to teaching. They provide the necessary structure for the complicated journey of the martial artist. And yet what's also striking is the freedom they grant the follower. Among the twenty rules there are few absolutes (like #2, "Never attack first in karate") and many relativities: "Know yourself first, then you can know others" (#4), "Don't assume what you learn from karate can't be used outside the dojo" (#8), "Don't think that you must win; remember instead that you don't have to lose" (#12). Funakoshi's rules prod the martial artist to see things differently, to question assumptions, and to find his or her own way. To study and investigate, cultivate the spirit, assess new situations and react intelligently; to be mindful of change, open to opportunity, and above all, to be patient. The Niju Kun are an invitation to learn, reflect, and grow.

If you happen to be familiar with Gichin Funakoshi's *Twenty Guiding Principles,* the tone and substance of an e-mail like "9 Safety Tips for Women" is especially jarring—the contrast between the work of an unrivaled master and the worst kind of amateur hour. The Niju Kun assume that people develop power when they explore new paths, not when they *always* dress or act a certain way. In fact, Funakoshi's only use of "always" comes in his twentieth and final guiding principle, "Always create and devise new things." His emphasis is clear, urging the *karateka* to remain open to new possibilities. How different from the standard self-defense advice for women, which orders us to squelch all our best impulses. The only thing the two documents have in common is their assumption that the reader lives in a constant state of deadly peril. This makes sense for an Okinawan who lived through the Meiji Restoration, but seems rather extreme for us.

Whatever era we happen to be born into, living in accordance with rules is vastly different from merely obeying them. The former allows growth; the latter does not.

If I hadn't fallen in love with karate, I might never have become conscious of that distinction. And if I hadn't had Sensei Suzanne as my teacher, I might never have noticed that many of the rules I was told to respect actually didn't respect me.

I handed out a lot of advice in my inaugural self-defense class: If one technique doesn't work, try a different one. State what you want. *Do something.* It was the same advice Sensei Suzanne had given me, and it harmonized with the spirit of karate, not with the hysteria of women's "safety tips." This, I decided, was a way I could take Gichin Funakoshi's admonition to heart: "Don't think that what you learn from karate can't be used outside the dojo." I might not have much luck teaching the Niju Kun to someone like Anna, or any other random gathering of Girl Scout leaders, but I could help them see the value in Funakoshi's approach to life—even if they didn't know that's what I was doing.

I myself was terribly lucky, all things considered, to have discovered Funakoshi's art. The average woman might not want or need karate in order to live her life relatively free from fear. But I sure did. As with my roundhouse kick, I had energy, but I lacked discipline. I needed something to steady me, something strong, in order to step out into the darkness and confront my fear.

Don't be afraid of the dark – grab darkness by the throat, kick its ass, push it down the stairs, and laugh at its haircut.

これもかなり乱暴である。（あまりうまいとは言えないが）
詩的なイメージを使うことによって、読者は自己の恐怖心と対峙し、
できる限り軽くあしらうことを求められている。

I'M LEARNING MY first new kata since I returned from Hawaii, and the lights have just gone out.

It's winter; I've been home for six months now. The air in the dojo is frigid; the ten-year-old carpet rasps my bare feet like pack ice. A half-dozen grim little lightbulbs provide the only illumination in this vast, whitewashed warehouse, but I'm used to the dimness. I understand that better lighting would cost money the school doesn't have, that this is a women's karate school, and that women and poverty often occupy the same spaces. So I know where every lightbulb is without even looking up. I've trained myself not to hit them with Arnis sticks or the long staff during weapons practice. I'm careful because I don't want showers of tiny, hot glass fragments spilling over me and embedding themselves in the ancient carpet, and also because I have no desire to face Sensei if I am careless enough to break a lightbulb in her dojo.

Sensei is about to teach me Gekisai Dai, a kata created in the 1930s by Miyagi Chojun, the founder of Goju-ryu karate. Now, as I work toward my brown belt, the last step before *shodan* (black belt), I'm learning more advanced kata. Kata are choreographed technique sequences, usually performed solo, wherein the *karateka* mimes a fight with an invisible opponent or opponents. Beginners' kata are fairly simple—perhaps twenty steps, including eight basic blocks and twelve punches. After yellow belt they become more intricate, mixing hard and soft styles, requiring techniques we don't practice every day. It's no longer a simple task to visualize what my imaginary opponent is doing—block his front kick, punch his midsection. Now I have to broaden my scope, to examine each movement I perform for clues as to what it might mean in an actual fight.

I'm excited about learning Gekisai Dai, thrilled to begin something new, even though it is about thirty-five degrees in the dojo tonight and I've been at work all day and my son will be asleep in bed by the time I drag my ass back home.

Gekisai Dai is a *mokuso* kata. Before you perform it, you close your eyes (*"Mokuso,"* the instructor tells you) and meditate. Then Sensei says, *"Yoi"* ("Ready"), and we open our eyes. And then the lights go out.

Darkness falls early in December, even in Texas, and apart from the reddish glow of a traffic signal that seeps through the corrugated plastic windows, it is inky black in the dojo.

A fuse has blown, Sensei Suzanne deduces instantly. She knows the building's every electrical quirk, and though we have a spare fuse, our landlord has locked the fuse box because someone keeps stealing the fuses out of it (we're not located in the best of neighborhoods). Now we have no heat and no light; nothing at all but a space in which to train.

I can't see Sensei shrug, but I don't have to. "Well," she says, a disembodied voice in the blackness at my right elbow, "you'll just have to learn Gekisai Dai in the dark."

I have always been afraid of the dark.

For an instant my mind snaps back to a warm summer night years ago, not long after I got married, when I came home and found a note from the police on the front door. Scott was still at school, the street was dark, and I had to unlock the door and turn on the porch light to read the note. It informed me that a neighbor at the end of our cul-de-sac had been raped the night before by a stranger who climbed to her second-floor window, cut a hole in the screen, and assaulted her while her young son slept in the next room. No suspect was in custody. Residents were asked to call the police if they noticed anything unusual.

I stood at the door then, in the pool of light from the porch lamp, and knew that if I spent any time at all thinking about this news, I would return to my car and go somewhere else, somewhere brightly lit and well peopled and safe, because I would be too afraid to do anything else. So instead of thinking about it, I went inside. I started turning on lights and methodically stomping through every room in the house, opening doors, sweeping aside the coats in the closet, the drapes in the living room; kicking piles of old boxes to see if they yelped; peering under furniture. The dogs followed me from room to room, mystified but eager to play along.

There was no one there, and I was glad of that, and yet a small part of me felt let down. I had challenged the darkness, and it retreated to fight another day. I just wanted to get the battle over with.

And now, I think as I shuffle my feet along the arctic cold of the dojo floor, here I am again, in the dark. Once again I'm about to fight an opponent who isn't there.

Gekisai Dai begins with familiar stances and techniques. At the outset there is a left pivot into *sanchin* stance, with a high block to ward off a blow as I turn toward my opponent. Sensei's voice describing each movement echoes in the dark and I can execute the techniques because I've done them before in other kata. Now she tells me to step forward into *zen* stance, with a face-level punch. After this I step back into *kiba dachi,* horse-riding stance, with a low block. Three stances in three counts: the emphasis is on maintaining stability through changing states; hip movement; generating power from the ground. I perceive the effects of the kata on my body more than usual because I am blind to everything else.

With the opponent on my left presumably neutralized, the sequence repeats on the right, against a second attacker: block, punch, block. Then I move forward, three slow steps in *sanchin* stance, with slow center blocks, breathing with the powerful abdominal tension called *ibuki.* In the dark, I can't see what I'm doing, but I can picture it in my head. I know where I am, I think.

Then Sensei sends me into the kata's first combination, and now I am truly beginning something new. I step in with a front kick, an elbow strike, a backfist, and a downblock and lower punch. This flurry of techniques is followed immediately by a sweep with my rear foot, a 180-degree pivot, a lunge forward with a knifehand strike to the neck, and a *kiai,* my voice barking out into the pitch-black cold. Now I am back in *kiba dachi,* a deep, low stance that loads potential energy into the large muscles of the legs. As I step forward again into the blackness, following Sensei's instructions, I am feeling my way with every nerve in my body—feeling the cold air on my face as I move through it blindly, feeling with my feet in the dark, not sure if I'm stepping in the right direction. Sensei Suzanne is a few feet away on one side of me, Jan is on the other, yet I am completely on my own.

I have no idea what I'm doing as I block invisible strikes and strike imaginary opponents. I've never done this before, possibly no one has ever done this—made these grand, emphatic gestures for the very first time, into the darkness. It is puzzling and profound and curiously beautiful, and as I move forward through the kata, tracing an unseen path on the floor, I start to feel, strangely enough, like I was born to do this—to listen, interpret, guess, and at the same time move with absolute certainty. What I look like is irrelevant; there is only how I feel. And I feel very powerful, there in the cold and the dark.

Fighting the darkness is seldom as easy as turning on the lights. More often, you have to go into the dark to meet what's there. Sometimes you have to fight the unseen on its own territory. Karate allowed me to do that, and to revel in the fight. I spent a long time preoccupied with the fear of darkness; of nameless, formless dangers. Karate, when I stumbled into it at Sun Dragon, gave me weapons with which to carve a path into the darkness, into the heart of fear. It gave me something to do in the dark besides tremble. When I finally went into the darkness without flinching, bringing my own power with me, the darkness changed. It wasn't foreign territory anymore. It became just as much my country as anyone else's; a place to explore, to learn in—to fight in, if I had to.

• • •

When my friend Laura's mother died, my childhood fear of the dark turned into something much deeper and more tangible. Her death was (as I now know, having studied the subject) statistically unlikely: a random, deadly encounter with a complete stranger, probably a serial murderer. The killer left a phone message with a local real estate agency expressing interest in buying a house. Laura's mother happened to be the agent on call that evening. She went to meet the potential client, telling her family she'd be back by dinnertime.

When it grew dark, Laura's father drove out to the vacant house the caller had asked about and found his wife's body. Her attacker probably hit her in the head with something heavy. The evidence indicated that she fought back. She had been stabbed multiple times, sexually assaulted, and strangled.

According to the FBI, out of maybe three thousand women murdered in an average year in America, perhaps five hundred to a thousand are killed by strangers. There are about 150 million women in this country, so that puts my chances —or yours, or your mom's—at around one in 150,000 in any given year. It's a pretty long shot.

But it's still the equivalent of ten jumbo jets going down annually, filled with mothers and daughters, wives and sisters. It happens. Women like Laura's mother disappear off the face of the earth, sentenced to death simply because they are women and some men consider them disposable.

That's darkness, and I stood in it when I heard about Laura's mother. I stood in it again later, on my front porch on a summer night, with a note from the police in my hand. I walk through it every time I cross a parking lot at night, or lock myself into my campus office when I work late. Darkness hides murderers and muggers and rapists, and it draws its veil across our lives in a hundred other ways—ways less likely to end up on TV but a lot more sinister. About two-thirds of the women murdered in America are killed not by strangers but by husbands or boyfriends. Girls are twice as likely as boys to be sexually exploited. Over half of sexual assaults are never reported. There's more, a lot more; you can look it up if you want. If you're female, you don't have to. You know it in every bone of your body, because you've spent your life locking doors and windows, avoiding certain parts of town, circling the parking lot to find a spot under a light. You've endured sleazy comments, groping hands, obscene phone calls, jealous threats, and insults. You've observed that date rape drugs can be bought online. ("Orders arrive within three days in discreet unmarked parcels.") You walk around looking mean all the time in the hope that pushing people away will keep you safe. You read idiotic e-mails that advise you to avoid overalls and crash your car on purpose, and you think, Well, maybe that's reasonable. You carry Mace, or a gun, or wonder if you should, because you know the darkness is all around you.

Women are half the world's population, yet we huddle inside our burrows, noses twitching, afraid to venture out into the open. We live like prehistoric humans once did, in fear of predators, loath to leave the fireside, to come out of our caves. Human beings are generally safe, now, from cave bears and saber-toothed tigers. And still, half of us cower and fear the darkness.

There's a primal place inside all of us that is full of very dark things indeed. But it's dangerous only if we fail to explore it. Every human has an innate capacity for violence and I, for one, am glad of it.

One afternoon, years before I took up karate, I was walking the dogs on a local hiking trail when two men on bikes blew past us from behind, breath rasping, their expensively shod feet pumping up and down. Those feet were too much for Memphis, who was a good dog but unfortunately also a sheepdog. All sheepdogs have a thing about feet. Feet in motion provoke herding dogs irresistibly to follow, and not only to follow but to give precise and imperative directions, usually with their teeth. Before I could yank back on his leash, Memphis lunged forward and seized the second biker neatly by the ankle, eliciting a yell and a thud as he came off his bike.

I have to say, no one throws a bigger hissy fit than a man wearing spandex. Of course, no one likes being bitten on the ankle, either. I was mortified by what my dog had done, and apologized. I completely understood the biker's fury, even though he wasn't bleeding. You'd expect someone in that situation to be mad. But you might not expect them to do what this guy did—something I believe he did solely because I was female. He told me he was going to pick up a rock and split my dog's head open with it.

Now, I understand anger all too well; I get angry every day. But I don't like bullies. I had been sympathetic, and apologetic, until this guy threatened violence. And not just violence against me, but against my thirty-pound dog. Honestly, how big a coward does a man have to be to threaten a woman's *dog*?

There was something about the sheer jackassedness of it, the rank egotism of a full-grown man bellowing at a woman he has never met, describing the violence he's about to do, that flipped a switch somewhere inside me. In that moment, I got tired of hiding in my cave and decided I would rather just fight the fucking bear.

"You know what?" I told the enraged biker. "There are plenty of rocks around here. If you want to split my dog's head open, you're welcome to try." I was pretty sure he wouldn't, but I was acutely aware that I was outnumbered, in an isolated place. I had my dogs, it's true, but aside from their ankle-biting skills they weren't much of a backup plan. I own dogs for comic relief, not for protection. So while I thought the guy's threat was ridiculous (he was riding a carbon frame bike with full suspension, for one thing—not a great way to flaunt one's hooligan credentials), I was, absolutely and literally, ready to rip his face off if he tried to touch me or my dog. And I'm pretty sure I looked like it. The two bikers regarded me as if they had suddenly noticed a big warning label on my forehead—DANGER: LIGHT FUSE AND GET AWAY. The one who hadn't been bitten finally muttered, "Come on, man, let's go." And after a little more blustering, they did.

The man in spandex limped away with dog slobber on his ankle and a lot of unexpended testosterone. I, on the other hand, was shaking, sick to my stomach, and light-headed. For days I wondered if I should stop going to the park alone. Curiously, I didn't wonder too much about what might have happened if a fight had ensued, despite my lifelong habit of mapping out disastrous scenarios. There are plenty of things I'm afraid of, many of which I haven't even dreamed up yet. But fighting itself isn't one of them. I'm not even afraid of losing fights. I've lost lots of them; I expect I'll lose more. I couldn't care less. All I ask for, all I really want, is a chance to do some damage.

There's something unhealthy about that attitude, I know. It could land me in a lot of trouble, and it's unlikely to make the world at large a more peaceful place. But it's what I am. The darkness doesn't just surround me; I contain quite a bit of it myself. Whatever it was that uncoiled inside me in response to the bike rider's threat, that stood up and snarled, wasn't going away. And I wouldn't want it to go away. It might be a dangerous thing, but I think I'd be even more vulnerable without it.

Since that ugly encounter on the hiking trail, I've spent a lot of time exploring my own capacity for violence, measuring and testing and hopefully learning to control it. Fortunately for me (and everyone else), I've been able to do that in the structured, disciplined space of the dojo.

Here is what happens to an opponent in the second movement of Gekisai Dai:

The kata has begun with an attack from my opponent. In accordance with Gichin Funakoshi's admonition, "Never attack first in karate," my opening movement is defensive: turning to block his punch. (I try, as Sensei Suzanne taught me, not to always assume my attacker is male, but my personal experience has made male attackers much easier for me to visualize.) Once my assailant has initiated the conflict, I'm free to attack, so on the second count, I step forward and punch him in the head.

Let's look at what goes into that punch. On the previous move, I have chambered my right hand in a tight fist, up under my armpit. My biceps and triceps are tensed, ready to explode outward again, and as I step forward with my right foot, my shoulder lags just a little bit, preserving some energy, creating slightly more distance between my fist and my target, in which to build speed and momentum. The stance I'm moving into, *zenkutsu dachi,* requires me to drop my weight and push forward with my left leg, throwing most of my body mass straight into my opponent behind my punch.

If I time the technique correctly, and articulate all the complex body mechanics properly, my fist will carry all the power of my arm, my back and trunk muscles, the extra inertia from my shoulder as I finally allow it to travel forward, and an additional boost of energy from my hip, which rotates like the shoulder but with a smaller radius.

All of this upper-body power is bolstered from below by the thrust of my left leg, which has gone from flexed to fully extended and is, at the moment of impact, braced firmly against the floor behind me. The principles in play are identical to the architectural concept of the flying buttress, but the physics are reversed: instead of redirecting the lateral force of massive stone walls downward into the ground, my leg is directing force *from* the ground laterally *into* the target. In a way, I'm hitting my opponent not merely with my fist, or even my entire body, but with the Cathedral of Amiens.

To hell with driving your car into a wall; *that's* the way to fuck up an attacker.

And that's just the first punch. In the remaining eighteen moves of the kata, I'll strike my hapless attacker, or his accomplices, eleven more times. Every single one of those strikes, if properly landed on a real human, could kill him. *One blow, sudden death.* And Gekisai Dai is pretty tame, compared to some kata.

Karate is full of this disturbingly specific violence. Indeed, that's the essence of the art. Logically, I suppose I should be horrified by this. And yet when I perform Pinan Sono Ni, and visualize myself plunging a spearhand into someone's throat, grabbing his trachea, and then breaking his jaw and possibly his neck with an upper forearm block, what goes through my mind is not horror, but a grim sense of accomplishment.

Could I really do this to someone, I wondered as I worked my way through the rest of Gekisai Dai's precise destruction? The biker who threatened my dog, or the rapist who failed to appear in my apartment? Could I drive my fist into their skulls, or crush their tracheas, or mutilate them in some other way?

I'm pretty sure I could. I hope I never have to. And I don't suppose it would be easy, or leave me the same person afterward that I was before. But I'd rather be a different person and still be alive than not be a person anymore.

Gekisai Dai ends with three double punches, to the chest and ribs—a solid ending, not especially gory, but emphatic.

"Naore," Sensei Suzanne says when we have reached the last movement, meaning, "return to ready stance." I step back into *heiko dachi,* balanced, feet apart, fists clenched, ready for the next kata, the next opponent, the next challenge. Ready for whatever comes out of the darkness.

Push yourself past your limits; then let your friends push you further.

限界を超えるために、自分で自分を駆り立てよう。
そこから先は、今度は友達に背中を押してもらおう。

TESTING FOR BLACK belt is a lot like getting married, except you have to fight all the bridesmaids. You wear white, your friends and family are all invited, the venue is decorated with flowers, and there's a party afterward. Also, you're terrified most of the time, and the photos are usually disappointing.

Promotion tests, like a lot of terrifying experiences, share a sameness—time stretches out endlessly, and the lack of escape options feels paralyzing for so long that eventually it just becomes a bore. Every time I test for a higher rank, I know I'll be dry-mouthed and nervous and not sure what to do next; indeed, not exactly sure what the hell I'm doing at all. I know I'll be tired before I even start the test; they make sure of that. I'll experience moments of heart-stopping panic—when I will know with absolute certainty that I can't do what is asked of me—utter confusion, disorientation, hyperventilation, nausea. That's the whole point of the test, to make you cope with more than you think you can.

After five or six tests, though, the novelty wears off, and though the discomfort and panic remain, they're familiar sensations. You almost start to feel nostalgic about them, the way survivors of the London Blitz have fond memories of sleeping in the subway tunnels. You don't become entirely sanguine about testing, but you acclimate to it.

The gamets, however, never lost their novelty.

I still don't know why we called them *gamets*. The term wasn't, as I originally assumed, related to *gamut*, a word that is itself frequently confused with *gauntlet*, as in "running the gauntlet," which is kind of what a gamet was like. No one even knew if *gamet* was a karate-specific term, like *osu*; as far as I could tell, it didn't mean anything in standard Japanese. All I really knew was that the gamets Sensei Suzanne put us through—a series of nonstop sparring rounds against multiple opponents—were a kind of miniature version of Kyokushin's fabled Hundred Man Kumite (*kumite* meaning "fight"). The Hundred Man Kumite has been attempted by only a handful of Kyokushinkai, and finished by even fewer. (And several of *them* had to be taken straight to the hospital afterward.) The gamet was supposedly our way of honoring this tradition.

But the origin of the term *gamet* remained a mystery, like so many elements of our Kyokushin training at Sun Dragon. We were never formally affiliated with any of the schools left behind after Mas Oyama's death, so it was typical of our peculiar relationship to Kyokushin that we followed the gamet custom without any sure knowledge of its origins. We were used to observing certain protocols as received wisdom, though it was often unclear from whom we had received them, or when or why. Explanations were sparse, and they sifted down from Sensei Suzanne through the senior students like gossip in a small town. Because Sensei had been known to change the explanations from time to time, there could be two or three versions of any given ritual or technique in play simultaneously.

"The two-punch combination on the sixth movement of Tsuki No Kata"—I asked Gina and Jan before class one night—"is it low/middle, or middle/low?"

"Low/middle," Jan said, at which Gina got the pained expression that many of us wore during such discussions, and said she'd learned it as middle/low.

They looked at each other, and at me, and shrugged. Sensei must have changed the sequence at some point, presumably to correct an error. But how had she determined that error? Who was the ultimate authority? Sensei's former teachers? The British branch of the IFK (International Federation of Karate)? The blurry mimeographed book of Kyokushin kata that Sensei kept in her desk, which was, for some obscure reason, written in German? No one could say.

Our mission was clear, our lineage murky. The Kyokushinkai of Sun Dragon were like a community of shipwreck survivors on a desert island who persisted in assembling every seventh day, on what two-thirds of the company were fairly certain was Sunday, to sing poorly remembered hymns. We had our faith, and very little else, but it was enough.

I tested for my Kyokushin black belt two years after returning from Hawaii. I may not have known why a gamet was called a gamet as I prepared for my test, but I knew what I was in for. I'd been introduced to the gamet tradition soon after I joined Sun Dragon during my graduate school days, when an exceptionally large cohort of advanced students went up for promotion. Joy and three other students tested for green belt, Gina for her brown belt, and two women, Karen and Jan, were black belts candidates. I knew Jan pretty well by this time. She'd kept me updated through a succession of alarming-sounding girlfriends, various body piercings, and a job in customer service that was a decidedly poor fit for her skill set. That summer she tried to persuade me to go to Nevada with her to dig for opals. "The trip will pay for itself!" she insisted, but I had to finish writing my dissertation, on perceptions of the actress in the Victorian marriage-plot novel. (I now realize I should have gone opal-digging instead.)

I was glad not to have to fight in Jan's black belt gamet. I was only a yellow belt at the time, and I had no firm idea of what a gamet involved, but I knew what sparring with Jan was like. I'd taken some beatings from her that were so disorienting that when I went to take a shower afterward, I was surprised to find that my sports bra wasn't, in fact, turned inside out.

The outset of Jan's test was much like all the others I later witnessed or participated in at Sun Dragon. The candidates lined up in rank order: brown belts, then green, then yellow, blue, and white. Everyone demonstrated basic techniques, combinations, kata, self-defense, and whatever else Sensei had dreamed up that day. Sometimes she'd pull people out of the audience and make the candidates teach them something from the curriculum. Every once in a while—just often enough to make us wonder if this was one of those times—she'd have the testers break boards. After a couple of hours of good, clean fun along these lines, the white and blue belts bowed out, and it was time for the gamet.

There was a distinct change in the atmosphere at this point. The entire student body assembled out on the training floor, and Sensei also summoned all the spectators who had been sitting along the walls of the dojo. She gathered everyone into a ring, maybe twenty feet across, and then she gave a little speech.

"The gamet is a Kyokushin tradition," she began—she didn't go into further detail—"but it isn't required for promotion. It's entirely voluntary. All the women fighting today have chosen to gamet. We're here to test them, to give them this gift of a challenge to their spirit and their physical endurance.

"Please be supportive," she went on, in the way that only Sensei Suzanne could, which implied that anyone who wasn't supportive would leave the room in a bucket. "This is a celebration of what our students have learned. What they're about to do is really hard. It may look frightening to those of you who haven't seen it before. Rest assured, we're going to take care of one another."

Then she called a green belt candidate into the ring, looked at her clipboard, and read out the name of the first opponent, who bounded into the ring much more enthusiastically than the candidate had. The fighters detailed for the next few rounds jogged eagerly on the sidelines, ready for their turn.

"Face me; bow," Sensei said to the fighters, and then, "Face your partners; bow." She held her hand up, suspended between the two women for a moment, then dropped it and said, *"Hajime!"*—"Begin!"

I knew what to expect from Kyokushin sparring by now, so what I saw didn't surprise me too much, but I wasn't prepared for what I heard. The minute the gamet started, there was an instant roar of encouragement from the onlookers, a solid wall of noise. For the first couple of rounds it was hard to even distinguish what anyone was saying. It took a minute before I could pick out a few comments, things like "Go, Joy!" or "Nice kick!" or "That's it! Follow up!"

I've never been much of a cheerleader myself, but at Sun Dragon you weren't allowed to watch quietly; anything less than full-throated support was considered rude. So I started shouting along with everyone else, little realizing that I would have to keep doing this for the next hour and a half.

Pretty soon it became clear that gamet sparring was different from regular sparring. The pace was faster, the punches harder, and there were none of the lulls that usually punctuate casual sparring. The circle was kept tight around the fighters, so they couldn't back away from each other to buy time. Sparring is always exhausting, and you learn to look for any opportunity to take a breath, plot strategy, or just enjoy not being hit for a couple of seconds. In a gamet, the opponent's job was to deny the tester any and all such opportunities, and Sensei watched the fighters like a hawk to make sure there was no respite for the candidate. "Push her, Denise," she would say. "Don't let her rest. Get in there. Make her fight." If a candidate started to flag, there was coaching, from Sensei and from the audience: "Keep your hands up!" "Use your feet!" "Push her back!" Whenever the candidate landed a good shot there was cheering and whistling.

After two minutes of intense combat, Sensei called out, *"Yame!"* ("Stop!") Both fighters were windblown and red-faced, and the one who wasn't testing bowed gratefully out of the ring. The candidate had about three seconds to catch her breath before she was bowing to her next opponent, hearing *"Hajime!"* again, and fighting some more.

A major logistical challenge for any gamet was procuring enough people to fight the candidates. At this particular test, the seven candidates fought a total of forty-five rounds, and the school had only about twenty-five students altogether, many of them, like me, not yet advanced enough to participate. Sensei fought a few rounds herself, but she still had to think creatively to fill out the roster. So Jan and Karen, who went last, ended up fighting their even-numbered rounds against each other, and odd-numbered rounds back-to-back against multiple attackers. Their ninth and final round was something of a scrum; Sensei simply emptied the stands and sent everyone wearing sparring gear into the ring. When it was over, Jan told me, "By the end, I thought Sensei was going to tie a pork chop to my ass and turn a pack of wild dogs loose on us."

Sensei might well have done this if she hadn't been a vegetarian.

My own Kyokushin black belt test took place three years after Jan's. It was comparatively free of drama, unlike my yellow belt test, during which I was unable to speak due to a viral infection my son had given me; or my brown belt test, where I got stabbed in the eye with a rubber knife (entirely my own fault; you can't block sloppy against a knife). This time, I was sweat-soaked and limp after twenty minutes, precisely as expected. I managed not to get stabbed during the self-defense portion of the test. I made it through the kata section, which is especially long for black belts, including several iterations of Sanchin Kata. Sanchin is always a high point during tests, at least for the audience. It's performed with *ibuki* breathing and dynamic tension, the goal being to keep your abdominal muscles engaged while breathing deeply and efficiently. Theoretically, this makes you less vulnerable to an impact. To test the theory, Sensei would send a team of advanced students out onto the floor during the kata to punch the candidates in the stomach. They would also check the testers' stances by kicking their shins and calves. It was more fun to watch than it was to undergo, but it sure did reveal who was breathing correctly, and who wasn't. If you were breathing correctly, you didn't fall over.

On my path to black belt, I'd survived two gamets of my own, for my green and brown belts, and fought in quite a few for other students. But when two or three hours of my black belt test had ticked away, and all the other material had been covered, my heart still gave the same familiar, horrible little lurch as Sensei Suzanne said, "OK, everyone who has sparring gear, put it on and meet me in the back. If you're gameting, stay warm."

In the changing room, those of us preparing to gamet nervously strapped on our shinguards and gloves, looking taut and pale, and trying to laugh at the jokes of the lighthearted nontesters. "This is the fun part!" someone was sure to say, or more helpfully, "It's almost over!" Jan or one of the other old-timers might wax nostalgic: "Ah, I remember my first gamet. We had a guest instructor who offered to fight a few rounds, and the woman broke my cheekbone."

The stories of past gamets never lost any color in the retelling, but there were actually pictures of the infamous fracture and black eye Jan sustained at her green belt gamet. Everyone had seen them. They were hard not to think about as you slipped your mouthpiece between your teeth and ducked under the dressing-room curtain onto the training floor.

If you weren't testing, you headed to the back of the dojo, where Sensei stood with her clipboard, handing out assignments—who would fight whom, in which rounds, and what their jobs were. (The jobs were usually one of three things:

tire them out if you're fighting early in the match; in the middle rounds, keep them moving; if you're in at the end, make them look good.) If you were gameting you turned in the other direction when you came out of the changing room, toward the front of the dojo, where the gamet would take place. You stretched your legs self-consciously, trying to stay loose; maybe you threw a few halfhearted kicks that didn't fool anybody. The gamet candidates formed a tense knot of concentrated let's-get-this-over-with misery in stark contrast to the carefree group in the back, who were laying out the battle plan. Gamet candidates studiously avoided asking themselves, Why, exactly, did I choose to do this?

For a green belt gamet, you fought five consecutive rounds, or ten minutes total. For brown belt, it was seven rounds; for black belt, nine. In theory, that meant facing five, seven, or nine opponents, but the exact number could vary, depending on how many people showed up with sparring gear and how Sensei was feeling. If she ran low on advanced belts, she might send two yellow belts in together to round out a match. You never knew, in advance, exactly whom you would fight. You could request certain people ahead of time, but it wasn't until each person faced you in the ring that you knew who your gamet opponents were.

I had specifically requested Jan as one of my gamet partners. Sensei sent her in for the opening round, and explicitly tasked her with knocking me over, which Jan did about three seconds into the match. I had learned a thing or two on my way to black belt, though, and I did not go down alone. On our way to the floor, Jan punched me in the head a couple of times, but as we landed, I managed to reach her inner thigh, which I pinched viciously—not a legal sparring technique, but once you're on the ground, in my opinion, you're no longer sparring. Also, I was betting Sensei Suzanne couldn't see what I was doing.

Jan yelped—in point of fact, I'm ninety-nine percent certain she swore, a major faux pas in the dojo—and bounded up off the floor. I did, too, naturally. Getting back up was, after all, the whole point of the test and the gamet. For the past three and a half years of my life, I'd been making myself into someone who got back up every time she went down.

In a gamet, you always got back up, whatever it took, because the people around you were willing you to get up. I like to think that experience will serve me well if I ever find myself in a similar situation, minus the cheering crowd. After all, when you always *have* gotten up, it stands to reason that you always *will.*

Jan and I fought out the next two minutes like we were in the center of a tornado—a loud, chaotic, but very supportive and nurturing tornado. I enjoyed myself hugely, and I think Jan did, too. She was laughing, but then, she always did laugh when she was fighting.

I didn't enjoy the eight succeeding rounds nearly as much. In fact, I remember very little about them—who stepped into the ring to fight me, how many punches I took, whether I landed any myself at all. No matter how long you were scheduled to fight, your second round was always the point when the gamet really started to suck. You'd just done one intense round of sparring that you were reasonably happy with, and you knew, with absolute certainty, that you could not do four or six or eight more rounds like that one. You had no air in your lungs. Your legs were already weak from the previous hours of testing. Your hands did not respond with anything like the kind of speed they needed to block, let alone throw a punch. Your uppermost thought was, *Uh-oh. Maybe this wasn't such a great idea after all.* (This is the exact same thought I've had both times I've gone into labor.) It became abundantly clear that the next eight or twelve or sixteen minutes of your life were going to hurt, and there wasn't much you could do about it.

So you did what you could. You covered your head, blocked what you saw coming and absorbed what you didn't, and tried to take a shot at your opponent if the opportunity arose. You tried to remember how to breathe. You rationed your kicks to avoid burning the extra oxygen required to lift your legs above waist level. This was not exhibition-style sparring at all. It was a much bigger challenge—coping with an opponent when all your resources were expended.

Fighting takes an awful lot of energy. It takes creativity. It takes persistence. Even if you like to fight, you'll eventually reach a point where you want to stop. The whole point of the gamet was to push the candidate—who had to enjoy fighting, or she would never have reached this point in her training—to the point where she wanted to stop. And then make her keep fighting. It felt like the exact opposite of empowerment, while you were in the midst of it. But when you reached the other side—when Sensei called out *"Yame!"* and you stared dumbly at her, your lungs heaving, waiting for the next opponent to appear in front of you, and then grasped the fact that there were no more opponents, that it was over, you were done—then it felt a lot better.

And by the time you regained control of your breathing, and took off your sparring gear, and drank about a gallon of water, and lined up to receive your new belt—then, it felt awesome.

• • •

You always learn something about yourself when you're tested. My dissertation defense, for example, which had occurred between my green and brown belt tests, was a lot less fun than a gamet, but still instructive. At some point as I looked around the table at the impassive faces of my faculty committee members, I thought, *What a shame that I can't hit any of you. Because this test would be over a lot faster if I could.* That was the moment I realized I probably wasn't destined to make a living writing scholarly articles about Jane Austen novels.

People try to test us every day: strangers, employers, children, telemarketers. Some tests we don't have much choice about—the illness, the job loss, the betrayal. Others we choose. During my black belt gamet, I discovered that not only could I get back up as often as I needed to, I could give my opponent something to think about while I was still on the ground. And I found out what happened when I didn't think I could fight anymore: I kept fighting. My gamet provided indelible proof that, regardless of my skill level as a *karateka,* no matter how much fear I carried around with me, I was a fighter.

When you're tested, you find out who you really are, and who your friends are. The pictures of me taken in my new black belt after the gamet aren't perfect, but I like them better than my wedding pictures. I'm surrounded by friends I trust, who took care of me and were willing and able to challenge me. I look tired but happy, which is how everyone looked after a gamet if they weren't clutching an ice pack. And sometimes even then.

The gamet at Sun Dragon was a truly exceptional ordeal, and it was an extraordinary gift—one that could be given only when a whole lot of people put vast amounts of time and energy into making it happen. They had to train with you, sweat with you, show up at your test, and be willing to spar with an exhausted fighter who had very little control—a dangerous activity. They had to be ready to tie a pork chop to your ass if necessary—whatever it took to push you past any limit you had set for yourself. No one but your friends could force you over those walls, into new territory.

We are connected by the distance between us.

我々は、互いの間の距離によってつながっている。

IN MARTIAL ARTS, the term *mai-ai,* or "range," refers to the distance between you and your partner. It's a physical construct with temporal and emotional elements. *Mai-ai* combines the ideas of the space between two opponents, the speed with which each can close the distance, and their choices about when and how to do so. Speed, control, and timing are critical for managing *mai-ai* successfully. The interval separating you from your partner is relative, and fluid. If you're faster than your opponent, then you are, in effect, "closer" to her than she is to you, because you can cross the distance between you in less time. If you can dominate emotionally and intimidate your opponent, you can increase the physical space between you by making her back away. If you're deceptive, you can lure her in. Or you may be able to disrupt her timing, making her nerves react just a beat too slowly or too quickly. It's a tricky dance; you and your partner have to cooperate in order to fight, but at all times you're in direct competition, each seeking to subtly manipulate the *mai-ai,* to control the distance—in all its dimensions—between you.

When you engage in this dance with someone, especially when you do so night after night, over a period of years, you learn a tremendous amount about her, about yourself, and about relationships in general—the distance between people, how we increase or decrease it, and how we successfully manage change and transition in our lives.

It was a typical Wednesday night at Sun Dragon, not long after my black belt gamet: advanced class was under way, sparring was the entirety of the lesson plan, and Sensei Suzanne was kicking my ass back and forth across one end of the dojo.

Sparring with Sensei Suzanne was always a special challenge. Her status as my teacher made her intimidating to begin with, and she was also, as you'd expect, a formidable fighter. On this particular night she was pushing me harder than usual. I had just earned my black belt, and she didn't want me resting on my laurels.

As usual when I sparred with Sensei, I was trying to control the *mai-ai* by alternating between two extremes: (1) resisting the urge to run away screaming, and (2) making suicidal frontal attacks in an effort to seem aggressive. Not surprisingly, it was hard to strike a balance.

For the most part, Sensei fought in a typical Kyokushin style, moving in aggressively. She had plenty of power and commitment, and her reputation preceded her. I found it petrifying, which I probably could have adapted to, eventually, if fear had been the only consideration. Constant, predictable aggression gives you something to work with as you manage *mai-ai*. You can slip past an aggressive opponent's techniques and use her momentum to add force to your own strikes. You can fade back for a while until she's overconfident, and then surprise her with a sudden reversal. If your opponent is big and mean in addition to being aggressive, the match might not be much fun. Still, you have options.

Unfortunately, Sensei had trained in Aikido as well as Kyokushin. The *tenkan* turn—a 180-degree rear pivot fundamental to Aikido throws—was her not-so-secret weapon. That night she executed *tenkan* over and over by stepping in toward me, straight on my center line. As I was preparing to block a high punch or a kick, she would suddenly twist, swinging her rear leg behind her, and spin past me, mere inches from my shoulder. From my perspective, she simply disappeared just as she got within striking range. And as I stood there wondering where she had gone, she would wallop my temple with a backfist.

Every time she did this, I would whip around to face her, looking, I'm sure, like a bird that has flown into a window. *What the hell was that?* I would think. *I didn't even see it.*

"You didn't see that, did you?" Sensei would ask. And I would shake my head, partly to indicate *no,* and partly to dispel the ringing in my ears.

"That's *tenkan* turn," she would say. I knew what *tenkan* was; we had practiced it in drills plenty of times. But I had no clue how to react to it when it was used on me. Over and over again, Sensei flitted past and blindsided me with the same technique. I wasn't getting the lesson, but she kept trying to teach it to me.

Timekeeping was fairly casual when we sparred during class. Four or five pairs of students would be in action at once, waiting for Sensei to tell us to stop and change partners. She usually did this every three minutes or so, but if she was involved in an interesting match, the round could stretch out to ten minutes or more. I don't know how long she spent trying to beat the idea of *tenkan* into my head that night. Eventually she decided I wasn't going to miraculously figure out how to defend against it, and called, *"Yame!"*

Time for a new partner, and a new way of addressing *mai-ai.*

Jan, as I've already intimated, was an aggressive opponent, though less terrifying than Sensei Suzanne. She was also wily, however, and she moved more like a boxer than a martial artist, with a boxer's footwork and economy of motion. One of her favorite ways to manage *mai-ai* was to circle around me, just outside of striking distance, like a sheepdog working the herd. This meant I had to keep pivoting to track her movements, and inevitably as I turned I'd expose some vulnerable point, and she would barrel in on me. If I was fast enough, I could shift off center and avoid her. Sometimes I was fast enough, but more often I was dizzy from all the circling.

Jan's most fearsome weapon for managing *mai-ai,* though, was her capacity to neutralize force. As a newly minted black belt, I expected great things from myself in the sparring ring. Or failing that, I assumed I should at least be able to push people around a little bit now. I had some power at my disposal. My black belt was proof, and I had earned it in part by fighting Jan.

Yet that night, the same thing was still happening that always happened when I sparred with Jan. I would punch or kick her, *hard,* and it would have no effect (unless she laughed). This was disconcerting because, apart from the obvious shock of seeing an opponent laugh off my best offense, it disrupted my timing and gave Jan control over the *mai-ai.* Usually, when you hit a normal person, there's a brief pause, even if only for a fraction of a second, while her body adjusts to the application of outside force. The better the fighter, the shorter the pause. Jan never seemed to react at all, and I was bitterly disappointed that even as a black belt, I couldn't make a dent in her.

I had no idea how to deal with the way Jan's freakish absorbency affected my own body. Typically, that instant when you land a blow, and your opponent is absorbing it, is also a moment during which your own body adjusts to the exchange of force—the moment where your roundhouse kick finally discharges all that energy that would spin you around in circles if you had missed. When I kicked Jan, the energy didn't feel like it was passing into someone else. It just sort of disappeared—*phht*—like it had been swallowed up. As if I were kicking molasses. It brought me to a dead stop, like a motorboat when you cut the engines, and left me bobbing in the water.

If earning my black belt had made me any better at sparring, it wasn't showing tonight. All the power I'd worked so hard to acquire was fizzling. And it didn't help to get mad about it, because the harder I hit Jan, the more she laughed.

That laugh was indicative of the way Jan fought, and of why she fought, too. Her benevolence in the ring was just another way she controlled the *mai-ai*. Jan could have quickly and easily beaten down everyone in the dojo except Sensei Suzanne, but it wouldn't have been any fun for her. Jan wanted to have fun. And she wanted her opponent to have fun, too.

Even though, on this particular evening, I was frustrated that being a black belt wasn't all I had imagined, I was still having fun. Jan had superb control over her own power, so when she did clobber me, it hurt a lot less than it could have. As a result, I was willing to fight far less defensively than I otherwise would have. With Jan, I didn't veer between panic and self-destructive onslaughts as I had in my round with Sensei Suzanne. Instead, the *mai-ai* felt open and flexible, and I had a chance to try new things—shifts in stance, combination kicks, tempo changes. I knew I wouldn't suffer instant annihilation for doing this, and I also knew that Jan would keep me honest by busting me if I got sloppy. I felt safe experimenting, because the worst that could happen (what *always* eventually happened) was that Jan would end up in my face, slugging me pretty much at will. Whereupon I would do my best to imitate her and let the force of each blow pass through me, into the ground, dissipated.

We could connect or disconnect; we could engage or leave; we could sink power shots into each other's guts or dance around each other just out of range. It was all the same game. Take it or leave it, Jan's sparring style implied; but I knew taking it would be more fun.

And it was, until Sensei Suzanne called out *"Yame!"* again, and I bowed to Jan, and found another partner.

Sparring with Joy, who earned her black belt a year before I did, was a completely different enterprise from sparring Jan. Joy didn't approach *mai-ai* as aggressively. She controlled the interval between herself and her partner with exceptional precision, enabled by her flawless technical execution and an impressive ability to improvise and change the rhythm of an exchange. I didn't know anyone else who fought like that, and Joy's sparring style perplexed me for months, until she mentioned that she had been a dancer before she started karate. Then I understood what I had been noticing: she managed *mai-ai* like a dancer. Her years of dancing had endowed her with the footwork to go wherever she wanted in relation to a partner. Dancing had also given her the ability to move an opponent around at will. Joy let her opponents think they were leading and she was following when, in fact, she was calling all the shots.

That night, it was tempting to think that Joy, who is younger and slighter than me, was one of the people I might be able to push around a little. I wasn't tempted long. Joy wasn't a hard hitter—a round against her usually left me feeling like I'd been pummeled by a butterfly—but she could hit hard when she wanted to, and that night she wanted to. Instead of dominating the *mai-ai,* I felt as if I were at a job interview, applying for a position I was manifestly unqualified to fill. Our interaction was characterized by a respectful give-and-take, but Joy was clearly in charge, and she picked apart my defense with an executive's attention to detail. She also —this is a trait I've since noticed in other trained dancers— smiled the whole time.

I would move in behind a punch, and Joy would evade it while simultaneously repositioning herself perfectly to either kick me (if she chose to move away) or punch me (if she preferred to stay close). She wasn't especially deceptive in her attacks. Directness typified Joy's interactions inside and outside the dojo, so I could usually figure out what she was going to throw at me before it was too late. But she was relentless, and full of ideas: if I blocked her opening kick, she was ready with a head/body punch combination, and if I managed to duck one and parry the other, she would step nimbly around me and start punching from the other side. Unlike Sensei Suzanne, Joy didn't disappear. She was always right there, connected to me. Her control of *mai-ai* reflected her dancer's sense of partnership. You'd see very similar interval management in a Fred Astaire and Ginger Rogers dance routine, if Ginger Rogers punched Fred Astaire in the nose every few measures.

I'm not a dancer myself, and never will be, so while I didn't enjoy the bruises I was collecting on my forearms and shins that night, I felt a certain gratitude to Joy for giving me an inkling of what it must be like to dance. Sparring with her reminded me that while my goal in a sparring match was to control the *mai-ai,* I could benefit just as much, in the long term, from experiencing how the other person controls it.

I couldn't have predicted that, in less than two years, I would be addressing Joy as Sensei Joy, when she would be using the same talents she employed to manage *mai-ai*—her precision, focus, and executive ability—to run Sun Dragon.

When Sensei called *"Yame!"* again, Joy and I bowed to end our match, and I turned to face my final partner of the evening.

KJ was still a brown belt at that point. She had joined Sun Dragon the year after I did. Like Jan, KJ played full-contact pro football for years—beginning with the Austin Rage in the WPFL (number 68), and later for the Outlaws in the National Women's Football Association. KJ was a key member of her team's offensive line, and when she sparred she started every round as if she were exploding off the line of scrimmage. Now that she's a second-degree black belt, KJ has developed more control. But back in those days, sparring with her always made me feel that I was of only passing interest to her; her real goal was to trample over me and sack the quarterback. She controlled *mai-ai* exclusively through forward energy, always closing, crushing, pushing me back, rolling over me.

You can still see her forward bias when she teaches footwork drills during sparring class these days. "The three basic moves are scoot, slide, and step," she'll tell the students. "'Scoot' means moving forward three to six inches." She demonstrates this by surging forward about two and a half feet. She honestly isn't aware that she's moved this far; that's just what three inches feels like to her.

KJ's reliance on forward motion should have been exploitable in a sparring match, and I did my best to use my fledgling black belt skills. Certainly backing up and running away wouldn't work; she would have just chased me down, and then she'd have hit me at a higher speed. If I had been allowed to grapple, I'd have had her in the palm of my hand, because one thing KJ couldn't do well was change directions. If I caught or jammed her foot during a thrust kick, I had a good chance at toppling her backward. Alas, grappling was not allowed.

A better fighter than I would have controlled the *mai-ai* in that match by working the angles to evade blows and moving in and out of range. I couldn't do that; not for very long, anyway—it required even more energy than backing up, plus I lacked the patience. I dislike being bulldozed, and it makes me angry, so I tried to foil KJ's management of the *mai-ai* between us by simply planting my feet and refusing to move at all. Instead of letting her build momentum by crossing the distance between us, I stayed in close. This was sort of nihilistic (and guaranteed some heavy damage), but it did let me land a punch now and then. It wasn't a very smart way to handle *mai-ai*; it resulted in a lot of what we call "clashing," which is pretty much what it sounds like.

"Your problem," KJ told me when we broke off for a minute to adjust our shin guards, "is that you think you weigh two hundred and forty pounds."

Sparring brings out the essential elements of your personality, and the truth is that I'm stubborn and I don't like to share. I know perfectly well I don't weigh 240 pounds, but I'm carrying at least a hundred pounds of ego. And if I couldn't control the *mai-ai* with KJ, I wasn't going to let her control it, either.

Curiously, when we're not sparring, KJ and I have always had the most jovial of relationships. We find each other endlessly amusing. These days, after years of sparring each other, we interact effortlessly in front of a class, regardless of which one of us is supposed to be teaching. KJ's enthusiasm for her art is loud and infectious, and my penchant for providing color commentary during my every waking moment creates a natural counterpoint.

"Straight into the gut," she'll tell the advanced students as we work on knife attacks. "If you want, you can give the blade a twist at the end." She demonstrates, grinning, and everyone says, *"Eww,"* quietly. Then I point out, "It's the only way you're gonna get the knife back," upon which they all say, *"Eww"* loudly, while KJ chortles loudly. "Suction," I explain simply to the revolted students, and the expression on their faces leaves KJ helpless with laughter.

Sparring with her now is nowhere near as overwhelming as it was on that night so soon after my black belt test. By the time we finished our round, I felt like I'd been run over with a potato picker, and I was glad to bow out and say good night to all my partners. They had taught me a lot that evening, and I knew I'd be feeling it for days.

I reached home around nine o'clock, cranky and sore, dissatisfied with my performance and pissed at the world. My legs were like rubber and I could feel bruises developing on my forearms and shins where I had blocked punches and kicks, and judging from the stiffness in my left leg, somebody had driven an elbow into my thigh as I was trying to kick her.

Scott was sitting at the kitchen table grading papers.

"Good class?" he asked. I snarled noncommittally and hauled my reeking bag of sparring gear past him to the laundry room.

Marriage is another relationship requiring a nuanced understanding of distance and timing. Scott and I have been negotiating our *mai-ai* for over two decades now, employing a lot of honesty, sporadic yelling, and occasional adult supervision. Where my karate training is concerned, though, the give-and-take between us has been entirely in one direction: whenever I need time or reassurance or a kick in the pants, Scott supplies it. It's ironic that my training at a feminist karate school has depended, in large part, on a man's influence.

But not just any man. Scott is that rare kind of husband who knows when to support his wife and when to get the hell out of her way. If I grumble that I really don't want to go to karate on a given night, he'll say, "So don't go." But if I worry that I shouldn't go because one of the kids has a fever, or extra homework, or has recently started referring to me as "what's-her-name," he'll say, "The kids are fine. I can handle things. You need to go to karate."

"You need to go to karate." If I had a dime for every time my husband has said that to me over the years, I could hire my own personal security detail and stop worrying about defending myself. I'm never quite sure how to respond when he says it. "Don't tell *me* what I need," I sometimes bristle; at other times, I'm deeply touched that he cares about what I need and is willing and able to push me toward it.

Most of the time, I just think: he's right. I *do* need to go. For his sake and the kids' as much as my own. For all the time that karate has prevented me from spending with my family, and in spite of the stress it has sometimes contributed (especially before tests), it's indisputable that my training has led directly to fewer slammed doors, damaged walls, and raised voices in our home. As Scott explained it when Dave was a toddler, "If Mommy's crazy, no one is happy."

I sometimes wonder if Scott's own halfhearted relationship with the martial arts contributes to his unwavering support of my training. He has a green belt in Tae Kwon Do from his college days. He's a natural athlete and could easily attain black belt proficiency in almost any style with relative ease. But he never could submit to other people's discipline for very long. He was kicked out of the Marines during boot camp for what they called "flagrant disregard for the law"—though he had never been arrested for anything in his life. When I press him for details, all I hear is a vague story about "getting a lot of speeding tickets," which hardly seems like something the United States Marine Corps would make a fuss over.

And you can say what you want about the military's recruitment standards; I have to admit they were right on target with their assessment of Scott. Much of the conflict in our relationship has stemmed from his flagrant disregard for all kinds of things: his steadfast refusal to wear a watch; his conviction that a man can pull on a pair of shorts and be fully dressed; his belief that fresh air will somehow cure his hay fever. It has taken twenty-five years for us to reach agreement on some basic standards of propriety, such as that people should wear shoes when going to dinner at a restaurant (*even if they have outdoor seating*), and try not to get more than one speeding ticket per year. We've learned to peaceably disagree on smaller points and save our energy for interactions that might actually improve our relationship rather than just leaving us both bruised.

When I emerged from the shower that night, Scott tactfully avoided the subject of sparring class. With the wisdom of long experience, he focused instead on bringing my blood sugar back up.

"Dinner's in the oven," he said, gesturing toward the kitchen.

"Thanks," I mumbled, gathering up the plate and collapsing at the table. Scott's cooking was just one more way he supported my training, and I was grateful for it, even though it often meant eating oddly gritty baked potatoes or pasta that clung together in tough, vinelike lumps.

"How was your day?" I asked, feeling guilty, as I always did, that it took me until nine o'clock at night to ask him this.

"Great," he replied. "I bought a new bike."

Scott travels by bicycle whenever possible, which is good for the environment but not for the bike. He is not gentle with machinery. He disdains all gears but the very highest, and being built like a speed skater, with overdeveloped quads and long legs, he's able to apply so much force that he breaks chains and strips gears with depressing regularity. A couple of times he's actually broken the crank arm off the pedal assembly—just snapped a three-quarter-inch-thick piece of titanium in two. His latest bike had recently succumbed to the outrageous stress and developed a crack in the frame.

"Oh good," I said. "How much did it cost?"

"Kind of a lot," he hedged. "I went with a heavier frame. The shop said it should last longer."

I reserved comment on that. I don't doubt that the bike

shop's owners were being honest, but Scott's purchases must have already put several of their kids through college.

"Did you pick out a new helmet?" I asked, trying to sound casual. Scott's bike helmet was a frequent point of contention between us; he didn't like to wear it and was prone to "forgetting" it in the driveway. I had backed the station wagon over the last one a few days earlier.

"Well, they're expensive," he said, which told me everything I needed to know. Tired though I was, I began gathering my energy for another round of the bike safety argument.

"I'm quite willing to spend the money," I said.

"Yeah, but I don't really need one," Scott assured me. "You know I hardly ever ride on the street. And it's not like the cops will give me a ticket. There's no law that says you have to wear a helmet."

"I'm more worried about simple physics," I said. "You know it doesn't matter how careful you are; one driver on his cell phone is all it takes."

"Yeah, I know," he said, nodding in the placatory way that never fails to enrage me.

Appealing to his sense of self-preservation wouldn't work. Scott considers himself immortal. I couldn't off-balance him that way. Instead, I tried working the angles.

"You have to consider that you're a father now," I reminded him. "If your brains end up splattered across the road, it's not going to suck for just you."

That shot hit a little closer to home. Scott takes fatherhood seriously. In fact, it's almost the only thing he takes seriously. But he batted down this attack. "Good helmets cost fifty or sixty bucks," he pointed out. "And I just spent five hundred on the bike."

Ouch. That set me back on my heels. My job at the university paid well enough to cover our student loans, and Scott was teaching. We weren't poor graduate students anymore. Still, five hundred dollars would have to be artfully filleted out of our monthly budget.

Suck it up, I told myself. *Redirect the damage. Let it go into the ground.*

"A helmet is a good investment," I suggested. "You can't buy any other form of life insurance that cheaply. And we save money on gas when you don't drive, so it ends up being a net savings."

I was definitely scoring points now. With his fiscal responsibility argument blocked, Scott went on the defensive.

"Helmets are a pain in the ass," he grumbled. "They make me sweat, and I can't see as well when I wear one."

He's tiring, I thought. *Press the advantage.*

"Tell me, when Dave is old enough to ride a bike, are you going to make him wear a helmet?"

"Of course," he said, as I knew he would. Once you've cradled your child's tiny, fragile skull against your chest, you don't send it out into traffic unprotected.

"And if Dave asks you why *he* has to wear a helmet and *you* don't, what will you tell him?"

"Well, I'll probably have to start wearing a helmet then," he admitted.

"Isn't that kind of hypocritical?" I asked. "You'll set an example for him when he's older, but not now? You want him to *think* you wear a helmet, but you don't want to *be* who he thinks you are?"

I could literally see the impact as the shot went home. Scott's eyes narrowed for an instant, as if he were absorbing a physical blow. I would have felt bad for him if the stakes hadn't been so high.

"I guess you're right," he conceded.

"So you'll buy a helmet tomorrow?"

"It looks that way," he said glumly.

"And you'll *wear* it?"

"Yes."

"Thank you," I said. "And thanks for dinner."

"There was no way I was going to win that argument, was there?" he asked after a moment.

"No," I agreed. "You don't have a black belt."

What you're good at is less important than what you're good for.

何が得意かは、どのように役に立てるかほど重要ではない。

A LOT OF RELATIONSHIPS involve people seeking advantage over each other. Healthier relationships involve a search for mutual advantage. And then there are still other relationships that exist solely because we want to help someone else.

The year after I earned my Kyokushin black belt was marked by turmoil and change — in the sparring ring, where I continued to learn every lesson in the most painful way possible; at work, where I had a new boss, a new office, and a new set of administrative roadblocks; and at home. Scott and the kids were fine, but in the summer of 2004, my mother called. At work, in the middle of the day — a sure sign that something was terribly wrong. Her voice shaking in disbelief, Mom told me that my sister Cathy, who was thirty-eight at the time, had just been diagnosed with advanced ovarian cancer. My mother, a cancer survivor herself, as well as a nurse, went over the odds with me: with immediate surgery and chemotherapy, Cathy had about a one-in-five chance of living to the age of forty-three.

My sister is seventeen months older than I am. As children we shared everything—toys, bath time, the tiny crawl space behind the backseat of the family car, where we rode on top of the luggage during vacations. We occupied a separate social class from our three older siblings, Peter, Ellen, and Paul; the rest of the family referred to us collectively as "the little girls" until well after I was married.

Cathy and I also shared a bedroom and a lot of fights. I was a slob and my sister was not; my willingness to live in my own filth quite understandably incensed her. Since annoying my sister was one of the few ways I could have any measurable impact on the world back then, I took great delight in the pigsty that was my half of the room. (This behavior, you'll be glad to know, built up a vast reservoir of karma that came back to me years later in the form of a husband and children who are rather casual housekeepers.)

My sister, true to our shared heritage, did not respond to my provocation with silent rage. In fact, she may be more responsible than any other person for my inclination to fight. She certainly gave me my earliest training. Cathy and I fought constantly, quite literally tooth and nail, and for most of our childhood she was bigger and stronger than I was. ("You weighed forty pounds *forever,*" my mother often recalls.) When push came to shove, which it did approximately three or four times a day, I usually lost out to my big sister. I did leave her with some interesting scars, though.

This dynamic changed as we grew older. Ironically, I gradually became, at five feet four, the Amazon of the family. These days, I tower over my mother and both sisters, who ask me to reach for things on high shelves when we visit—much to the amusement of my husband, who has to walk doubled over through Mom's kitchen or risk being decapitated by the low-hanging geranium near the sink.

I also beefed up, especially after I started training in martial arts. I have shoulders that defy typical women's clothing and, as one definition of the mesomorphic body type politely puts it, a "slightly defined waist." Cathy has never weighed over a hundred pounds, and I could now bodycheck her into next week. Had we not gotten past our childhood squabbles, I would be poised to wreak a terrible vengeance upon her.

But we are long past them. By our teenage years, family life was more and more chaotic at our house, and Cathy and I prudently learned to fight as a unit rather than adversaries. As I surged ahead of her in bulk, I took on a semiprotective role in our relationship. In part, I was trying to pay off a debt of many years' standing. Though she once dealt out plenty of abuse, Cathy was always just as generous with more valuable things, especially information, that most vital component of survival. Advice on how to handle difficult teachers she'd had the year before, explicit directions for passing my driving test, instruction in the social protocol of the drinking aged—everything my sister learned about functioning in the outside world, she passed on to me.

Now she probably had less than five years to live, and I was powerless to help her.

We had tickets to take our son to the circus the week of Cathy's diagnosis. I didn't feel much like going, and thought about staying at home until my husband pointed out that (1) my son wanted both his parents with him so he didn't have to sit next to a stranger; (2) the Greatest Show on Earth isn't exactly cheap, nor does it offer refunds; and (3) elephants always cheer me up.

I do love elephants, and their slow-moving, deliberate power seemed doubly appealing in light of my sister's illness. So I went to the circus hoping the elephants might ease my mind, at least for a while. But as it turned out, it wasn't the elephants that captured my attention. It was the trapeze act—specifically, the catcher.

The catcher in a trapeze act is always a big guy, not lithe and balletic like the flyers. He doesn't attract attention. You hardly even see his face, because he sits with his back to the action most of the time. When he does drop down to catch, he's upside-down, and all you really notice are his arms. It's not, on the whole, a glamorous job.

The flyers are the main attraction, and that afternoon the audience watched, mesmerized, as they did flips and twists, swooping from the bar to the catcher's arms and back to their platform, where they posed and smiled and waved.

But I just watched the catcher, and the catcher just caught the flyers.

He caught them upside-down and forty feet in the air. He caught them elegantly when they did their stunts well. He caught them inelegantly, but safely, when they messed up, overrotated, undershot. He was also responsible for telling the flyers when to jump from their bar to his hands and when to release his hands and return to the bar. If you listen carefully during a trapeze act, you can hear him: "Ready!" he calls just before the stunt, and then "Hep!" when it's time for the flyer to let go. The flyers depend on him for this; sometimes, they get so focused that if the catcher doesn't say "Hep!" they'll never let go of the bar.

It made me wonder what leads a man to this career, hanging upside-down like a bat, before thousands of people, with a perpetual drumroll ringing in his ears, catching people. It's a ridiculous job, really, and it probably doesn't pay very well, considering the risks. But without the catcher, the flyers couldn't fly. Everything, everyone, depends on him. The catcher is the one who's always there; he's the one who makes it the way it's supposed to be.

I left the auditorium wishing everyone had a catcher. Especially my sister.

Cathy had surgery. Her pathology report was grim, and her doctors rushed her into chemotherapy just three weeks later.

"I will never complain about having curly hair again," she said, as she went online to look for wigs. She bought several, all of them with straight hair, because she said she wanted to see what it was like for once. She bought scarves. She lost weight she really couldn't afford to lose. She made friends with other ovarian cancer patients at the oncology clinic. "They make us all come for chemo on the same day," she told me. "It's too depressing for the other patients to see us there."

I couldn't do anything to help her, but at least I knew she was surrounded by others who could.

There are many ways to catch people. In fact, that urge to catch—to step in and help, rescue, defend, protect, heal—has always been a big part of my own makeup. How else can I explain the fact that I, one of the least social people you'll ever have the awkward experience of meeting, spend my spare time teaching strangers to look me in the eye? From very early on in my life, the moment I developed any sort of power to defend myself—even if it was just the ability to tell people what I thought of them—I felt a strong compulsion to use it on behalf of others. Admittedly, it's not the same as being a trapeze catcher. It's the best I can do, given that I get dizzy way too easily even when I'm right-side up and I have bursitis in one shoulder.

If even I—miserable, misanthropic wretch that I am—want to help people, then that urge must be a near-universal trait. And, in fact, if you know what to look for, you'll see that this is true: we're all catchers at heart, even though it may take a catastrophe to make us act on the instinct. What impulse launched the ad hoc flotilla that carried thousands of New Yorkers off Lower Manhattan on 9/11? What made people imperil themselves for strangers, and turn *toward* danger that day? What transformed yacht owners (not typically the first people I think of when I hear the word *altruistic*) into rescuers?

"Most people are good." I learned this simple phrase from Irene van der Zande's Kidpower curriculum, which I use for children's self-defense workshops. Sometimes I have to remind myself that it's true: we hear so much hysteria about "stranger danger" and nameless serial killers that it's easy to lose sight of the simple fact that most of us are decent and well intentioned. A great many people do render aid in emergencies, and intervene when they witness violence, and most of these people are strangers to those they help.

Of course, just because people *want* to help doesn't mean they know how. Their helpfulness may manifest itself as forwarded safety e-mails or handgun recommendations. That's why we make a point, in self-defense workshops, of showing students how to elicit the help they need from bystanders. I hadn't had time, in the single hour I spent with Anna and the Girl Scout leaders, to delve into this portion of the curriculum, but it's an important lesson: during a violent or potentially violent encounter, strangers can be enlisted, unwillingly if necessary, in your fight for safety.

Much of what the empowerment method teaches about dealing with an attacker also works to secure aid from bystanders—skills like being loud, or saying explicitly what is going on and what needs to happen (*"Let go of me!"*). Creating a disturbance and drawing attention can convert passersby into witnesses. Witnesses, even if they don't lift a finger to help, can be powerful allies. People tend to behave very differently when they know they are being watched.

And clear, assertive communication can do more than just attract scrutiny. It can tap directly into people's instinctive urge to help you. The key is to establish a connection between fellow humans, because the more we feel personally connected to someone in trouble, the harder it is to ignore our instinct to help. So making eye contact with people outside the zone of conflict is a good tactic; it establishes a relationship, however fleeting, between you. Giving direct instructions ("You—call the police!") is also effective. If you speak directly to one person, you can short-circuit the phenomenon known as "diffusion of responsibility," where no single person in a group wants to be the first to act. When you give directions, you relieve bystanders of the burden of deciding whether to intervene, or how. "I wasn't sure I should get involved," they might say if they witness two people scuffling in a parking lot. If one of those people yells to them, "Call the police, I'm being mugged!" there's no room for doubt about what they should do.

In the months after my sister's cancer diagnosis, as I thought more often and more longingly about rescue, it occurred to me that I'd been sharing information like this in workshops for a while but neglecting half of what I ought to be teaching. If I want to harness the general human proclivity to help others for my own self-defense, I reasoned, then it's pretty clear that I likewise have an obligation to help others. And most of the time, that's not going to be as clear-cut as calling the police because someone tells me to. Now that I was reasonably confident in my ability to keep myself safe, I wondered, how could I expand the scope of my safety to include other people?

Teaching self-defense was one way, obviously. I knew how helpful I had found my introductory self-defense class. Making that experience available to more women was aid I felt qualified to give. Still, I felt I should be doing more, or should be prepared to do more, if the need arose.

It wasn't merely that I felt a duty to reciprocate for the altruism my own safety might one day depend on. It wasn't just the logical conclusion that I'm safer when everyone around me is safer. Rather, I felt very deeply—as I watched Cathy's fight with cancer, saw her spirits flag and her strength dwindle—that I *needed* to help people in real, tangible ways. That if I wasn't helping others, something inside me would be wasting away, too.

It was a tremendous evolutionary shift from my earlier preoccupation with my own safety. Training at Sun Dragon, I had learned a lot about violence, and about preventing it. And I had learned a lot about myself as well. Finding ways to intervene when someone else is in trouble can be risky, and often messy; I knew that. But my sister's illness showed me that the urge to protect is a basic, essential part of our humanness, and we deny it at our own peril. It connects us to our fellow humans, and when we act on it, it connects us to a better part of ourselves. If I never tried to protect others, I might stay safe myself, but at what cost to my humanity?

• • •

My sister contacted the MD Anderson Cancer Center in Houston shortly after her chemotherapy began, to see if she could join an experimental stem cell study they were running. Their answer: we don't know if you'll be a good candidate for the stem cell therapy, but please come. Send your X-rays. Bring your pathology report. We will do everything we can to help you.

And, true to form, Cathy immediately insisted that *I* come down to Houston—while she was in the midst of a grueling chemotherapy regime—and go to MD Anderson for my own screening, since her cancer, plus our mother's, put me at high risk for the disease. Bone-thin and wearing a wig, but still just as bossy as she was at age eight, she walked me through the whole day's tests, introduced me to people she'd already met in the huge medical complex, and gave me firm directions about the blue ID card the hospital issues to everyone they treat. "Now, you *keep that card,*" she instructed me, as if it were a high-quality fake ID. "If you're *ever* diagnosed with cancer, you can come back to MD Anderson and you'll already be in their system and they can put you straight into a treatment program."

My sister was reaching out to catch me even as she herself fell.

Of course, self-defense instructors aren't the only people to have noticed the power of altruism. Predators of all kinds are experts at manipulating our instinct to help. In fact, almost the entire point of the "Just Say No" workshop activity is to teach people to think twice before acting on that instinct. I puzzled over this apparent conflict for a long time: How do you choose a safe path between hyperdefensiveness and naive do-goodism?

I decided to start small. I already had plenty of low-risk opportunities to protect others. Some of them I thought of as common courtesies, and subsequently neglected, like using my turn signal, yielding to pedestrians—not driving like an asshole, generally. I began to pay more attention to the everyday things I did that could put people at risk or provide them some measure of protection. One morning I traded seats on the bus with a young woman who was being verbally harassed by the man next to her. He looked at the book I was reading —Anthony Herbert's *Military Manual of Self-Defense*—and lapsed into silence for the remainder of our time together.

I pumped Sensei Suzanne for information on de-escalation and intervention strategies. These were part of the Sun Dragon curriculum but received less emphasis than defensive tactics because of the time constraints in our standard three-hour workshops. There were some basic principles to keep in mind, Sensei explained. Unless you're witnessing something obviously illegal, don't take sides when you intervene. You have a better shot at stopping conflict if both parties consider you impartial. Consider distraction and disruption as alternatives to direct intervention. My seat-swapping tactic was a good example of that, she said. And look for ways to allow everyone a dignified exit. If someone can back down from a fight without losing face, he or she usually will.

Most important, she urged me to keep practicing de-escalation and intervention in small ways, just as I'd practiced making eye contact with strangers on the street after my first self-defense workshop.

I started trying. I found it every bit as hard as I'd expected. But it was still the right thing to do, even if I wasn't hearing a lot of thanks for my efforts. A couple about to come to blows outside the movie theater didn't thank me when I asked if everything was all right. In fact, they shifted their ire to me and told me to fuck off. Which was, I decided, still a better outcome than a fistfight between the two of them. Offering myself up as a common enemy wasn't exactly the kind of distraction I had envisioned using to short-circuit a conflict, but it worked. And at least I let them know someone was concerned. At least I tried.

Still, I had no illusions that I was cut out to be a professional catcher. I needed to do what I could, and that included admitting my limitations. This was made plain to me after class one night, when two people—who weren't even associated with the dojo—had a noisy altercation in our parking lot. Being hypervigilant, I was the one who noticed the commotion and called the police. But it was Amy, the young woman who had joined Sun Dragon while I was in Hawaii, who went out to the parking lot and spoke calmly to the couple. Amy had been even more profoundly impressed with Sensei Suzanne and the empowerment approach than I had—so much so that she had quit her job and gone back to college to study social work. Now she listened to both people involved in the argument, asked them enough questions to determine that no one was in immediate danger, and gave them her phone number in case they wanted to talk to someone later. She didn't solve all their problems, but she kept them, for that one night at least, from hitting the ground, hard.

Amy's actions taught me a basic truth about violence reduction: we tend to want to act heroically against violence, when more often, what's needed is simple courage. The difference is plain. Heroics make you look cool. Courage more often makes you look silly, at least puts you at risk of looking that way. But that was exactly the kind of skill I'd been learning at Sun Dragon all these years. Now I was seeing just how many ways there were to apply it.

Lots of people become catchers, though they don't all join the circus. It takes a special kind of person, and a lot of training, to do it well. Doctors, lifeguards, social workers, firemen—people drawn to the catching trade spend years learning how to help and protect others. But catching people is hard work, and no matter how good you are at it, you won't catch them all. It takes a toll. High blood pressure, depression, PTSD, drinking, drug use, domestic violence—all are more common among those whose job it is to protect others. We're shockingly bad at taking care of our protectors, who are, in turn, notoriously bad at taking care of themselves.

Protecting makes you a bull's-eye for bullets, insults, germs, and plenty of other bad stuff. And the job requirements can tie your hands in strange ways. It's a curious fact, for example, that carrying a weapon can actually make you more vulnerable in a conflict, because it limits your options for responding. As I've learned while teaching self-defense, many of the most basic self-defense tactics are useless when you're armed. If someone grabs me by the throat, I might try to break their hold by clasping my hands overhead, stepping back, and pivoting. An armed peace officer can't perform this basic maneuver, because it would allow the attacker to grab the officer's gun. And the gun doesn't help you much once you've been grabbed by the throat, either, because it's hard to unholster a sidearm, take off the safety, aim it, and fire when you can't breathe. It seems unfair, but even the tools of the trade can become a burden for the protector.

We rely on professional catchers. Most of us can't do what they do. It's too difficult and important and imperfect.

I couldn't spend the bulk of my working life seeing the worst of human nature, knowing that there's only so much I can do about it, and that it's not nearly enough. In my darker moments I wonder if we created professional catchers not so that people will be caught, but so the rest of us don't have to worry about catching them.

When you're a catcher, the expectations are high, and people notice your performance only when you screw up. We're quick to condemn the CPS caseworker who doesn't document the bruises, the doctor who writes the wrong prescription. We want our protectors to be superheroes, but instead they're all too human—and a good thing, too, or why would they give a damn about mere mortals like the rest of us?

I was on my way to a coffee shop before dawn one morning, hell-bent on knocking out some dumb project or other, when I happened on an extraordinary moment: A police car, lights flashing, drawn to the side of the road near a highway overpass. An empty parking lot yawned blankly on one side; on the other, a medical office's electronic billboard flashed messages about pain relief into the dark. The place was deserted. And standing on the sidewalk, by the open door of his patrol car, was a police officer carrying a child. A toddler, no older than two, wearing pajamas. The policeman was holding the child on his hip, the little head tucked snugly under his chin, taking a few steps one way, then another, swaying a bit in between—the classic gait of an adult soothing a child who ought to be asleep. There was no one else around—no cars, no people—and I slowed down as I turned the corner, taking in this curious scene. Beyond the police car, back behind the medical clinic, loomed a row of apartment houses, dark and silent now. Somewhere among them, I realized, there must be one with its front door ajar and a sleeping adult inside who would soon awake to the panicked awareness that the child who was supposed to be safe in bed was not.

Somewhere in that apartment complex, someone was about to have a very bad moment, a moment that might have turned into a very, very bad rest of their life, except that the police officer driving past had seen this child—this predawn wanderer, trapeze flyer, opener of doors, explorer of highway overpasses—and caught him. He was holding him, as catchers do, and would continue to hold on to him until it was safe to let him go. Soon, another officer would arrive to help him walk through the apartment complex and find the unit with the open front door.

If I'd left the house a little earlier, I wondered, before the policeman drove by this corner, would I have even noticed the child? What if he'd been in the street, in the path of my not-yet-caffeinated driving? What kind of nightmare might this day have turned into? But instead, before I finished my coffee, the child would be back where he belonged, his parents' heart rate almost back to normal, the official incident report completed and filed.

And I thought as I drove off, I'm sure that guy has days when he wishes he wasn't a cop. But I'll bet this isn't one of them.

I still have my MD Anderson ID card, eight years after Cathy's initial diagnosis. And my sister is now, incredibly, cancer-free. She was caught by the remarkable network of professionals at the hospital in Houston. In many ways it was a routine case: the doctors there confirmed her diagnosis and staging, but they also discovered that her initial pathology report had misinterpreted the slides of her cancer cells. The form of cancer she had was under intensive study by researchers at the center and was known to respond well to certain medications—different ones than she had been told to take. They gave her new prescriptions, sent her to specialists, and talked her through the schedule of CT scans and tests she would undergo regularly for the next five years. It was exactly the kind of thing a specialized, well-funded research and treatment hospital exists to do. But it was also a spectacular, death-defying catch in midair, and just thinking about it, even now, takes my breath away.

I'm still cancer-free, too. But if that ever changes, I'll know exactly what to do, because my big sister explained it all to me.

Remain centered, no matter how many building permits you have to obtain.

この意味はよくわからない。正直なところ、この章はあまり注意して読まなかったのだ。要点は何か家庭における和についてのようだが。

LIFE WAS BUSY and complicated for quite a while after I earned my Kyokushin black belt. My sister's cancer diagnosis came just months after the birth of our daughter, Lilly, and for a year or two I found myself focusing, by necessity, on my family. The mundane domestic problems of sleep deprivation, laundry, and maintaining the household's supply of red wine occupied me more or less completely, and my karate training took a backseat. Then, one day, when Lilly had learned to walk and promptly displayed a talent for plowing into sliding-glass doors, I awoke to the realization that our family of four had outgrown the "starter home" we'd been living in for over a decade.

I doubt anyone just up and decides, "Hey, let's spend eighteen months with a gaping hole in our house and a washing machine in the dining room. And let's *borrow money* to do it!" Most of us would not willingly choose to live amid large piles of Sheetrock. No one looks forward to phone calls from the city's building-permits staff. We certainly didn't. But as my time in Hawaii had shown me, the question of where I belong is integral to my mental well-being. Luckily, since I had returned to Texas, I had gained a deeper understanding of concepts like centering, commitment, and leverage, and I had enough confidence to tackle this new challenge fearlessly.

We had bought our house, a three-bedroom, one-bathroom 1950s tract home, before Dave was born. It had been a rental for ten years before that, which was why we were able to afford it even though we were graduate students—it was a hovel when we moved in: green shag carpet, busted-out windows, and an impressive collection of old porn magazines that cascaded down from the attic when my husband opened the trapdoor to check the insulation (the last set of tenants also left a grow light in the carport). The yard was hard-packed dirt covered with a thick layer of broken glass and motorcycle parts. Despite the ten years we'd spent trying to erase all evidence of past inhabitants, the front lawn still coughed up a spark plug or two every spring.

We had, technically, enough space for a family of four. Dave had his own bedroom and Lilly seemed perfectly happy with a crib in the office, because whoever was in there trying to work became a captive audience. So the only sticking point was the bathroom.

As Lilly's potty training loomed ahead of us, and Dave, along with all his numerous neighborhood friends, turned eight years old, I decided that I was no longer willing to share a bathroom with children. Any children. This may sound selfish, especially if you don't have kids, but let me explain something about eight-year-old boys, in case you've never lived with one: they can do things to a bathroom that defy all the laws of physiology, gravity, and probability, at least as I understand them.

Now imagine an entire tribe of eight-year-old boys using a single bathroom for an entire day. *Now* imagine trying to potty-train a toddler in that same bathroom.

Exactly.

We couldn't create a bathroom out of thin air (or so we thought). The only option seemed to be moving to a bigger house.

This was near the height of the national housing bubble, so the good news was that our house was worth a lot more than we had paid for it. The bad news was that every other house on the market was likewise overvalued. We couldn't sell our house, in its quirky but suddenly trendy midcity neighborhood, and buy another, bigger one nearby. If we wanted a larger house, we would have to move outward, toward the suburbs on the outskirts of Austin. This would require longer commute times, to work and to karate. By that point, though, time spent in my car seemed preferable to time spent in a bathroom that looked and smelled like an Algerian prison. We started house hunting.

Or rather, I started. Scott was horrified by the mere thought of the suburbs, and while he freely admitted we couldn't go on much longer as we were (he was using the same bathroom, too, after all), he held out hope that we'd stumble upon some little fixer-upper nearby with a second bathroom. I knew better. When I went running through our neighborhood, my footsteps were dogged by the whine of tile saws from dozens of nondescript houses, where all of South Austin's wannabe real estate moguls were hastily remodeling the existing single-bathrooms.

My old friend Patty—the same friend who had helpfully pointed out that Hawaii was an active volcano—suggested I look at a new development near her in southwest Austin. Driving along the attractively curved streets on a Saturday afternoon, we surveyed an alluring suburban enclave for the upper middle class. The supersized houses were pristine, the trash cans were invisible, and every garage held at least one high-end sport utility vehicle, freshly waxed, like the plump, shiny seed of a ripe fruit. The immaculate lawns, Patty told me, were kept that way by small armies of non-English-speaking laborers of indeterminate nationality who descended weekly to mow, trim, fertilize, and weed.

"If you don't keep your yard up, the neighborhood association sends you a warning letter," Patty explained. I looked at the identically landscaped yards, each with a newly planted twig of tree on one side, each tree held bolt upright by two ramrod-straight guide wires. I thought about our front yard, with its archeological bounty of motorcycle parts.

We parked near a couple of FOR SALE signs and walked along the blinding white sidewalks. You could see the builder's floor plans repeat themselves over and over down the street: The Savannah. The Grand Oaks. The Majesty. The Savannah II (third bath, kitchen upgrade). The air was thick with bourgeois privilege and deed restrictions.

We finished up at the brand-new public swimming pool, which was spectacular. Lap lanes, a kiddie pool with a fountain, ample parking. All the children there looked unnaturally clean. They literally glowed in the sunlight, especially the blond ones, of which there seemed to be an abnormally high percentage. I wondered if they'd been irradiated.

I came home vaguely depressed. The dizzying array of available houses, mortgage options, and real estate agents was overwhelming. We hadn't even started moving yet, and I already felt uprooted.

"Find your center," Sensei Suzanne told me for the hundredth time that night. We were working on *zenkutsu dachi,* the long, forward-weighted stance used in a lot of our kata, and Suzanne was testing our stability by grabbing our belts and trying to pull us off-balance.

Centering is an elusive skill, particularly for the beginning *karateka.* Being centered is easy to feel, hard to describe. It requires a subtle understanding of multiple concepts. I initially thought of my "center" as the center of my body's physical mass; my center of gravity. That's similar to the martial arts concept of the *tanden,* a specific point located just below and behind the navel. The *tanden* is not only where energy is focused and transmitted through your physical body; it's the source of your *ki,* your combined physical and spiritual energy. The *tanden* is where you breathe from, and into. It's where they hit you when you're doing Sanchin Kata during a test.

Centering also has to do with your location in space. When you are physically centered—no matter what stance you're in—you're balanced, poised upon a certain spot, with your feet, hips, shoulders, and head aligned so that you have many potential ways to move, and all your energy available for use. This makes you quite dangerous and also hard to move. When I feel physically centered, I feel immovable, not because of my strength but simply because I am where I'm supposed to be.

We practice centering in karate every time we begin or end a kata or other exercise. On the command *"Yoi!"* you breathe in, drop your center by bending your knees slightly, and circle your arms outward to gather energy. Then, as you exhale, you block downward with both arms, shifting your feet into a strong parallel stance.

"When you perform *yoi,*" Sensei Suzanne told us, "you're claiming your space. You're establishing yourself on that particular piece of earth, and signaling your commitment to fight from that spot, no matter who tries to move you off of it."

Finally, being centered is a state of mind. No matter how fast a wheel spins, its centermost point remains still. When you put yourself in that space mentally, everything around you can be in motion, but you will be at rest. When you're centered, you have time and space in which to think. You make better choices. And when you decide to act, you can move with intent, free from the influence of all the activity around you. That's what a karate instructor means when she tells you to "move from your center."

One way to find your center is to be knocked out if it. This is what Sensei Suzanne was doing by pulling us out of our stances. When we lost our balance, we could feel where our center was supposed to be.

My sojourn in Hawaii, I decided after it was over, had been a rather drastic de-centering exercise. A less dramatic way to locate your center is to turn inward, and find the stable places, the things that sustain you, the parts of yourself that don't change. I was mulling this over one evening as I went for a walk in our neighborhood. It was a lovely day in early spring, but instead of seeing the mountain laurels in bloom or the bluebonnets flourishing in people's unmowed yards, I was noticing that there weren't any sidewalks on our street; how the pavement sagged and buckled, and the trees leaned drunkenly over fences and driveways. Most of the garages had been converted into apartments in flagrant violation of local zoning ordinances, and the cars parked in front of them tended to have body damage and cinder blocks where their wheels should have been. A couple of streets away, by a house with a goat shed and three goats in the backyard, I ran into a neighbor I had seen before in passing but had never stopped to talk to.

I'm not sure how I managed to live for so many years in our neighborhood without meeting Crazy Stan. "Hi, I'm Crazy Stan," he said, extending his hand to me, in much the same way that Buck Owens used to say, "Hi, I'm Buck Owens," when *Hee Haw* came on every Saturday night. "I live at the dead end of Jubilee Street." Stan was wearing a black cowboy hat and riding a red mobility scooter, accompanied by a moth-eaten golden retriever and a young Cavalier King Charles spaniel. We were heading the same direction, and it seemed rude to draw attention to my perfectly functional legs by walking faster than he could drive, so we strolled along together for a few blocks, making conversation.

Stan said he'd been living in this neighborhood for forty years, which meant he'd moved in when the houses were relatively new. He introduced me to his puppy, Charlie, and told me the history of the Cavalier King Charles spaniel. He then proceeded to ramble through a considerable chunk of the life of King Charles II, including the Conventicle Act, the Great Plague and the Great Fire, and the king's mistress Nell Gwynne's famous remark, "Good people, you are mistaken —I am the *Protestant* whore." I was spellbound. This is not the kind of conversation you hear very often while walking around my neighborhood. My neighborhood is known for noisy keg parties and lots of accidental shootings, not for its expertise on Restoration-era politics.

I sensed that Stan could be lucid enough if he wanted, but

that he'd spent some time in lucidity and found it a dull place. He was a fascinating person, even though he'd slip off into Carlos Castaneda territory every now and then—hell, some of the English professors I worked with talked just as crazy. If Stan knew even half the people he said he did, I could see why his memory might not be so good. Doug Sahm, Townes Van Zandt, Roky Erikson—they weren't an especially abstemious crew; even by Austin standards they might be said to have lived indulgently during the 1960s and 1970s.

We'd traveled a good half-mile, at a snail's pace, when Stan told me he'd adopted his yellow dog, Lemondrop, from the pound. He stopped his scooter squarely in the middle of the street to give this story his full attention:

"I had these two ducks that ate all the flowers off my tomato plants," he began. (This was the moment when I made an important discovery about myself; namely, that I am constitutionally unable to walk away from any story that begins, "I had these two ducks.") "So I took the ducks to the animal shelter," Stan went on, "to see if they couldn't find better homes for them. And while I was there I went past pen number five-two-five, and this dog came up to the gate and said to me, as plain as day, 'Listen, buddy, you've got to get me out of here.' And I said, 'What's a nice lady like you doing in a joint like this?' And she said, 'I don't want to talk about it; I was framed. Bribe the warden if you have to.'

"So I went to the people there, and told them I wanted to adopt the dog in pen five-two-five. And they asked me, 'Mister, have you really thought for very long about whether you want to adopt that dog?' And I said, 'Well, I was walking past her pen just now and she told me I had to get her out of here.' And so they let me take her home.

"And I'll tell you," Stan went on, "before she got to that

dog pound, somebody'd taught her a bunch of police dog tricks."

I wasn't sure what to make of that statement—perhaps the dog had a talent for sniffing out illegal drugs?—but just then Lemondrop, who was both as sweet and as sharp as her name would suggest, grew tired of standing around listening to Stan talk and casually circled to the other side of his scooter, where she jammed her nose against the joystick, sending Stan lurching forward down the street. "You see what I mean," he said over his shoulder. "She knows how to get what she wants."

I watched the three of them head off toward Jubilee Street. The dogs wound back and forth dangerously on their leashes as the trio progressed, and Stan's scooter veered out into traffic in a fashion that I found alarming, but they all seemed perfectly at ease. The dogs matched their gait to the speed of the scooter; they were obviously happy and doing exactly what they most wanted to be doing in all the world. When the spaniel puppy tired, he hopped onto the scooter's foot plate to hitch a ride.

I walked home in the twilight, and for once, all the neighborhood's tile saws were silent.

Shortly after my meeting with Stan and his dogs, a real estate agent named Cecilia took me back to Patty's neighborhood to show me some of the Savannahs and Majesties from the inside. Bare of furniture, the houses looked even more alike than they had from the outside. We walked from one echoing "great room" to another. ("No, this is the *media* room," Cecilia corrected me, smiling. "*That's* the great room in there, leading to the gourmet kitchen.")

As we progressed from house to house, she reeled off the amenities in the area—the wonderful schools, a bike trail, and the pool, which I'd already seen. The nearby shopping center had a *two-story* Starbucks, she chirped, and the local ice cream shop offered soy-based ice cream and nondairy, fat-free sorbets.

Back at our cars, we met a resident out walking her yellow Labrador puppy—a puppy that I knew, as soon as I saw it, would be named Marley. The dog walker exchanged pleasantries with us while the Lab sniffed my feet, and then started her own sniff test, subtly sounding me out as a potential neighbor. My husband and I worked at the university, I offered; our kids were eight and one, a boy and a girl. She nodded approval, and deemed me worthy of a tepid, well-manicured handshake.

"This is Marley," she said, as the puppy chewed happily on one of my shoelaces. "He's about to start obedience school, aren't you, Marley?" Marley wagged his tail.

"I just met a dog the other day who knew how to operate a scooter," I mentioned.

"Really?" Cecilia asked. "Like, a service dog? For the disabled?"

"Kind of," I told her, suddenly wishing I hadn't brought it up. "She belongs to my neighbor Stan. Crazy Stan, he calls himself."

Marley's owner arched an eyebrow at me.

"Kind of a typical Austin ex-hippie," I said apologetically. "I don't suppose you have many neighbors like that around here."

"Oh no," the woman laughed. "We don't have anyone crazy in *this* neighborhood."

I don't know, I thought, contemplating the limestone planters that stood sentinel along the sidewalk, one square box in front of each house. *I'll bet a lot of you need therapy.*

On my way out of the enclave, I drove past the shopping center the real estate agent had extolled, with its towering Starbucks, and pulled in to take a look. A couple of doors down from the lactose-free ice cream parlor, I noticed a Tae Kwon Do studio with a magnificent display of tournament trophies in the window. Inside, a children's class was going on; they must have had twenty or thirty kids in there, I reckoned, dressed in spotless uniforms. I eased the car past, trying not to gawk as I took in the vast, polished training floor, the stacks of expensive tumbling mats against one wall, the row of benches full of spectators. The floor-to-ceiling windows had a sheen of wealth and complacency that made me long for the solid heft of a brick in my hand.

Back on the highway, covering the five miles to my neighborhood (which took about five minutes at this time of day but would no doubt require more like half an hour during rush hour traffic), I saw a sales billboard for the subdivision. IF YOU LIVED HERE, YOU'D BE HOME BY NOW! it taunted cheerfully.

No, I wouldn't, I thought, and drove on past it.

I was on my hands and knees in the home office the next morning, cleaning up one of those obscure messes that really could have come from either end of the dog, when I found my center.

"So, what were the houses out by Patty like?" Scott asked, coming in with a cup of coffee (having stalled just long enough, I noted, to make sure the worst of the filth had been removed).

"Big," I said, sitting back on my heels. "Nice. Empty."

"What's the neighborhood like?"

"I would rather cut my own eye out with a broken bottle than live there," I replied.

"Told you so," Scott said.

I ignored him and went on, "Furthermore, the smallest houses I looked at were around twenty-five hundred square feet. That's more than double the size of this place." I gestured meaningfully at the floor. "The number of bathrooms is irrelevant. I can't clean that much carpet."

"Well, if all we need is an extra bathroom, and maybe a bedroom, why don't we just build them?" Scott asked.

I should mention here that my husband did work on construction crews throughout college, and built his own vacation cabin in New Mexico. His doctorate in sociology tends to make me forget these more basic capabilities. Also, I admit, I was nervous about turning our home into a do-it-yourself project. For one thing, Scott was far too eager to get started.

You would understand how I felt if you'd ever seen his feet. There is no polite way to say this: my husband has the feet of a cartoon hillbilly. They are long and bony, with toenails that don't quite match the shape of the appendages they are supposed to cover, and his toes jut out at odd angles, hinting at a history of profound (you might say flagrant) disregard for safety regulations. He sees no use for shoes, even when he is mowing the lawn or kick-starting a motorcycle. He walks barefoot everywhere—across blazing parking lots and burr-infested fields; I'm sure he could manage hot coals if there were something interesting to see, do, or talk to on the other side of them.

When he wants to, Scott can work harder and faster than anyone I've ever seen. When our neighbors needed to replace their roof, and the workers ripped off the old shingles and then didn't show up the next day, he pulled out his old tool belt, climbed up a tree to the top of the neighbors' house, and had the new roof framed, decked, and capped with metal panels in one afternoon. He did all this barefoot, including the parts that involved power tools.

So I'll admit he's an awfully handy person to have around in an emergency, but Scott is not what you would call a detail man. His preferred medium is plywood and two-by-fours, not cabinetry or molding or any of the niceties that builders call "finishing." When he replaced the window over our kitchen sink, he had the old window out, the new frame roughed in, and the window installed in less than an hour. It was two years before he finished taping, floating, and painting the three square feet of drywall surrounding the window.

But at this point, we were running out of options, and Scott and I both knew it. One of our neighbors, in a similar bind, had received a bid from a contractor to add a bathroom for a cool fifty thousand bucks. We didn't have that kind of money. We just had Scott, and his feet, and our wits. But now I knew what we were doing: we were claiming our space.

We devised a plan of battle, initially envisioning a blitzkrieg assault that would put a new roof over our heads by the time school started in the fall. Soon enough, however, we came to see that we were involved in something much more like siege warfare.

The opening maneuver in our campaign was to knock down the carport (city demolition permit: $60), but since the carport housed the water heater, that had to be moved to a temporary position outside the kitchen window, necessitating some ad hoc rerouting of plumbing and electricity. Once that was done—summer was already well advanced by this time

—Scott went out and happily tore down the old, horrible carport, dispersing thousands of cockroaches out into the yard. Lilly, who was now a year and a half old, trailed behind him dragging a sixteen-ounce hammer and randomly pounding stray pieces of asbestos siding. ("Don't worry," Scott reassured me. "It's not friable.")

Next, the old concrete slab beneath the carport had to be broken up and hauled away, a job we turned over to the Haupt brothers, a pair of local contractors. Ernie and Ben took out the slab on a July afternoon when the temperature hovered well over a hundred degrees, renting a jackhammer and busting up the concrete, then carting the pieces out to their truck in a wheelbarrow.

The Haupts were probably in their late sixties, and I watched in amazement as they took turns with the jackhammer out in our backyard. Whichever brother wasn't blasting away at the slab would smoke a cigarette and drink an RC Cola, then heave a bunch of concrete chunks into the wheelbarrow and trundle it around to the driveway. By the time he returned, the other brother would be ready for a cigarette, and they would swap tasks. They worked in a cloud of tobacco smoke and cement dust, sweating profusely, and I was convinced that at least one of them was going to have a stroke. But they never even slowed down. In fact, in the months they worked for us, the Haupt brothers missed a total of one day on the job, and that was the day their mother died. And they *told us in advance* that they wouldn't be in that day. Their mother was in the hospital, they informed Scott one afternoon, and likely to die within twenty-four hours. And die she did, the good woman, as if contractually obligated.

Once Ernie and Ben had hauled away our old carport slab and buried their mother, they engineered our new foundation (city permit: $80). Before they could pour it (which they did themselves, parking a rented cement mixer in our driveway and hauling the wet concrete around back one load at a time in their trusty wheelbarrow), the incoming water lines had to be rerouted, and new drains installed ($200 for the plumbing permits), which necessitated the digging of an eighty-foot trench around the house from the backyard to the main sewer line in front. Also, our plumber Don informed us, the kitchen drain pipe really ought to be reconnected to the city line. The previous owners ("the slumlords," as we affectionately referred to them) had apparently grown tired of repeatedly unclogging it and simply disconnected it from the main drain, routing all the dirty water into what was essentially a miniature graywater zone beneath the patio.

"That might explain the fly problem out here every summer," Scott observed, as the plumber's crew shoveled several hundred pounds of grease-coated rocks and sand into a mound in the backyard.

When the plumbing crew had finally extended the new drain trench all the way around the house to the main sewer line in front, they discovered (when Don accidentally stepped on the pipe and crushed it) that it was made of Orangeburg pipe, a 1950s wonder material that was supposed to last forever but ended up disintegrating after about fifty years, since it consisted of nothing more wonderful than cardboard soaked with creosote. So the main sewer line also had to be dug up and replaced. And somewhere in the middle of all this, Don disappeared.

"I don't know what the hell is going on with the plumbing," Scott told me, the fourth or fifth time I asked him why no one had shown up to put in the new pipes. "Don doesn't answer his home phone. His voice mail is full. Ernie thinks he might have gone to Mexico." For days, Scott stomped around the house fuming about all the work he could have done by now if the pipes had been put in on schedule. I thought back over my objections and reservations about this project; the difficulty of working with subcontractors, the time required, the stress. But for once I kept my mouth shut. We were in too deep for me to say anything now.

One night Widget, our tiny, intrepid, alligator-hunting dog, walked out into the yard and vanished for several hours, responding to our repeated calls with only muffled barking. Eventually I went out searching for her with a flashlight, and pulled her, coated with mud from head to tail, from one of the trenches in the front lawn. She had evidently fallen in and, being too short to jump back out, had wandered around like a forlorn infantryman on the Western Front, unable to find her way out of No Man's Land.

Centering had shown me that renovating our house was the right thing to do. Strategy and sheer brute endurance had taken us this far in the project. If we wanted to make it through to the end, I decided, I would have to use another skill I had learned in the dojo: leverage.

The basic wrist release is a beautiful illustration of the possibilities of leverage. We talk about wrist grabs a lot in self-defense classes. Grabbing someone's wrist can be a low-level form of assault. It's a common way for people to try to control others against their will. Someone might grab your wrist to keep you from walking away from an argument, for instance, or to physically pull you in a direction you don't want to go. There are several varieties of wrist grab (same side, opposite hand, two hands on one), and there are dozens of ways to escape one, almost all of which work by exploiting the weakness of the thumb.

Opposable thumbs are an evolutionary breakthrough, but they're hardly foolproof. The simplest wrist release we teach for self-defense involves winding your contested hand laterally around the forearm of the person who grabbed you, moving inward toward her torso—the way a snake would climb up the branch of a tree. The mechanics are simple. The long bones of your forearm, and the metacarpals of your hand, create leverage against a concentrated point on your attacker's body: her thumb. Even if she has very strong arms and hands, odds are that her thumb will be overpowered, and that's all you need to release your wrist from her grasp.

Leverage can help you free yourself from an undesirable situation like a wrist grab; you can also use it to control an attacker. In our karate curriculum, we teach a fundamental wrist-locking technique, *kotegaeshi,* as it's known in Aikido. It's a tremendously subtle move that requires years to master, but even in very crude form it's an effective way to control an opponent. It involves "reversing" the wrist—folding the palm inward, toward the inner forearm, and simultaneously rotating the hand to the outside of the body. This can be a painful technique, even when done properly, but it doesn't have to be cruel. It lets you control a person by giving her one, and only one, option for avoiding pain.

The time had come to apply some leverage to our plumbing situation. "Give me the estimate Don wrote up for us," I told Scott, and settled down in front of the computer to look for the professional equivalent of our plumber's thumb. And I found it, too: the Texas State Board of Plumbing Examiners. Don's billing form had his license number printed on it. So I composed an earnest letter to the board, expressing concern over their licensee's whereabouts, safety, and (I made it clear this was strictly a secondary concern) professionalism. I explained all the ways we had tried to contact him, the dates on which we had last seen and heard from him, and the completion dates he had listed in his estimate. I sent a copy via certified mail to the board's main office and a second copy, also certified, to Don's home address.

Don called forty-eight hours later, profoundly apologetic, and the drains were finished by the end of the week.

"Leverage," I told Scott. "You find the right place to apply pressure, and you make it obvious which direction they need to go to avoid pain."

Slowly, the addition took shape. Scott framed three rooms on the new slab: bedroom, bathroom, laundry room. The Haupts helped him engineer the roof join, always a tricky bit of work. Then the city inspectors started showing up to look at the plumbing and the wiring, finding problems in direct proportion to the moods they happened to be in that day. (I don't know what it is about electrical inspectors, but they all seem to be going through really ugly divorces.) Scott installed the windows and doors, and enlisted some friends to hang the drywall. The Haupts installed the new bathtub and shower.

And finally, one morning in August—a year after we had thought we'd finish—Scott and I triumphantly, if wearily, moved into our new bedroom and dragged Lilly's crib out of the office to her new room. I hung fresh towels in the new bathroom and hummed cheerfully as a parade of children filed in and out of the old bathroom, slamming the door as they went.

True, it had taken eighteen months. The new cabinets

weren't painted yet and we weren't sure what we wanted to do with the floors, so they were still raw concrete. And the addition, of course, made the older part of the house look shabbier than ever.

But it was space: new, clean space that could be closed off and made private and, I hoped, kept clean. And it was ours. Scott and I sat on the bed that morning and surveyed our new kingdom.

"Now we just need to install the trim around the doors," I observed.

"Sure," Scott agreed. "But first I want to put up a shed in the backyard. I need somewhere to store my tools now that we don't have a carport anymore."

"How long will that take?" I asked.

"Not long. I'll just pier-and-beam it and knock together a frame with the studs I saved from the carport."

The fact that the shed was finished that same week but the molding still hasn't, after five years, been installed sometimes irks me. But when it does, I go out and walk around the neighborhood. Then I come home and take a bath. I fought hard for that bathtub, and it's quiet there. It feels like where I'm supposed to be.

Everybody wants to have adventures.
Whether they know it or not.

誰もが冒険したいと考える。本人が気づいているか否かに関わらず。

THE UPHEAVAL OF our home renovation mirrored what had been going on with my karate training in the year or two after I got my black belt. I got pregnant just a few months after the gamet, and though I trained through most of my pregnancy, I still struggled to reorient my body and brain to karate after Lilly's birth in late 2003.

It's always odd to resume training after a break, whether the layoff is due to pregnancy, injury, illness, or just life getting in the way. The dojo is still a familiar place, but your body feels stiff and foreign. You perform the same movements you've done thousands of times, and they come out all wrong. After childbirth, you also have the surreal effects of sleep deprivation to contend with (changes to your reaction time, your vision, hearing, balance, and short-term memory), plus the radical reconfiguration of your hips and pelvis, which are central to most of the action in both pregnancy and the martial arts.

I was focused on trying to make my side kicks come out the way they did before I'd had a nine-and-a-quarter-pound baby, so it took me a while to notice a change in the atmosphere at the dojo. For one thing, Sensei Suzanne was gone more often. She had always traveled periodically, to teach elsewhere, to visit family, or to study in India or other out-of-the-way places. But now she was in a serious relationship, and she was gone more often, for longer intervals.

Jan, looking for a new challenge, had finally parted ways with Sun Dragon, and was pursuing a black belt in Shaolin Do Kung Fu. Gina had finished her PhD and taken a job in Boston, which left Joy as the school's senior student. In the past, senior students had been charged by Sensei Suzanne with leading warm-ups and basics. Now, Joy was teaching the whole class, almost every night.

"Where's Sensei tonight?" I would ask. "Dallas" was always the answer. She's in Dallas today; in Dallas this week; she'll be in Dallas pretty much all month.

There were hints, murmured comments, and strained, uncertain looks among the students. Sensei was not one to keep secrets or spring surprises (she didn't need to), so I saw no cause for undue alarm. But something was clearly in the works.

"Everybody wants to have adventures," Sensei Suzanne used to say whenever she taught a self-defense workshop for teenagers (this was part of the conversation she preferred to have without parents in the room). Unlike a lot of teachers, who are apt to bombard teens with warnings, cautions, and admonitions, Sensei made a point of acknowledging their desire, and their right, to explore. As a parent herself, she said you'd have to be willfully blind to think for one second they're *not* going to explore. Go ahead, try new things, she told the kids. Meet new people, and learn about other ways to live your life. The purpose of self-defense isn't to stop you from having fun. It's to help you find ways to do so safely and intelligently.

But Sensei understood, too, that the need to have adventures doesn't end in adolescence. She knew that change is a necessary part of our growth throughout life. So, following her own advice, she had begun carefully laying plans for her own adventure, which was this: retiring.

When she made the formal announcement that she would be leaving and Joy would become Sun Dragon's head instructor, some students were distraught. A few were angry. "How could Sensei just *abandon* us?" a frustrated green belt fumed in the dressing room afterward.

"Yeah, and leave all this?" I mused, looking around at the moldy rafters, the leaking water cooler, the yellowed, curling linoleum.

As strange as it seems, given my history of panicking at the slightest whiff of change, the news of Sensei Suzanne's impending retirement was a huge relief to me. Sure, I was sad, and a little shocked, at the thought of losing the teacher who had taught me so much. And it's not that I wasn't anxious about what would happen—to the school, to us, to my grip on reality.

But I harbored a much deeper worry, and that was for Sensei herself. For fifteen years she had lived the most basic spiritual lesson that karate teaches: The "empty hand" (*kara te*) is one that shares freely. Even in the martial arts, you rarely meet people who embody the philosophy the way Sensei Suzanne did. Anyone can be generous when they have plenty to share. She was generous when she had nothing to give. One winter when she was reduced to living in the dojo's office, she let a homeless guy camp out in the building's unused garage because he had no safe place to sleep.

I don't mean to depict her as a saint. If I did, she'd kill me. But Sensei Suzanne had made Sun Dragon her life, and she impoverished herself in the process. I don't think she ever regretted that choice; still, the sacrifices she made were, quite frankly, appalling. She had no retirement fund, no health insurance, no Social Security contributions to her credit from all those years of work. She rarely had enough income to give her any kind of cushion. Her school had done so much for so many people, including me, and I felt more than a little guilty about the precarious nature of her existence.

Not that I could say anything to that effect. Sensei made her own choices, and she would not have thanked me for telling her how to prioritize her life. But I had heard her talk for so long about the importance of self-care that I was truly happy to see her taking this step. To feel any other way would have been selfish.

Like the other black belts at Sun Dragon, I had already been through plenty of challenges purposely devised by Sensei Suzanne to test me: gamets, board breaking, last-minute teaching assignments, unscheduled public speaking appearances, and ad hoc lessons in electrical grounding systems, just to name a few. From that perspective, her departure looked like just one more difficult, irritating, ill-timed, messy, but valuable training exercise. We all knew it would be good for us, if we survived it.

Sensei had a long experience with adventure, and she moved into this one as purposefully as she did everything else. She planned to relocate to Dallas, where her partner lived, and she needed steady work when she arrived. So she dusted off her master's degree in chemistry, earned a state certification to teach high school science, and found a job in the Dallas public school system. She started the dojo on the road to nonprofit status and promoted Joy to the title of Sensei, and then she left us. That part couldn't have been easy for her, but Sensei liked to do hard things.

Sensei's final gift, after everything else she had already bestowed, was to give us the adventure of running Sun Dragon without her. She did not ask us if we wanted this gift. She just gave it to us. As I said, she was a very generous woman.

Within months of the change in leadership, the dojo's roof was leaking, the plumbing had erupted, and we were fighting a pitched battle with the rats. Faced with this string of calamities, we had no choice but to figure out how to function as a team. It could easily have been a disaster—a bunch of strong-minded women, trained to be vocal and assertive, figuring out how to run a project they were all deeply invested in emotionally. We might have ended up like the women's lay ministry group at my mother-in-law's church, notorious for its infighting (my mother-in-law attributes the excessive conflict to the simple fact that all the good Episcopalian ladies in the women's lay ministry are, astrologically, Leos).

I'm pretty sure the reason we were able to pull it off—to keep the school running, and remain friends, instead of turning into a bunch of backbiting shrews—was that we were used to hitting one another.

Addressing Joy as *Sensei* was the first big change we confronted when Sensei Suzanne left, and it went deeper than just the use of the title. This was someone we had trained alongside, as peers, for ages, and we couldn't simply erase our former friendship from our memories. Yet now, as our instructor, Sensei Joy required our formal respect. We had to establish a new relationship with her, one that reconciled our past informality with the current realities of rank.

I reminded myself of this often when we were adjusting to the new arrangement at the dojo. Every time Sensei Joy told us to do something a certain way, and it occurred to me that there might be a better way to do it, I would remind myself of how Joy moved in the sparring ring, of the certainty she brought to everything she did, and of the results she got. And most of the time, this prompted me to keep my helpful suggestions to myself, and just say *"osu."*

The exact number of black belts who were training at Sun Dragon at that time is hard to calculate; people had an annoying tendency to marry, move to Central America or Europe, and have babies (not necessarily in that order). Apart from Sensei Joy, there was a core of us who, largely by default, were left to assume the role of senior students. KJ, Denise, Amy, and I would not, perhaps, have been anyone's preferred candidates to take on so much responsibility. As a group, we were long on camaraderie but conspicuously short on decorum. But we had already been through a lot together. And we each brought some unique talents to the project. Above all (in keeping with the Sun Dragon tradition), we were the ones who were there. It was us or nothing.

We certainly didn't look like the kind of crack squad you'd assemble if you needed to save a karate school. Of the four of us, KJ was the only natural athlete, and she also had an infectious enthusiasm that we sorely needed at the time. She approached the new reality at Sun Dragon the same way she sparred: by rolling forward and crushing every obstacle in her path. KJ started helping Sensei Joy teach the adult classes, and became the de facto leader of the senior students as we rallied around the project of keeping the dojo afloat.

Denise was a mild-mannered speech therapist who had earned her black belt two years after I did. With her glasses and flyaway, prematurely graying hair, Denise bore a more-than-passing resemblance to Sensei Suzanne. Temperamentally, though, they were polar opposites. Denise was the least alarming person I'd ever met, and if the word "unflappable" didn't already exist, I'd have to coin it to describe her. Even on days when her client visits had gone badly—which, for Denise, meant she'd had to call the police *and* emergency medical assistance—she was calm and matter-of-fact about life. It was only after we'd known each other for a long time that she revealed her past as one of a notorious group of antiapartheid protesters arrested on the University of Texas campus in the early 1980s for forcibly occupying the president's office.

"You were one of the UT Sixteen?" I asked, awestruck. "You guys were, like, heroes!"

Denise was more circumspect. "Well, the judge didn't think so," she recalled. "I had to spend the whole summer doing community service. But, you know," she said philosophically, "this is Austin. I did my service at Barton Springs Pool, at the admissions gate. I watched people get high and play Hacky Sack. There are worse ways to spend a summer."

Denise began helping out with the children's classes and some of the self-defense workshops. She was especially well suited to teach the class Sensei Suzanne had pioneered at a local women's addiction-recovery center. The women there were the kind of population Sun Dragon existed to serve. They didn't have time or money to study karate, but they were desperate to regain a sense of control over their lives, and self-defense was a basic skill that many of them could use every day. Working with people in this situation requires a special kind of instructor—these were women with a lot of personal problems—but Denise went about it the same way I imagine she locked down the president's office at UT, with imperturbable competence and the simple conviction that she was doing the right thing. And, as she pointed out, her arrest record gave her instant credibility with her students.

Amy, who received her black belt in the final gamet Sensei Suzanne presided over at Sun Dragon, was the baby of the black belts. Because she had joined Sun Dragon while I was in Hawaii, she seemed even newer to me than to everyone else. The feeling was mutual. "I was always confused about where you came from," she once told me. "When you came back from Hawaii it was like a fully fledged green belt had just dropped out of the sky."

Amy had absorbed Sun Dragon into her life more fully than any of us. When she enrolled at the dojo, she had been a midlevel computer systems administrator. By the time Sensei Suzanne departed four years later, Amy was on her way to a social work PhD and had essentially made the reduction of societal violence her life's work. Like all grad students, she was busy and poor, but she volunteered to teach the children's classes, as well as some of our self-defense workshops.

I would have liked to teach regularly, or to assist more often at self-defense classes, but my work schedule and family made that close to impossible. I figured I might be able to help with the rats, though.

The rats had invariably shown up when Sensei Suzanne was out of town. They had a sixth sense about her. As soon as she was beyond the city limits, we'd hear them scurrying around in the rafters over the office. Sometimes, if classes ran late and they grew tired of waiting for us to leave, they would venture out above the main floor, peering down at us from the ceiling joists.

Sensei Suzanne had always peremptorily poisoned the rats, karma be damned, as soon as she returned to the dojo, but we were young and squeamish. I offered to bring in the humane rat trap I had acquired in Hawaii (rats had been a bigger problem there than sharks, as it turned out).

The night I volunteered for the dojo's rat-catching duties, Scott came out in the backyard to help me look for the trap. Together we waded through the mountain of junk in the crawl space beneath his new storage shed, where I vaguely remembered seeing the blue and white Havaheart box.

It was a warm, humid night, as nine out of ten nights in Austin are, and I was tired and sweaty and hadn't eaten since lunchtime, nine hours and two karate classes ago. Also, we had spent half of black belt class swilling water off the bathroom floor with dirty towels.

"Fucking rats," I muttered, tossing empty suitcases furiously across the yard like the gorilla in that old luggage commercial. "Fucking plumbing. Fucking leaks. Next thing you know the roof will be caving in on us. The rug is taking water from above *and* below; we'll never get it clean."

The sad truth is that while my attitude at the dojo (and especially in front of junior students) was very much in the "Keep calm and carry on" spirit, at home it was a different story. As I'd worked toward my black belt, I'd become much better at integrating the focus and calmness of the dojo into the rest of my life. But in these circumstances, I wasn't quite up to the task. This test wasn't like a gamet. It wasn't like any of the other tests we'd undergone. This one had no definite end point. Every time we surmounted one obstacle, something new emerged to throw our training, and Sun Dragon's existence, into doubt.

Doubt is not a happy place for me.

Scott, unlike my sparring partners, has to live with me whether I'm wearing my black belt or not, and he was the one who bore the real brunt of the stress I was feeling about the changes at Sun Dragon. He's a former bad boy himself and understands selfish behavior as well as anyone, but even he has limits to what he can tolerate.

That evening he watched me fling objects haphazardly out from under the shed, interrupting my venting only after I heaved a weighty metal toolbox up from a dark corner.

"Hey, my socket-wrench set!" Delighted, he deftly removed it from my hands before I could throw it anywhere. "I was wondering where that was."

I gave him a look that was fortunately lost in the dim light, and viciously kicked an old office chair.

"You know," Scott observed, "you don't have to do any of this if you don't want to. If it's making you so unhappy to keep training, just stop."

"I *can't* 'just stop,'" I snapped. "Not now. I mean, the school would function just fine without me; they don't *need* me, but I'd feel like I'm leaving at the worst possible time if I go now. Like a rat leaving a sinking ship," I added, as I spotted the blue silhouette of a rat on a battered white cardboard carton. "Here it is."

Scott lifted up a stack of mildewed Forest Service maps. I yanked the trap out from under them and tossed it behind me onto the lawn. As it landed, an enormous brown cockroach, fully three inches long, burst from the Havaheart box, scrambled past my left foot, and disappeared under the trash cans.

"We need to spray out here," Scott observed. "They must have found somewhere to hide when we tore down the carport, and moved back in afterward."

"The exterminator charges seventy-nine dollars per visit,"

I reminded him bitterly. "That's about a month's tuition at the dojo. We sure could use that money; Lilly's preschool is raising its rates again."

"Hon," Scott said, his voice rising just a little, "when we lived in Hawaii and you weren't training at Sun Dragon, you were miserable. That's why we came back to Austin, remember? Now you're here and you have Sun Dragon. Does that make you happy or not? If it doesn't, then for heaven's sake, stop going. But *you* have to make up your mind. I'm not going to tell you what you should do. Is that what you *want* me to do? Make the decision for you? Because I won't do that. All I can do is support you once you decide. And I'm sorry if that's not enough for you. That's just the way I am."

"That's why I *married* you, dumbass!" I shouted in exasperation. (Keep in mind, this is what we sound like *after* years of marriage counseling.)

He didn't say anything.

"Look," I told him, thoroughly ashamed, "the problem is that I don't know exactly what I'm fighting for now. I'm a black belt, but I'm not really needed as a teacher. I don't know how to make the school solvent; I can't fix the plumbing. Other than trapping rats, what am I good for?"

"Trapping rats is important," Scott pointed out reasonably. "And anyway, you don't have to solve every problem by yourself. Sun Dragon has been around for a long time. It's part of Austin. Other than Suzanne, the people who make the school what it is are still there. It's going to survive, in one form or another."

"I hope so," I said.

We stood out there by the shed a while longer, slapping at the mosquitoes attracted to our neighbors' backyard Christmas lights (a sure sign, during the summer months, that you live in South Austin), listening to the buzz of the cicadas and the intermittent chirps of the geckos that eat the cicadas. Out on the highway, a siren started up and the neighborhood dogs joined in like gospel singers on a refrain. Something rustled in the compost pile. Too big for a rat, I judged; it was probably a possum, looking for eggshells.

"Do you remember," Scott asked after a moment, "earlier this year when Joy brought that instructor down from Minneapolis to teach a seminar at Sun Dragon?"

"Sifu Koré," I said. "Sure."

"You told me something she said—about those moments in your practice when you forget what you're doing and you don't know what's supposed to happen next, how those moments are gifts."

"Yeah," I recalled. "Because when you don't know what to do next, you can do anything. She said the more experienced you become, the rarer those moments are, and that they let you open up to new possibilities. And that's really important."

"Well, I think you've hit one of those moments," Scott said. "You don't know what's going to happen next, and you don't know what to do."

"And I hate that."

"But you don't have to."

As usual, I thought: he's right.

Everybody wants to have adventures. Sometimes we just forget how.

We never completely vanquished the rats, but we did achieve a sort of détente with them. I set the humane trap on one of the ceiling joists, over the office (we didn't have a ladder, so KJ had to hoist me up in the air while I baited it). The rats avoided it entirely, but they seemed to get the message.

At any rate, after that they stayed out of the dojo while classes were in session, which was all we wanted—a time-sharing agreement, really.

The plumbing continued to sulk and threaten and throw the occasional tantrum, but we became adept at locating leaks and unclogging drains. And Sensei Joy somehow maneuvered the landlord into replacing the dojo's roof, a huge and unexpected boon, which instantly cut our flooding problems in half. With slightly dryer carpet underfoot, we forged ahead, encouraging the junior students and rubbing the rough edges off our new relationships with one another.

We often act as if women, once they reach a certain milestone—finishing college or marrying or becoming mothers—are through exploring and changing. The reality, I think, is that most of us don't *start* growing up until sometime in our thirties. It's not an age for caution. In many ways it's the best time to have adventures. And I've learned that when you find yourself in the midst of one, you have three choices: you can embrace it, run away from it, or suffer through it. They're all viable options, but the first is the only one that's any fun.

Sometimes the only way forward is to go back and start over.

時に、前進する唯一の方法は、最初からやり直すことだ。

ONCE WE HAD settled into our new roles at the dojo, Sensei Joy took a careful look around her and determined that Sun Dragon could not survive much longer on its established business plan of independence, poverty, and imminent disaster. She then resolutely set about the monumental task of stabilizing the dojo's income.

What we needed most were white belts. While experienced students are the backbone of any martial arts school, the white belts are the lifeblood. A dojo requires a constant stream of new students, because karate is a grueling discipline. Not everyone who tries it loves it enough to keep coming back. You need a lot of people who are willing to try it in order to support the few who end up loving it.

We advertised in local newspapers, online, and on the radio. We offered new students free uniforms, discounted tuition, and two-for-one, bring-a-friend! specials. Usually these efforts would net a couple of fresh white belts, but not enough, and most of them didn't stay long.

One obstacle to new enrollment was our beloved but increasingly derelict dojo. Prospective students would find our Web page, get excited about karate, come in for their free trial class, and then take one look at—or, more likely, one whiff of—the dojo, and decide, well, maybe they'd rather try yoga after all.

Upgrading the dojo wasn't feasible until we had more revenue. Revenue comes from students. Prospective students were repulsed by the dojo. And so on.

Sensei Joy brought the collective wisdom of the black belts to bear on this problem during advanced class one evening, with mixed results. "Let's hear your ideas," she encouraged us, as if we might actually have some. We did our best. Amy advocated a membership drive, pitting our current students against one another to see how many friends they could sign up for a class. KJ offered to pay for an ad in the program distributed at Austin Outlaws' football games. Denise suggested we offer discounted rates to people who worked at social service agencies. "Or any public sector workers, really," she said. "Bus drivers and mental health caseworkers—they all need self-defense skills on the job."

No one paid any attention to my suggestion, which was that we stop trying to persuade people to visit the dojo and simply hunt them down in the streets, using tranquilizer darts and perhaps nets. "What? Can't you see how perfect it is?" I asked when they just stared at me blankly. "Go out to Sixth Street on a Friday night and bag half a dozen people while they're drunk. By the time they sober up, we have them in a *gi* and out on the floor, and if they ask questions we'll tell 'em they've already signed the paperwork."

"Well, it *does* sound like fun," Denise conceded, "but don't you think there would be liability issues?"

"Gold's Gym has been doing it for years," I insisted. "How do you think they meet their sales quotas?"

Sensei Joy sighed one of her long-suffering sighs, which had grown increasingly frequent in the past year.

"We just did a membership drive in March," she reminded Amy, "and we had two students sign up, which was great, but it's too soon to do another one. KJ, I think it would be wonderful to have an ad in the Outlaws program, thank you. And Denise, please feel free to offer a tuition discount to anyone you work with, and I'll mention that, too, when I contact other organizations."

She was too diplomatic to say anything about my plan.

With her black belts devoid of (lawful) ideas, Sensei Joy was left to solve the problem on her own. The solution was not simple; it called for long-term strategizing. And it ended up requiring, as had Sensei Suzanne's departure, a series of elaborate transformations for everyone concerned.

By 2006, about a year and a half after Sensei Suzanne's retirement, Sensei Joy had finalized her plans, and she revealed them to me at Special Training, an annual National Women's Martial Arts Federation (NWMAF) meeting that is half summer camp and half high school reunion for female martial artists. She pulled me aside at lunchtime in the cafeteria, where I was trying to figure out what, if anything, I should eat in advance of the one-thirty open sparring session, and asked if we could talk about the school.

For reasons I will never quite understand, I had been invited the year before to join Sun Dragon's board of directors. The board was created by Sensei Suzanne before her departure, when she converted the school into a nonprofit organization. When I joined, the board consisted of me, Amy, Joy, and anyone we could talk into attending who might have some vague idea of how to strengthen the school. It was as a board member that I finally became privy to the bald numbers underlying Sun Dragon's precarious existence. It was an eye-opening experience. I had always known the place was run on a shoestring, but I had no idea how thin and frayed the shoestring was. So when Sensei Joy told me, over our trays of generic cafeteria salad, that she had a plan to put the dojo on solid financial ground, I was all ears. As my advocacy of tranquilizer darts indicated, I was willing to try anything to help the school.

What Sensei Joy had decided, she told me over the clatter of forks and plastic trays, was that Sun Dragon needed to affiliate with a national martial arts system. This would allow several things to happen. All of us black belts would finally have some meaningful training goals. Until now Sun Dragon's curriculum had effectively ended at black belt, so we had been spinning our wheels for some time in terms of our skills development. Sensei Joy and I had labored for months over the twenty-seven moves of Seienchin Kata, a complex kata from the Okinawan Naha-te tradition. We sweated over it night after night in the murky dojo, but so many of this advanced kata's techniques were unfamiliar to us—*yumi uke,* the archer's block, was unlike anything we'd ever done; the rising elbow block, *jodan hiji uke*, how was that supposed to work? The turns were strange, the angles confusing, the movements obscure in purpose. We had no one to turn to for clarification. I ended every session feeling defeated and uncertain, and also a little guilty for being so hard for Sensei Joy to teach.

We had brought in a series of guest instructors in other

styles, like Sifu Koré Grate from Minneapolis, but we knew this wasn't a long-term solution. Joining a national system would also give us some organizational and business experience to call upon as we worked out the economics of the school. And we'd gain a more formal, hopefully more impressive, institutional affiliation to point to when new students considered joining our school.

In theory, it sounded quite logical, and even easy. The catch was this: we were Kyokushinkai.

Several groups claimed to be heirs to Mas Oyama's legacy, but there was no single, thriving national Kyokushin organization to which we could turn for training, recognition, or advice. Moreover, the individual Kyokushin schools we knew about, apart from Sun Dragon, scared the pants off of us. We thought *we* were tough; some of those people still fought bare-knuckled, and all of them were heavily male dominated. They were not overly concerned with violence prevention, safer communities, or women's empowerment.

The uncomfortable truth was that while the art of Kyokushin fit very well within Sun Dragon's mission, Sun Dragon would not fit at all well within Kyokushin.

So Sensei Joy, as was her wont, had maneuvered around this particular block. "I've been talking to the ladies from Thousand Waves," she explained, shoving some defeated-looking carrots to the side of her plate. Thousand Waves Martial Arts and Self-Defense Center was a dojo in Chicago, whose directors, Nancy and Sarah, were longtime members of the NWMAF. Moreover, they had been friends with Sensei Suzanne for many years. Thousand Waves *did* have a mission of violence reduction and women's empowerment. And it was a member of the World Seido Karate Organization.

Seido karate, Sensei Joy went on, is derived from Kyokushin, and the two styles are very similar. This is because Seido was founded by Kaicho (Grandmaster) Tadashi Nakamura, who was once Mas Oyama's senior student. Most of the kata and techniques in the two systems are almost identical, but the spirit of Seido, Sensei assured me, was quite different from the Kyokushin ethic of "one blow, sudden death."

Kaicho Nakamura had been a champion knockdown fighter in Kyokushin, and a national hero in Japan as a young man after defeating a Thai kickboxer in an international tournament in the 1960s. But after twenty-plus years training and teaching in Kyokushin, he grew concerned about the direction he saw the art of karate taking—its focus on finding the biggest, best, and toughest fighters, and developing them into champions. Kaicho, as he was referred to within the Seido system, felt that this was unhealthy for the people practicing karate and for the art itself. It was too insular, too limited; it turned karate in on itself and made it into something most people wouldn't even think of trying.

So Kaicho founded his own karate system, Seido (meaning, "Sincere Way"). His goal was to make a place for the spirit of *budo* in modern society. *Budo*—"the way to stop the spear"—is the traditional term used to describe all Asian martial arts. As its definition implies, such arts are rightfully concerned with self-defense and self-mastery, not with the domination of others. The way of *budo* should be open to everyone, Kaicho felt, not just a few elite fighters. And so the mission of the World Seido Karate Organization, Sensei Joy summarized, was to help weak people become strong, not merely to help strong people become stronger. Seido even had its own nonprofit arm, a foundation that raised money for charitable causes like the Red Cross and domestic abuse intervention.

Seido's founder clearly understood the same strengths and

weaknesses in Kyokushin that we had run up against, but unlike us he had a lifetime of experience making sense of them. It sounded like a perfect fit for Sun Dragon, and I said so. Sensei's relief at my enthusiasm was palpable. If the rest of the board agreed, she told me, the leaders of Thousand Waves would help her formally request permission to begin training in Seido, with an eye toward eventually transitioning Sun Dragon—the whole school—into the Seido system. She would make periodic trips to Chicago to train at Thousand Waves until she could test for her Seido black belt, and Jun Shihan Nancy would come to Austin to meet with the rest of the Sun Dragon black belts.

I could already tell we were moving into higher realms of our art—the titles were different.

That autumn Sensei Joy began training in earnest for her Seido black belt test, and we all happily cheered her on. Until, that is, she broached the subject of Jun Shihan Nancy's impending visit to Sun Dragon, to start us on our own road to Seido black belts. This was the point where reality set in for the rest of us, because having meaningful training goals was one thing; preparing to test for black belt in a new style in nine short months was something else entirely. True—KJ, Denise, Amy, and I had black belts in Kyokushin, but those had taken years to earn. The Seido curriculum, we were discovering as Sensei Joy attempted to master it, was complex and detailed. A student joining Seido as a white belt could expect to take four or five years to learn it all. We were going to do it in less than one.

The insanity of the whole project really hit home the night Amy announced she'd been diagnosed with multiple sclerosis.

Sensei Joy had seated us all in a circle on the floor, saying Amy had an announcement.

"So, you all know I've been having problems with my balance for a while," Amy told us. We had noticed this, and knew also that she'd been experiencing tingling sensations in her arms and legs, and some other worrisome symptoms. We knew she'd been seeing doctors and undergoing lots of tests.

"There's no single test that proves you have MS," Amy went on. "All they can do is evaluate your symptoms and rule out other causes. And in my case, they've now ruled out everything except MS, so that's my official diagnosis."

No one knew what to say. I waited for someone else to contribute something compassionate and wise, but they didn't, so I just said what I was thinking, which was "Well, that sucks."

Amy laughed and said, "I agree. And I've promised myself that this won't stop my karate practice. With MS," she went on, "staying active is important if you want to stay mobile. My neurologist says that if I keep training, the odds are good I won't end up in a wheelchair."

"We'll do everything we can to help you stay mobile, Amy," Sensei Joy promised her. "And I know several women in the NWMAF with limited mobility, so if it comes to that, we have resources we can draw on to help you continue your training."

"And, you know," Denise pointed out, "if you ever *do* end up in a wheelchair, you could get one of those monkeys." Denise works with a lot of disabled kids, so I don't think she was trying to be funny, but for some reason, a helper monkey for Amy struck all of us as a brilliant idea. By the time we had exhausted the possibilities of having a monkey in the dojo—"Maybe he could figure out where the rats are hiding," KJ suggested—the mood had lightened considerably.

"I just want to reiterate," Amy said, as she struggled to her feet, refusing the outstretched hands we offered her, "that I'm still going to finish my doctorate in social work, and I'm still planning to test for my Seido black belt along with the rest of you."

"Osu," we all said, knowing that Amy would be at the test if she had to be carried into the dojo on a stretcher.

Amy's announcement also settled some questions for me. I had been sharply conflicted about making my own personal leap into Seido. With my kids, an ever-more-demanding job, and an aging body, this black belt test seemed like a much bigger challenge than my first one had. And I was nervous about testing with so little preparation. It all reminded me of that recurring dream, where I was back in school and about to take a final exam in a class I hadn't known I was enrolled in. That dream always made me wake up sweating.

But Amy's news put my doubts into a whole new perspective. Even if you have multiple sclerosis, Amy was showing us, you can do almost anything you put your mind to. And if you *don't* have MS, well, then you sure as hell don't have any excuses.

Sensei Joy successfully tested for her Seido black belt at Thousand Waves in April, and a few months later, KJ, Denise, Amy, and I lined up in the dojo on a Friday night for our first class with Jun Shihan Nancy.

Jun Shihan offered us some comforting words about the stylistic similarities between Kyokushin and Seido. She complimented us on the regularity and volume with which we responded, *"Osu!"* at each pause in her remarks. Then she said, "Let's start off with some basic punches." (*"Osu!"* we said.)

On her count, we did ten middle punches, *chudan tsuki,* in our best style: elbows in tight and driving behind the punch, hips solidly beneath the technique, feet rooted.

Jun Shihan looked at us thoughtfully when we had finished, nodded, and then said slowly, "OK, that was great. Your energy is fantastic. Now, in Seido, we like to employ what we call 'natural breathing.'"

We all laughed nervously. Sensei Suzanne had stressed forceful exhalation on most techniques, the way she had been taught. It wasn't as showy as some styles I've come across, where the artist practically whistles with every move. But it was noticeable. And it was, for us, automatic. We always breathed that way.

They didn't breathe that way in Seido.

We executed another ten punches, trying not to breathe so loudly this time. Unfortunately, after so many years of training with Sensei Suzanne, so many thousands and thousands of punches, so many breaths, we discovered we were no longer capable of breathing "naturally." We weren't even sure what the term meant. We would, it appeared, have to learn to breathe all over again. I determined not to think too deeply about the ramifications, filing this knowledge away for the time being with the mental note: *Breathing: dial it back.*

Jun Shihan watched us carefully as we punched and tried to breathe naturally. "Very good," she encouraged us. "Now I want you to think a little bit about your lower bodies. Seido's style encourages us to take advantage of the rotational energy in our hips. So try letting your feet pivot a little as you punch, and feel your body turn into the technique."

She was always careful, I noticed, to phrase her corrections as opportunities. And everything she was suggesting made perfect sense, in terms of application. Kaicho Nakamura had done a lot of full-contact fighting, and his style of karate was designed to let a fighter maximize his or her power. Pivoting the hips is a natural follow-through movement with a punch; it provides additional momentum and allows you to keep the base of your hips and legs under the punch longer. I tried to pivot the way Jun Shihan did, but my body, which I had trained for years to employ straight vectors of power, refused to pivot. I could lean forward (not a smart thing to do when trying to punch someone). I could bend my knees inward (also dumb). I could not pivot.

I tried; I really tried, through one set of punches after another. The energy in each punch would surge up my legs from the ground, and I would channel it through my hips into my punching arm, but the instant I turned my hip, the all-important link between the legs and the arms was broken, and the punch went nowhere. It was incredibly frustrating, like a spotty electrical connection.

As I was struggling, Jun Shihan peered back into the dim corner of the dojo where I stood and asked me, "Do you have an injury to your left arm?" In fact, I don't have an injury to my left arm; I have one to my right shoulder, which makes it tough for me to retract that arm strongly, and thus manifests in underextension of my left arm on some techniques. It's not too pronounced, unless I'm cold. How Jun Shihan had noticed it, from that distance, in that light, in the midst of all the fruitless gyrations I was producing as I tried to rotate, I had no idea.

"*Osu,* Jun Shihan," I said, and explained the injury, assuring her it was healed, and affected only my range of motion.

"All right," she said, and left it at that, but I could see her filing the information away. I knew Jun Shihan had a reputation as an excellent instructor, but that was the point at which I recognized that I was in the hands of an extraordinarily experienced teacher. Somehow, I had to believe she was going to find a way to teach me to breathe and punch properly. Just maybe not tonight.

"Why don't we move on to blocks?" Jun Shihan suggested.

When I staggered into the house at nine-thirty that evening, I could barely move my arms.

"Rough class, huh?" Scott asked as I dropped my gym bag on the floor and crawled toward the sofa. "You want a beer?"

"Just break the bottle over my head," I told him.

"You need a hot bath," he said, heading off to the kitchen.

It was an hour before I had enough energy to stagger from the sofa to the tub, and after lying there until the water grew cold, I still needed Scott to help me into bed.

"I'm turning forty in a few weeks," I said as I closed my eyes. "Is this what middle age is going to be like? Does it just hurt all the time?"

"Not all the time," Scott assured me (he's six years older than I am). "You'll be fine, I promise."

"If not," I muttered, "I can always get a monkey."

"You're talking in your sleep," Scott said as he turned off the lights. "Nighty-night."

Jun Shihan Nancy went back to Chicago, leaving us with encouraging words and an encyclopedic list of terms and techniques to memorize. At Sun Dragon, we had learned kata, and self-defense, and . . . well, punching and kicking, mainly. Sensei Suzanne had supplemented our Kyokushin curriculum with a little bit of Aikido training, and some Arnis, the Filipino stick-fighting art. But most of what we did involved simply hitting things, or one another.

Seido had all the punching and kicking, and the kata, but it also had a bewildering palette of prearranged technique sequences we needed to memorize: partner drills, solo drills with imaginary partners, and formal combinations of blocks and strikes. There was much more weight given to the process of memorizing movements, so that you could use them spontaneously when you needed them. Given that Kaicho had been a successful match fighter, it was hard to argue with this approach.

Sensei Joy, with her past experience memorizing choreography, had made it look pretty easy. It wasn't. The four of us junior black belts sweated over the Seido curriculum all through Austin's long, hot summer, as the dojo, under its new roof, reached Saharan temperatures. We kept a concerned eye on Amy, whose MS symptoms were worsened by the heat. We wrestled with the new vocabulary as much as we did with the techniques. KJ developed a habit of saying the name of each movement as we did it, which was a good learning method for her but quickly became very distracting for everyone else. *"Juji uke, hiza geri, yoko geri,"* she would hiss, until it was such a predictable part of Kihon Kumite Number Seven that I found it hard to practice on my own without hearing KJ's closed-captioning. I also found myself resenting all the new Japanese vocabulary. We had enough trouble remembering the techniques themselves, I thought, without worrying about memorizing the Japanese term for back-spinning foot sweep, *ushiro mawashi ashi barai* (which is pronounced just like it's spelled).

Still, if Seido was more demanding than our prior curriculum, it was also more forgiving.

When the day arrived (all too soon) for our Seido black belt test, the old and the new Sun Dragon were represented together at the judges' table: Jun Shihan Nancy, who would, if all went well, award our Seido belts; Sensei Joy, who had relentlessly shoved us forward on our torturous path; and Sensei Suzanne, who had flown in from Kansas City, where she and her partner now lived, to give her blessing to this new direction for the dojo.

The contrast between the past and the future, Kyokushin and Seido, became crystal clear to me during the *tameshiwari* (breaking) portion of the test, which Sensei Suzanne kicked off by telling us the following story:

"Mas Oyama was famous for fighting and killing bulls bare-handed," she began—a fact we all knew, and had been hearing about forever. "When Mas Oyama originally decided to fight a bull," she said, "it was a really big deal. This was how he planned to gain recognition for his style of karate, and his reputation and livelihood were riding on the results. And the first time he struck the bull"—Sensei demonstrated with a knifehand strike—"nothing happened. The bull didn't go down. So he hit the bull again, and again—nothing happened, and, in fact," she told us, "he got gored."

This was the first time any of us had heard that particular part of the Kyokushin mythos.

"And then he realized that not only was he about to fail, very publicly, at a task he had told the entire world he would succeed at," Sensei said, "but he was also very likely to die in the process. And then, in that moment, when he knew that everything was on the line—he struck a third time, and he killed the bull."

This was typical of the charming little stories Sensei Suzanne used to tell us all the time; it had blood, and shock value, and the moral was that you had to be committed one hundred percent to what you were doing at all times. She meant it to serve as a pep talk before we broke boards, and it certainly did give us something to think about. As usual, the test had been set up to tire us out as much as possible before we got to the *tameshiwari* portion, so we couldn't rely on power alone to accomplish our breaks. We had to demonstrate good technique, and we had to commit to the act.

But with our recent training in Seido, it turned out, we had a lot more technique to rely on. Make no mistake, commitment was every bit as important in Seido as it was in Kyokushin. "Nonquitting spirit" is essential to *budo,* and we had been hearing a lot about it in our new style. Still, when Jun Shihan Nancy told me I would be breaking my board with a horizontal *shotei,* or palm-heel strike, and I set up for the break, I saw (finally) the benefit of all that pivoting we had been urged to do. Instead of simply driving the technique out from my center and muscling through the board, as I would have done a year earlier, I was careful to put my hip into it (Jun Shihan watched carefully as I took my practice strike to make sure I was doing this). As a result, the break felt almost effortless. It was a subtle difference—engaging the hip behind the technique, rather than simply under it—but, in everyday parlance, it gave a lot more bang for the buck.

And it made me understand something that had never occurred to me before: commitment doesn't have to be a substitute for confidence. In the past, I had always relied on commitment when I had doubts about my ability. "I may not win, but I'm sure as hell gonna mark you" was my attitude, and while this berserker approach to life had carried me through some difficult moments, it finally dawned on me, in the middle of my second black belt test, at the age of forty, that there could be more to the concept than that. Commitment didn't have to spring from desperation; it could be part of a long process of preparation and intelligent planning.

I don't know why this hadn't been obvious to me all along; certainly I was seeing this kind of commitment practiced every day at the dojo, first by Sensei Suzanne, then by Sensei Joy, and by KJ, Denise, and Amy. But it didn't register for me until my hand went through that board. Preparation—not *worrying*—was the solution. Worrying was what I did when my exam-anxiety dreams woke me up and I lay in bed all night hyperventilating. Preparation was what I did in the dojo, purposefully, because I meant to be there, practicing, moving my body, checking my stances, following the patterns. *I should do more of that,* I thought, as the two pieces of my board clattered to the floor. *It works.*

At Sun Dragon, Sensei Suzanne had always awarded our new belts by untying the belts we'd started the test with and draping them around her neck, then tying on the new belts. (The untying of the old belt was a dramatic and touching moment with a utilitarian purpose: Sensei re-used our old belts to keep costs down for other students.)

At our Seido black belt test, we untied our own belts. These were white, since Seido requires black belt candidates to train in white belts for the last few months before their test. This serves as a reminder that a *karateka* is always, in an important sense, a beginner.

We sat in a row, in *seiza,* folded up our white belts, and laid them on the floor in front of us. Then Jun Shihan called us up, one by one, to receive our Seido black belts.

The tradition at Thousand Waves is to "break" a new belt as it's awarded. Taking each of our belts in turn, Jun Shihan Nancy held it up over her head, one end of the lengths of folded canvas in each hand, and snapped the belt taut with a loud crack, as if it had broken the sound barrier.

We hadn't fought a gamet—just a few rounds of sparring near the end of day—but this test, too, felt like a wedding. People cried, especially when Amy received her belt. There was hugging. Everyone was relieved it was over.

After the ceremony we all lined up to have our picture taken: four new black belts and our three teachers. Sun Dragon had moved from the Kyokushin era into the world of Seido. KJ, Denise, Amy, and I, in the photos from that day, look radiant. Sensei Suzanne looks genuinely happy. And Sensei Joy looks determined. She knew just how much more was still left to do.

Once a place becomes part of you, you can leave it without regret.

ある場所が自分の一部になると、
そこから後悔せずに離れることができる。

WE HAD ACQUITTED ourselves well, I thought, by earning our Seido black belts and paving the way for Sun Dragon to enter a new era. Sun Dragon had been a tight-knit community; now we were, more than ever, a family. And all of us were about to test our collective spirit of adventure and commitment even further the following year, as the school took its next step toward sustainability.

The Travis County tax rolls are mysteriously silent on the origins and market value of the building that housed Sun Dragon. The tax assessor apparently knows the property exists but doesn't seem to have much information about it, other than the address and its official status as "nonresidential." Sensei Suzanne's periodic habitation of the dojo was only one of the many things the tax assessor either didn't know about or preferred not to look into too closely. Things like the plumbing system, which must have been installed sometime in the late Pleistocene era, or the electrical wiring, which was only slightly more modern. The cavalier way we married the two systems wasn't pretty, either. To keep temperatures under a hundred degrees in the dojo, we relied on the "swamp cooler," a huge black box containing a fan squatting over a pan of water, which blew slightly cooler air over anyone lucky enough to be within ten feet of it. To fill the pan with water, we had to drape a garden hose over the dojo's rafters (alongside the electrical wiring) and down the wall to the cooler's spigot, which was unconscionably close to the ungrounded electrical outlet powering the appliance's 115-volt fan.

The standard daily activity in the dojo involved a considerably higher risk for electrocution than almost any other business would have incurred. It's basic science: A 115-volt shock to a person wearing tennis shoes and standing on a dry floor is usually harmless. However, if that person is sweaty and barefoot, her resistance to ground (which determines the severity of an electrical shock) is much, much lower—so low, in fact, that ventricular fibrillation is almost assured. In other words, whoever invented the swamp cooler might just as well have set out to create a bug zapper for karate students.

The city's reticence to check up on any of this may have simply been evidence of Austin's laissez-faire code enforcement. Maybe the inspectors were too busy complicating people's home renovations. Perhaps some simple bribery was involved. All I know is that the dojo's infrastructure would have given a nasty shock to any honest building inspector who'd bothered to take even a cursory glance at it.

But we got what we paid for. The rent our landlord asked of us was really more like an honorarium, a mere pittance compared to what Sun Dragon would have paid for a comparable space anywhere else. He settled for what we could pay because he liked Sensei Suzanne and wanted to support her school. Of course, he wasn't losing much by the arrangement; the building couldn't have been used, practically speaking, by many types of business. Really, without thousands of dollars of infrastructure spending to bring it up to code, it couldn't have been used *legally* by anyone. Still, we liked our landlord. He owned the adjacent sandwich shop that always donated food when we had a party at the dojo, and more important, its soft-drink machine was a ready source of ice whenever someone was injured during class.

So for over a decade, Sun Dragon's students managed to patch and mend and make do, or do without, as the building aged and sagged around us. But it was becoming increasingly clear, by the time we became a Seido school, that we couldn't keep this up forever. The building wasn't just scaring off prospective students anymore; it was starting to scare us. Plumbing failures grew more common, and more extensive. Wood we had painted and repainted was rotting at an accelerating pace. There was a general air of fatigue and impending doom about the place, and while there wasn't any blood actually running down the walls, the building was clearly telling us to *get . . . out.*

There was pressure from outside the dojo, too. In the years since Sensei had opened the school, the urban landscape around it had changed dramatically. The once-meandering traffic on Riverside Drive had become a torrent of buses and cars. Exhaust poured in through the open windows during rush hour, and the peaceful atmosphere degenerated into a constant drone of honks, tires squeals, and idling engines. New luxury apartment complexes rose on both sides of the dojo as the old ThunderCloud beer garden was swept up in the same red-hot real estate market that Scott and I encountered when our family outgrew its bathroom. Almost overnight, Sun Dragon's little pied-à-terre in trendy downtown Austin had turned into a potential gold mine for its owner. We learned that he was mulling plans for a large office building on the site where the dojo stood, and when our lease expired, he declined to renew it, accepting our nominal rent month-to-month instead. It was a nerve-racking arrangement. No one was happy about it, but I, naturally, worried about it nonstop.

Fortunately, our landlord moved at a typical Austin pace, which meant he still hadn't firmed up his building plans when the housing bust finally hit. (It's no coincidence that most of the big real estate projects in Austin are developed by Californians.) We had managed to hang on in the old dojo throughout this period, and as the property development whirlwind died down, we began to wonder if we might find a new school somewhere in the debris.

When I say "we," I mostly mean Graham.

Graham was not our first male student. Sun Dragon had always had boys in the kids' classes, and toward the end of Sensei Suzanne's tenure, she had allowed a few students' fathers to enroll in the adult program. So, after many years, I once again had male training partners (or, as I think of them, "the only men in the world allowed to hit me"). But Graham had been involved with the school longer than anyone else with a Y chromosome. When we originally met him, he was dating one of our black belts. He joined Sun Dragon as a student after they split up.

Graham had a quiet, bookish exterior, acquired in a series of harrowing Christian summer camps during his childhood in North Carolina. His law degree, his passion for dominoes, and his Southern-gentleman manners (really, he wouldn't have seemed out of character in suspenders) all belied his ability as a martial artist. Because, in addition to attending what he called "Jesus camp," Graham had spent a lot of his time in North Carolina training in Tang Soo Do, and he came to Sun Dragon with a third-degree black belt. His explosive spinning kicks—a hallmark of this Korean martial art—completely befuddled (and continue to befuddle) us straight-punching Kyokushinkai. But, though his stylistic background differed starkly from ours, Graham was one of those rare men who instinctively appreciated Sun Dragon's approach to martial arts and self-defense.

When we undertook the project of moving the school, I was serving as chair of the board of directors, which meant I showed up late to the meetings and quashed Amy every time she suggested a new membership drive. Something more was needed, and we were unbelievably fortunate to have Graham join the board shortly after I did. His efforts on behalf of the dojo, like his martial arts ability, were somewhat unexpected but extremely effective and perfectly timed.

In contrast to the rest of us well-intentioned doofuses on the board, Graham had bona fide business expertise, and once he no longer had a girlfriend, he had plenty of time on his hands. Following the vaunted Sun Dragon tradition, he perceived a need going unmet, discerned that he alone had any applicable skills, and stepped up to do what he could.

Our martial arts training had not prepared us particularly well for the soul-killing nature of interaction with commercial real estate agents. And the criteria for our search were stringent: Sensei Joy was adamant that the school remain in central Austin. We couldn't move too far from our existing students, and our mission obligated us to stay near the businesses, bars, and universities, where all kinds of people lived and worked. If we let Sun Dragon drift to the more economical suburbs, we risked turning ourselves into a studio school like the *dojang* I'd seen in Patty's neighborhood. We wouldn't be reducing violence or transforming lives. We'd be processing herds of upper-middle-class kids whose parents wanted trophies, not assertiveness, from their children.

Thus our real estate search, for many months, consisted of us board members craning our necks to spot RETAIL SPACE FOR LEASE signs as we drove to and from work. It mostly fell to Graham to turn our random efforts into a methodical process.

With bottomless patience, he called all the phone numbers we scribbled onto grubby gas-station receipts as we cruised past derelict shopping centers and boarded-up automotive garages. He visited filthy warehouses, took exact measurements and photos, and brought detailed reports to the board meetings explaining why each space was (a) too expensive, (b) too small, or (c) both.

This went on for months. Everyone but Graham grew frustrated and discouraged. Every time we found a place that met our specifications, it turned out to be beyond our means. Scott, trying to be helpful, pointed us toward several properties near the small university where he worked. This location was ideal because a university could be counted on to provide a steady stream of new students. One prime spot, in a glitzy new shopping center, was ruled out because it already housed a Krav Maga school with a noncompete clause in its lease. Another cool-looking old adobe building was revealed upon closer inspection to be a burned-out shell, which fazed Scott not a whit. "You could do a lot with this place," he remarked, tapping the charred ceiling joists. Graham measured and photographed dutifully, but he and the rest of the board were unconvinced. ("No way in hell" was how I voted.)

After that, Scott turned up a nondescript building next door to what had been a head shop back in the 1980s but now advertised itself as a supply store for the local pagan community. To save Graham from another fruitless trip, I told Scott to call and ask for details.

"It's cheap!" he reported back.

"What's wrong with it?" I asked suspiciously.

"Nothing, really."

I waited.

"The only thing is," he went on, as if he'd had a sudden afterthought, "the agent said tenants should expect some public nudity in the property's backyard during the full moon."

Nudity, like fire damage, didn't alarm Scott. I thought it might not bother the board too much, either, if the price was right. But I was reticent to send Graham, who still carried some baggage from his conservative upbringing, out to investigate with his measuring tape and camera. So I arranged a personal reconnaissance mission with Patty, using the promise of a magic shop next door to lure her. Patty has a passion for weird and out-of-the-way places. She once took her mother all the way to Europe to visit the Amsterdam Museum of Bags and Purses, and had recently regaled me with the story of her visit to the National Museum of Funeral History in Houston (where she bought a T-shirt with the slogan ANY DAY ABOVE GROUND IS A GOOD DAY). As I suspected, she was up for a trip to a magic shop.

The potential dojo was a nondescript storefront space, slightly rundown. Patty and I peered through the dusty windows at what had probably been a mortgage broker's office six months earlier. The carpet could come up, I figured. The size wasn't bad—nowhere near as large as the old dojo, but it was air-conditioned and nothing appeared to have been burned.

We couldn't tell much more from the outside, so I suggested, "Let's check out the magic shop," and led Patty up some rickety wooden stairs and through a door with a sign that read BLESSED BE! in faux-Gothic script. Inside, I immediately collided with a bundle of dried herbs hanging from the ceiling (yarrow, I guessed, based on the smell). Patty dodged the foliage but blundered into a lace-edged scarf draped over a bookshelf and, trying to untangle herself, backed into a beaded curtain that rattled menacingly. The air was fogged with the scent of Nag Champa, with an undertone of patchouli.

We stood still, afraid to move, and took in the shelves of tarot cards and candles, the dream catchers, the racks of tie-dyed skirts.

"Jesus," Patty muttered under her breath. "It looks like Stevie Nicks exploded in here."

"Namaste," said an owlish woman, who sat on a stool in the corner across from the door, working a pair of knitting needles. She wore a Juliet dress that had probably been quite cute on her when she'd bought it two decades ago, and she appeared to be knitting either the world's largest sock or a hat for an encephalitic baby. Whatever it was, it was pink.

"Hello," Patty replied. I blinked yarrow blossoms out of my eyelashes and smiled grittily.

"Can I help you ladies find something special today?" the woman murmured in the mellowest voice I'd ever heard in a sales clerk. When she spoke you got the impression that she was lying flat on her back. "We just received a new shipment of essential oils, and some fresh resins and incense. Or do you need tools? We have fabulous cauldrons, very reasonably priced." Her knitting needles continued clicking slowly and rhythmically, like a cow's jaws.

"Cauldrons?" Patty echoed.

"On the back porch," the woman nodded, making no move to stand up.

"Actually, we were just looking at the office space next door," I explained. "My karate school is thinking about leasing it."

"Oh really?" she said with polite interest. "What kind of karate school do you have?"

"Not Tai Chi," was what I wanted to say, since I suspected that was as far as her knowledge of martial arts would extend, but I gave her my thirty-second description of Seido, anyway. She nodded blankly, which seemed to be the way she responded to everything.

"Well, I hope you'll bring some positive energy to the place," she said. "The last bunch of renters . . ." She wrinkled her nose, sighed, and inspected her enormous pink sock with grave content.

"What kind of business was in there previously?" I inquired.

"Mortgage brokers."

"Ah," I said, and then had the sudden inane thought: wow, maybe I'm psychic.

"I'm Raven, by the way," the woman said, and nodded as Patty and I introduced ourselves. "This is a very *special* location," she went on. "A very powerful place, with the oak trees out back, you know, and the creek bed behind that. It's a dry creek, but it's a watercourse; that's what matters. Wonderful healing energy."

"Oh, is there a backyard?" I asked innocently (I hoped), while Patty detached herself from the scarves and beads and sidled over to a display of what looked suspiciously like voodoo dolls.

"Yes, it's a shared space," Raven explained. "All the tenants have access to it during business hours—the mortgage people used it for cigarette breaks—but our staff and customers have exclusive use after 6 P.M. We host rituals every month for the full moon, and all the usual holidays—Beltane and Samhain and the equinoxes. There's a calendar posted here." She gestured to a laminated card hanging next to the cash register.

I nodded, trying to think of a polite way to bring up potential nudity. Nothing occurred to me, so I stalled for time by asking, "What is that you're knitting?"

"A womb," she replied.

"A what?" I said, thinking perhaps a "woom" was some obscure medieval garment, like a snood.

"A womb," she repeated complacently. "You know, a uterus."

"Oh, of course," I said, and resisted the urge to point out that she appeared to have dropped a stitch up by the left Fallopian tube.

"What's it for?" Patty blurted out. We evidently had the same unsettling thought at the same time: maybe this lady is knitting an entire woman, like the serial killer in *The Silence of the Lambs,* but starting from the inside.

"I make them for female troubles," Raven explained, no doubt accustomed to this kind of response. "You fill it with willow bark, you see, for healing, or mistletoe for fertility." She held it up, a limp pink triangle, and I squinted at it, trying to look impressed.

"Do you like our poppets?" Raven asked Patty, who was gingerly turning over the little stuffed dolls stitched together out of plain brown and black cloth.

"They're very nice," she agreed. "Are they all the same?"

"The intent behind your choice is what matters," Raven

told her. "Beyond that . . . well, the smaller ones are easier to bury, but you can't put as much inside them."

"I see," Patty said thoughtfully.

"And while we don't *recommend* them for binding or revenge spells," Raven went on, "they have traditionally been used for both. 'An it harm none, do what ye will.' Have you had any bad relationships?"

"Oh, lots," Patty assured her.

"Well, if you'd like to cleanse yourself of any bad vibrations," Raven advised, "now's the time. Mercury's just gone retrograde."

We walked out of the store with a couple of packages of incense; a book on interpreting dreams, which I bought because Patty had practically ruptured herself trying not to laugh out loud at it; and poppets in three different sizes.

"When you told me there was a magic shop next door," Patty said accusingly in the parking lot, "I thought you meant a magician's shop. You know, top hats and disappearing rabbits and silk handkerchiefs. Not *magick* with a *k*. That woman should be burned at the stake for her fashion sense alone."

"I kind of liked her," I admitted. "She seems harmless enough."

"She just extracted thirty-seven-fifty from your wallet," Patty reminded me, and then repeated in Raven's nasal, singsong tones: "An it harm none, do what ye will."

"Aleister Crowley." I rolled my eyes at her. "That racist old windbag. Still, I'd rather have Raven for a neighbor than a bunch of mortgage brokers. If she and her friends want to run around nude in the woods now and then, I'm OK with it."

"Is the rest of your karate school going to feel the same way?" Patty asked.

I wasn't certain but was spared the bother of finding out. A few days later, Scott, who had made several friends in the city's building-permits department during our renovation, reported that the entire shopping center, including the magick shop and its healing backyard, had been sold to an investor from California who planned to tear it down and build a high-rise condo complex.

"It's going to have a rooftop Zen garden," he said, curling his lip in disgust. "They'll need it, too, because the ground floor is going to flood every time it rains if they build over that creek."

I felt bad for Raven and her customers, so that afternoon I dug out the package Patty and I had brought home, wrote *Cal-Urban Property Ventures, LLC* on a piece of paper, pinned it to one of the poppets, and buried it behind Scott's shed in the backyard.

"What are you doing, Mom?" Lilly asked, as she blew dandelion fluff into the face of our long-suffering Great Dane. She was four years old now, still walking into doors and finding other painful ways to test life's boundaries.

"Putting a curse on a limited liability company," I told her. "Child, if you don't leave that dog alone, I'm going to bite you myself."

"What's 'liability' mean?" she asked, scattering the rest of the dandelion seeds over the near end of the vegetable garden.

"'Liable' means you're responsible for something," I told her.

"So you're liable for me?" she wanted to know.

"Yes," I admitted.

"And Dad is, too?"

"Dad especially," I agreed.

"That's good," she said, "because I like him. Can I use the shovel?"

"No," I informed her, stomping on the poppet's burial site.

"Did you find a new dojo yet?"

"Not yet," I admitted. "But we will, sooner or later."

Graham found the new school.

It sounded almost too good to be true. Not only could we afford the place, but it was clean, had ample parking, no nudity, and was mere blocks from my house. The only downside, Amy observed, was its location in what she described as "the Vortex," a convergence of highway intersections in South Austin that is hard to navigate if you aren't intimately familiar with the area. But we would all quickly *become* familiar with it, I pointed out, if we were driving there four or five times a week.

The board convened at Graham's house one afternoon in early summer to discuss the lease and go over the numbers one last time. We were all a bit edgy. To meet our new rent obligation, the school would have to retain all its current students and add at least twenty new ones. We had a cash cushion that would carry us for about four months, but no longer. After that, we'd be falling behind with each passing day, jeopardizing the school's existence, not to mention Sensei Joy's livelihood.

It required a huge leap of faith, but here our training as *karateka* paid off in full. We had been well prepared over the years for the heart-stopping moment when we had to put the school at risk financially to accomplish the move. When "absolute commitment" has been the core of your training philosophy, you know damn well what you're going to do at such a time: you swallow hard and sign on the dotted line. *Osu,* you say to the forces of real estate, finance, and commerce. I will overcome this obstacle by moving forward.

The physical move was genuinely traumatic for some of our students, who loved the old dojo deeply. Those of us who had been in it the longest, and had done the most repair work on it, had more ambivalent reactions. We had our memories but were generally happy to leave everything else behind. Together, the students packed and moved a small portion of the gear that had piled up in the dojo and donated or threw away everything else: the moldy mats, the leaky water dispenser—even the swamp cooler went, sold off to a women's rugby team.

I'll admit I felt a slight twinge for the swamp cooler. For years, the deep-throated hum of its huge fan had provided the background to long stretches of meditation before and after class, becoming an integral part of what my body experienced as "peace." Part of me is certain that when I die and move on into the Great Tao, the eternal music I hear will not be the voices of angels, but the hum of the swamp cooler from the old dojo. To me it will always be the sound of infinity, one of the few things capable of soothing my restless mind. But we didn't need the swamp cooler anymore; we were moving to the promised land of climate control.

Meanwhile, the new space had to be converted from its old purpose, as a picture-framing shop, into a dojo. I kept Scott away from this process as much as possible, since there were only a few walls to be ripped out and rebuilt and a lot more detail work, like installing the equipment racks and sealing the new cork flooring. Scott did build some nice, sturdy benches in the changing rooms, which are not especially lovely to look at but are safely behind closed doors, where they don't mar the sleek polish of the new floors and wood trim in the main training area. Most of the visible work was done by the students themselves, and a team of contractors who evidently owed Sensei Joy one hell of a favor.

On our last trip to decommission the old building, I volunteered for the task of grappling fifty feet of garden hose down from the ceiling joists, and as I swayed erratically at the top of a borrowed stepladder, wrenching apart zip ties with a pair of rusty pliers, my hand came to rest on a jagged slice of rafter jutting out from the dry, ancient wooden beam. I sucked the resulting splinter out of my palm and then, tenderly, as if it were a piece of the One True Cross, I pried the chunk of wood away from the rafter and tucked it inside my *gi* top to take home, my own personal sliver of Sun Dragon history. I did have a moment while I was pulling it loose when I became acutely aware of the incredible fragility of the old place's bones and imagined that the removal of this one small piece might bring the entire building thundering down around my ears. Luckily, it did not.

I was conscious of that fragment of wood next to my chest as I clung to the ceiling joists in the middle of the soon-to-be-abandoned dojo. I'd earned two black belts beneath this decrepit lumber, in a process spanning almost a decade, and become quite a different person. How many other women had walked uncertainly under that beam to take their very first karate class? How many self-defense students had learned to say *no* beneath its shelter, to look a person in the eye?

There was a kind of magic in the place, I realized, something powerful—otherwise, I wouldn't have bothered to take a piece of it for myself. It wasn't a power that came from oak trees or creek beds; nothing inherent in the wooden beams or the brick walls. It wasn't the location at all. The piece of the building I was carrying home was mere sentiment. I already had a piece of the dojo inside me, all my own, that could never be taken away or lost. And the school, by now, had a piece of me. Because it was the people who had made this place powerful—Sensei Suzanne, with all the force of her own personality and talent; all the teachers who had grown and taken on new roles; every student who had dripped sweat on the vile and disgusting old carpet; every guest who had yelled herself hoarse at a friend's gamet. That was the magic that infused the dojo—and *that* could be re-created anywhere. All it would take was more of the same: More sweat, more people, more yelling. More work.

Moving the dojo required a lot of the kind of work I instinctively shrink from—the kind that taxes my weakest skills, like meeting new people, thinking about budgets, and making careful, informed decisions. But I was getting better at all of those things, because of what I'd learned at Sun Dragon. With the dojo safe in its new location, I felt I'd paid back a small part of my debt to the school.

I'd had a vague sense, when KJ, Denise, Amy, and I completed our second black belt test, that we had finished something, that the hard part was over. I understood now how wrong I'd been. Because when you are trying to change things, to build something new and important, the hard work never ends. Not if you're doing it right.

Parenthood is the most terrifying ordeal you will ever undergo. Enjoy it.

ここでは皮肉が用いられている。著者が言わんとしているのは、親になると多くの試練が待ち受けているが、それでも親であることを楽しもうと努めるべきであるということである。

WHEN SUN DRAGON opened in its new location, my daughter finally enrolled as a member of the Little Dragons preschool class. Lilly had always wanted to train with me and talked incessantly about her plans to do so ever since she was old enough to dress up in my sparring gear. Her enrollment in 2009, when she was five, was a great comfort to me, after so many years of having to explain to my peers that my son didn't take karate at Sun Dragon because he didn't want to. Finally I had a child who was doing what everyone expected a child of mine to do: karate.

Sun Dragon always had at least a few moms among its students. Some of them had come to us for their own training. Others became interested in karate after enrolling their kids in our children's program. Doris Ann, for example, had signed her son and daughter up, watched a couple of their classes, and decided, "What the hell, I might as well get a black belt, too." When Dave was little, I naturally assumed that things would work the other way around for us: that when my son was old enough, he'd train at Sun Dragon with me.

Alas, Dave wasn't interested in karate. At least, he wasn't interested in training at his mother's dojo (which, in retrospect, does sound a little awkward). Luckily, when he was in fourth grade, he and some friends visited a nearby *dojang* that taught a blend of Korean and Indonesian martial arts, very dynamic, with a lot of jumping and rolling. Dave took a trial class and enjoyed it, and I practically knocked our front door off its hinges rushing over to the *dojang* with the checkbook to sign him up. By the time Lilly started karate, he was closing in on his junior black belt, and already a far more talented martial artist than I would ever be.

I conscripted my children into the martial arts in part to quell my own parental anxieties. I wanted some reassurance that they'd be able to protect themselves when I couldn't do it for them. And I got that reassurance, although karate has undoubtedly done more to make my job as a mother bearable by changing *me,* not them. Just as airlines always tell you to put on your own oxygen mask before helping your children, karate has helped me function as a parent without hyperventilating all the time.

Because my lifelong worries about my own safety turned out to be nothing compared to the anxiety I felt as a mom on behalf of my kids. I don't want to belabor this point; if you have children you know exactly what I mean, and if you don't, you're tired of hearing people with kids yammer on and on about how no one but parents can understand parenthood. Still, it was a dreadful revelation: parenthood means plucking your heart out of your chest and sending it off to wander in a world full of reckless drivers, fire, sharp edges, electrical outlets, abandoned wells, perverts, and pools without lifeguards. It makes you vulnerable in ways you can't fully comprehend until you're in the midst of them. By the time you appreciate the danger, it's too late to turn back. So instead, I turned—once again—to the martial arts.

When my son was two years old, I witnessed him climbing out of his crib by gripping the side with both hands, slinging one leg over the rail, and feeling around with his toes for the arm of the adjacent rocking chair. After stabilizing his foothold, he swung his other leg over the side, felt behind him for the seat of the rocker, and slowly eased his weight down onto it, tipping the chair forward until it had balanced. Then he brought his feet together on the seat, letting the chair rock back again beneath him. Finally he sat down, slid off the chair, padded out into the hallway (where I was watching, mesmerized), and proclaimed, "Hey, guys! I just stopped sleeping!"

Dave was clearly destined to do great things, in either martial arts or cat burglary.

Lilly, on the other hand, may or may not make it to black belt but will almost certainly end up as either a civilian or military demolitions expert. I trained through most of my pregnancy with her, and prenatal exposure to Kyokushin might explain why my daughter weighed nine and a quarter pounds at birth, started life with a broken collarbone, and has been systematically destroying everything in her path ever since. If any member of our family is destined to drop a bull barehanded the way Mas Oyama did, it's Lilly.

To be fair, a lot of what she breaks is her own. When she was four years old, she broke her tailbone in ballet class. *In ballet class.* Wherever she goes, my daughter leaves a wake of toppled furniture, brimful dishes, shattered glassware, fragile objects teetering on the edges of things, and impossible piles of ruined toys. The first nine years of her life have been spent constructing, and falling into, one continuous booby trap, stretching from her birth to right now; as I write, she is about to tumble off the bar stool she is standing on while taking pictures of herself in the bathroom mirror, using the digital camera she has been expressly forbidden to touch.

Lilly's boundless exuberance is a stark contrast to Dave's innate self-control. It would be hard to imagine two more different siblings. (I sometimes think I *am* imagining them.) Unless, that is, you know their parents.

Dave is unmistakably my son, with my instinctive caution, my doubts, and my rationalism. He and I have an intuitive, sympathetic bond. Yet Dave's gender places him in a world I can never fully understand. He started out as a small child, just as I had, and his size was frequently remarked upon by the kind of parents who stand around the playground judging children like livestock at a county fair. "He's four?" they would say, eyeing him critically. "Wow, he's *small.*"

"Yeah," I always replied, "he's *mean,* though." I couldn't make the boy bigger, but I did what I could to inflate his reputation.

In fact, he wasn't mean at all, just possessed of an impressive stoicism. He was the victim of a biter in preschool, something we weren't even aware of until our neighbor, who teaches kindergarten and knows the signs, pointed out the telltale red semicircles on his arms and legs. "We had no idea he was hurt," his teachers told us apologetically. "He never cries."

You know the *really* weird thing about this incident? I'd be lying if I said I wasn't proud of my son when I heard this.

Lilly is very much her father's daughter: tall, noisy, and so full of energy she makes me feel anemic. Before she was born, I assumed I was capable of raising a girl because I *was* a girl, once. It doesn't even seem all that long ago. Yet I sometimes despair of finding any common language with my daughter. I have no idea how to warn her about the challenges we both face, as women. I'm not even sure we *do* face the same challenges; that's how different we are. This is frustrating because she shares half my DNA, and unlike Dave, she shares my gender. Lilly is more like me than anyone on the planet, except my own mother. And she's *nothing* like me. She doesn't resemble me physically at all, or anyone else in my family, unless you darken her eyebrows (which we did for her one and only dance recital). Then my mother's face, and my sisters', emerge and look back at me as clear as daylight. It's uncanny.

But apart from that brief glimpse, I often feel that Lilly and I may as well have evolved on separate planets. She doesn't have the same fears I have, and my fears for her haven't turned out to be at all what I expected. Lilly is a greater threat to herself than any external danger she might confront, and this has put a crimp in my plans for mothering her.

I'd always imagined that if I had a daughter, we would have long talks about personal power and believing in yourself; about gender roles, and resisting unrealistic expectations, and how society tries to limit and control us in ways that aren't healthy. Instead, most of my conversations with Lilly consist of tortured attempts to explain to her that (1) a third-floor balcony railing is not a jungle gym; (2) being unafraid of deep water is not the same thing as knowing how to swim; and (3) when the cat does that with her tail, it means she's about to scratch you.

I've never had to exhort Lilly to feel confident in herself.

And it's been even more disconcerting to see how the rest of the world reacts to my daughter's often unwarranted self-confidence—from the helpful strangers who return her to me at the grocery store, to the teachers who send home notes explaining the fresh Band-Aids on her knees, elbows, and forehead.

"She's quite the intrepid explorer!" they'll say, or "Lilly had a little too much fun on the swings today." There's no overt censure in their remarks, but they leave me bristling nonetheless. If she were a boy, I wonder, would people see any need to comment on her boundary-pushing, gravity-defying behavior?

One of the more ambiguous gifts my self-defense training has bestowed upon me is a hyper-awareness of the gender expectations surrounding both of my children. I can see how Dave's size and Lilly's boisterousness might color people's attitudes toward them. I worry terribly about how they might be forced to conform to bullshit social norms—much more than I would if I'd never enrolled at Sun Dragon and never gained a new perspective on things like high heels and short skirts. In a way, this awareness is much worse than ignorance, because although I can see the obstacles being placed in my children's paths, I can also see that, as a mother, there's not a whole lot I can do to mitigate the effects of society's relentless gender stereotypes.

Having a black belt only strengthens this perception. All the time I've spent training, fighting, meditating—it's all predicated on the belief that the only thing any of us can really change is ourselves. No matter how badly I want to protect my children, or shape them into certain kinds of people, I have to recognize the limits of what I can do. For the most part, my kids are the ones who will determine what happens to them, and who they turn out to be.

So it's a damned good thing that all three of us—Dave, Lilly, and I—train in the martial arts. That shared experience gives me a unique connection to each of my kids that I wouldn't have otherwise. Watching Dave and Lilly become martial artists themselves has opened a window into their lives, letting me share in their struggles and their victories much more intimately than I would have thought possible.

Watching your child excel at an activity you're good at yourself (or spend a lot of time trying to be good at, anyway) is a peculiar experience. I was already accustomed to seeing Dave's similarities to me; I see traces of myself in practically everything he does. But watching him practice martial arts is different. On Saturdays, after Lilly had finished her Little Dragons class, we would go to her big brother's *dojang* and watch the end of his class. I always found this unsettling, for some reason. Perhaps it's because I'm used to seeing him as a younger, less experienced version of myself, whereas his superiority in the *dojang* is painfully obvious; or maybe because one martial art is already so different from another (and within a style, individuals have their own interpretations of the same movements). Dave's system has much more spinning than I could ever handle, for one thing. And their curriculum is more complex. So when I watched Dave execute a balance form one morning, I was struck by how different all his movements were, his vertical and horizontal lines, his focus, his energy. Some of this was stylistic, to be sure, and a great deal of it was clearly an echo of his instructor's particular way of moving—which, like all good instructors, he had reproduced in his student.

Still, in the midst of all this difference, I could clearly see my influence on Dave. Every time I watch him at a test, I notice it. When he breaks a board with a flying side kick, I can see it in the way he lands, boom, perfectly collected physically and mentally because—hey, the job's done. When he runs up a padded post and jumps off to kick a target held seven feet in the air, I see myself in the exultation barely concealed beneath his mask of modest composure. Because, hell yeah, that's fun. Me being me, I see myself most of all when he's nervous, or misses a step, or doesn't do something as well as he thinks he should. There are moments where I feel as if I'm watching a video of myself, at a much younger age, performing techniques that I don't remember learning.

It's hard to describe the feeling, but it's pretty damn cool.

Watching Lilly in a karate class elicits different emotions. At her blue belt test I was struck by the way her face—normally an open book—sank into a stern mask of immobility when she stepped forward to address the judges.

"*Osu,* Sensei, my name is Lilly and I am six years old," she reported, her expression undermined just a bit by the trace of a lisp from her missing front teeth.

When I watched her perform her kata with the other kids, the way she moved was foreign to me. Her weight is centered higher than mine, over long legs. At the age of six she still lacked the flexibility and strength for the deeper stances that would let her shift her energy more efficiently. Kicks were harder for her, too, for the same reason: a higher center of balance and more mass to control than I had at her age.

Still, she looked wonderfully strong, and I could see how she would likely develop into a stunning martial artist. Her height and power will make her eventual grace all the more spectacular. I saw this with an odd remoteness, as though her beauty was nothing I could take credit for. Yet I knew the journey she was starting out on, because I've been on it myself, and I've seen so many other women who have made the same journey—some of them much more like my daughter than I am. And knowing those women made me feel much better about Lilly's future.

I have no idea whether she sees the same connection I do, between strengthening her body and creating a more stable place for herself in the world. But when I watch my daughter fighting to stay balanced as she kicks, or struggling to recall the next movement in a kata—then I know exactly how she feels. And I'm profoundly grateful for those moments, because they are so rare in our relationship.

Dave and Lilly's training has also shown me that I needlessly overcomplicate the problem of social pressures. Martial artists acquire all manner of skills, including the resources needed to deal with gender expectations or anything else the world might throw at them.

Not long after Lilly's blue belt test, I watched Dave perform in a demonstration at a neighborhood health and fitness fair. My son nonchalantly executed backflip falls, diving rolls, and spinning kicks. He broke boards, fought an adult student with the long staff, wielded *nunchaku,* and performed with the *bokken,* or wooden sword. (*When did he learn to use the* bokken*?* I wondered vaguely. *Did we pay extra for that?*) I wouldn't have been surprised if he'd pulled out a crossbow and shot an apple off someone's head, or sat down and field-stripped a Vickers .303. The kid knew his stuff.

The audience surrounding me consisted of eager children and their slow-moving parents, who looked like they spent a lot of time driving around in SUVs. And then I noticed a cluster of girls, maybe thirteen or fourteen years old, standing in the front row, watching Dave. They were silent. On their faces was an expression older than their years, older than time. It's the look women wear when they have just seen an unremarkable man do something remarkably well. It is a thoughtful expression.

When the demonstration was over, I listened to the applause and wondered, How many of you people think my son looks small *now*?

Being a mother has given me endless opportunities to put what I've learned in the dojo into practice. Lilly gives me daily (sometimes hourly) opportunities to employ forbearance and patience, two qualities that, as anyone who has spent more than ten minutes with me can tell you, I need to work on anyway. As her mother, I have learned not to ask about scorch marks in the microwave, or how many clothespins, exactly, were flushed down the toilet (the only possible answer—if the child is being honest—is "all of them").

I have learned that you can warn a child she is about to fall off the coffee table a dozen times to no effect, but if you keep your mouth shut, you'll only have to provide ice and sympathy once. I have learned to let the cats fend for themselves. This has not been easy for me. It takes nerves of steel. It takes faith. It takes guts. It takes most of the qualities you need to be a black belt.

Dave and Lilly, then, are just as much responsible as their father for my continuing journey into karate. For one thing, they give me reasons to get the hell out of the house three evenings a week. Given a choice between listening to them squabble over the television remote or being punched in the head, I'll take the dojo every time. But my kids also give me a reason to come back home when karate is over—and the motivation to return a better person than I was when I left.

See yourself clearly, and you won't dread the scrutiny of others.

明確に自分自身を見れば、他人の目はこわくない。

We cut off an ambulance on the ride in from the airport—an unmistakable indication that we were no longer in Austin. I didn't quite believe that our shuttle driver had done this, and I kept looking back over my shoulder at the ambulance as it hugged our rear bumper, lights flashing. Our driver acted as if the lights, the ambulance, and his rearview mirror simply didn't exist. We stopped at a red light, and the ambulance blasted its siren with a venom that was hard to misinterpret, but our driver was unmoved, and we sat, waiting for the green light and ignoring whoever was dying back there and I thought—Man, we just cut off a fucking *ambulance*; we are really in New York City.

We were in New York to visit Honbu, the world headquarters of Seido karate. I had become a Seido black belt two years earlier, in 2007, and ever since then I'd been told, "You need to go to Honbu."

Honbu was the mecca of Seido students, and a trip there was full of rituals. When you arrive at the Manhattan dojo, I had been drilled, you take the elevator to the second floor. As soon as you get out of the elevator, you bow and take off your shoes. Check in at the reception desk—show them your membership card. When you walk into the dojo, bow. Don't step over the line on the floor. Bow when you get to the changing rooms. Bow when you come back out. Say *osu* to everyone, and say *osu* plus the person's title if they outrank you. There was a different title for every level of black belt, and I knew only a few of them: five stripes on the belt indicated *kyoshi,* six indicated *shihan,* and nine stripes indicated you were looking at Kaicho Nakamura himself, the only person in Seido who held that rank. *Sensei* meant teacher; *kyoshi* meant advanced teacher. *Shihan* meant "master." *Kaicho* translated literally as "grandmaster," but it was a singularity. It functioned as Kaicho's name and title.

New York looked exactly like television had led me to expect it would, though with fewer Muppets. We arrived at Honbu slightly travel worn; Sensei Joy looking frazzled and pale, the two people from Sun Dragon who were testing the next day looking strained, and me, having just that moment noticed that my brand-new *gi,* which was brilliantly white when I packed it, had acquired a livid pink stain down one leg somewhere over the mid-Atlantic states—this despite the complete absence of any pink or red items in my luggage.

Our class that night at Honbu was the first time I had ever seen Kaicho in person. From photos, I knew he wasn't a particularly large man, but, in fact, when you meet him he comes across as plenty big. Even now, in his seventies, he looks capable of clearing a room. But I caught only glimpses of him that night, because for at least half the class he had us training with our eyes closed.

As members of the newest Seido school, in the obscure

province of Texas, we were already under considerable scrutiny. We had come all the way to New York explicitly to meet people, to join the Seido family more formally, and to let our new family get a good look at us. I'm generally desperate for attention, but I hate scrutiny, especially from competent people. The fact that I was wearing pink pants made me even more self-conscious. All I wanted was to be invisible. To disappear. So when the first kata was called out, and I heard the command *"Mokuso,"* a sense of resignation descended upon me, rather like what I imagine a captured spy feels in front of a firing squad. "At least I don't have to watch," I thought, and, in fact, closing my eyes was something like disappearing. I don't remember which kata we did; I have no idea how I kept from running into the people next to me. The entire class was just a long nightmare of blindly blocking and punching and wondering which way I was facing at the moment. We were allowed to open our eyes for brief intervals while we did many, many kicks, lying prone on the floor, and also when we did sets of push-ups on our hands, our knuckles, our fingertips, our thumbs and pinkies, and then our thumbs only.

It was painful, but I congratulated myself that at least no one had singled me out for correction, or outright derision. It was an experience I hadn't had in a long time, to be under the scrutiny of so many teachers with so much more experience. I hadn't missed it much.

Looking back on it, my first class at Honbu resembled nothing so much as an alcoholic blackout, with long gaps of confused darkness and an indeterminate amount of time spent rolling around on the ground in pain.

After an hour of that, it was time for meditation class.

I had been prepped for this, too; seated meditation, called zazen, is an important part of Seido practice, just as it had been in Kyokushin. So I knew how to line up, and sit *seiza* with my feet folded under me, and breathe, and keep my mouth shut. I knew my legs would go numb and my shoulders would lock up. What I didn't expect was that, in the meditation class at Honbu, no one ever said *"mokuso"*—at least not that I could hear. At Sun Dragon, I was used to training with my eyes *open,* and meditating with my eyes *closed.* It would seem, based on my observations, that they did it the other way around at Honbu. At any rate, I ended up meditating with my eyes open that night.

The second unexpected thing about meditation class at Honbu was that, while we were meditating, someone was playing a flute. A bamboo flute, it sounded like—spare and atonal. Against the backdrop of the Manhattan evening outside the dojo windows, it put me in mind of Thelonious Monk at the Five Spot on one of his mellower nights. And then, over the flute I started to hear a weird percussive slapping. It didn't sound like any instrument I was familiar with, and I live with a drummer, so I was truly puzzled. I'd hear the slapping from one part of the room, and then it would stop, and then it would start again a little farther away or a little closer. I couldn't see what it was, because the dojo was dark apart from a few candles. And besides, you're not supposed to look around when you meditate, even if your eyes are open. Even I knew that much.

It was distracting. The slapping would come a little closer, and then closer still—sometimes there would be long pauses between slaps and sometimes they would repeat fairly quickly. Always the same pattern: three loud, sharp smacks, then a pause, then three more.

Finally, out of the corner of my eye I caught sight of someone walking up and down the rows of students as we knelt there in the darkness. And whoever it was had a *kyosaku.*

In Zen practice, the *kyosaku* is sometimes referred to as the "stick of compassion." I'd heard the term but never seen (or heard) the implement in use, so it was lucky that I was doing an open-eye meditation because I was anxious to see who got hit and why. I tried to figure out how the slap-ees were chosen. All I could really see was that the person with the stick walked slowly around the room and occasionally paused to hit someone. It looked completely random, so I figured maybe he was like a mariachi; he went from one patron to another, and if no one made eye contact, he moved on. Or then again, I thought, perhaps there was some other unobtrusive signal that everyone was expected to know, like at an art auction. I sat very still, worried that if I twitched or scratched myself, I'd invite a whacking. Finally the *kyosaku* wielder (I never did see who it was—I didn't want to move my head enough to look up at him or her) stopped by the person directly in front of me. The sitter pressed his palms together and bowed (so *that* was the signal!). The stick wielder bowed back. Then the sitter leaned forward and to one side and received three whacks on his shoulder muscle. Stiff blows, but not too bad; about the way you'd hit a tough steak. On the third whack, the stick was rubbed briefly into the muscle, massaging it. The purpose, I knew, was to relieve tension in the muscle and focus one's mind. Then the student leaned to the other side and took three more whacks. Then more bows.

It didn't look so bad, and I knew that the *kyosaku* wasn't an instrument of punishment, so I relaxed a little. But now I was curious: who originally figured out that this was beneficial to students' concentration? That had to be an accidental discovery, don't you think? I mean, I'm a teacher myself. The first time you hit a student with a stick, I doubt you do it out of compassion.

Anxious to get the most out of my inaugural trip to Honbu, I wondered if I should request the *kyosaku* now that I knew how. I was used to being hit, after all, and being hit with a stick would add a new dimension to the experience. Plus, I had just sat on an airplane all day and was definitely stiffer than I'd have liked. But no one back in Austin had given me any advice for this situation, and I still had a few questions. If the *kyosaku* has already passed you, can you call it back, like a hot dog vendor at the ballpark? Is a gratuity expected, and if so, how much?

I decided to forgo the *kyosaku*. Instead, I just sat.

When we were done sitting, the flute silenced, the *kyosaku* retired, Kaicho gathered us around a whiteboard, and like a football coach at halftime, took us on a play-by-play analysis of what we'd just done. He drew two kanji characters on the whiteboard, one for *za,* which means "sit," and one for *zen,* meaning "meditate." He called our attention particularly to the first character, which depicts two people sitting on the ground. In zazen, seated meditation, Kaicho explained, these two people are contemplating each other. But don't make the mistake, he warned us, of thinking that meditation is about you contemplating someone else. The two people, Kaicho stressed, are "you, and *inside* you."

Of course, I'd been doing it all wrong, being mesmerized by the *kyosaku*'s journey around the dojo. I hadn't looked at myself at all. I had sat quietly just like everyone else, but I still managed to completely miss the point of the exercise. I vowed to do better next time. *Look inside; look at yourself.* That was why I was there. That was why I had been told, "You have to go to Honbu."

"How's it going?" Scott asked that night when I called home. He was about to set off with both children on a camping trip (which ended up being unexpectedly prolonged, I would find out later, after Lilly locked his keys in the car at thc state park).

"It was good," I said cautiously. "Meditation class was interesting."

"Lilly wants me to ask if you found the M&M's she gave you."

"M&M's?" I asked, a slow light dawning. "Were they red ones?"

I heard a muffled consultation on the other end of the line.

"She says she put them in your suitcase," Scott said. "For good luck."

The next day we checked out of our hotel, dragged our luggage (divested of M&M's) over to Honbu, climbed on a bus, and drove an hour north of the city for a Gasshuku, a weekend Seido retreat at Mount St. Alphonsus, an old seminary where obscure religious figures frowned and prayed and bled at us from the walls and all the bedrooms were named after saints—male saints for the men's wing, female saints for the ladies'. Seido students from all over the world were there, and we awoke every day at 4 A.M. to meditate, lining up in the darkness on a hill facing east.

This time, I did better. As I discovered when I put in my contact lenses at 3:55 A.M., looking *inside* yourself at that time of the morning sure beats looking *at* yourself. At four in the morning I barely recognized myself in the mirror. Even after a decent night's sleep, my eyes are tiny and pink, as if my ancestors swam into a cave thousands of years ago and never found their way out. Then, too, before sunrise and caffeine, the mind is predisposed to reflection. Why was I born? one asks oneself. What am I doing here, and why does St. Agnes look so pissed off? How is all of this making me a better person, exactly?

All in all, I found it fairly easy to look inside at 4 A.M., when everyone around me was still half asleep and the earth itself was only just rolling out of bed. Being outside helped, too. There was no flute; only the occasional drowsy chirp as the local birds clocked in. I have always, I realized as we knelt there, found it easier to look inside when I'm outside.

After the sun came up, we did karate, whole platoons of us spread over the seminary grounds. That second day I was in a kata class with about thirty other people, none of them ranked lower than black belt. All we did was practice Seienchin Kata, over and over—maybe ten or fifteen repetitions. I'd beaten my head against this kata many times back home at Sun Dragon, but never with a solid line of third- and fourth-degree black belts in front of me. It turns out you can pick up a lot of useful information that way, provided they let you keep your eyes open. Looking within yourself may be crucial to your development as a martial artist, I decided, but looking at other, more advanced martial artists sure as hell speeds up the process. Here was the flip side of the glaring scrutiny I'd suffered under in my first class at Honbu a couple of nights earlier. I learned more in that half hour than I'd learned in three years at home.

And there was something memorable about doing this out

in the open, in the same field we had contemplated earlier during meditation. Kata practice, like meditation, feels different outside, with your feet in the grass; your movements feel bigger, and your mistakes seem smaller. I felt like Almanzo in *Farmer Boy.* If Laura Ingalls Wilder's husband had practiced karate, I thought, this is exactly how he would have done it: barefoot, in a bucolic meadow overlooking the Hudson River.

My expansive feeling didn't last. Later that day, we did more kata, in an even larger group, on the side lawn of Mount St. Alphonsus. This time, an evil chance landed me in the very front row. Now there were no third- or fourth-*dan* black belts for me to observe. Much worse, I was now directly under Kaicho's intimidating gaze, and he zeroed in on my twitchy nerves like a chicken hawk on a big, fat Buff Orpington.

The language barrier made things worse. The problem wasn't that Kaicho's English was bad; it wasn't. I had no trouble understanding him when he spoke English. The problem was that his Japanese was good, and mine, honed in the linguistic backwaters of Texas, was execrable. All the Japanese terms I ostensibly knew, when pronounced by a native speaker, were completely incomprehensible. I tried to take comfort in the fact that at least the pink streak on my *gi* pants was now mostly camouflaged by grass stains.

It was inevitable; between the correctly accented Japanese, the sleep deprivation, and the knowledge that I was centered in Kaicho's crosshairs, I made a very basic error. As we executed a turn in a kata called Gekisai Sho, he stopped the entire class, more than a hundred students, and ordered me—*me*—to repeat the movement. Then he told me to do it again. And then he turned to the rest of the students and asked, "What's wrong?"

I was sure it must be something awful, but there was nowhere to hide now. I just stood there in my stance as students all over the field peered in my direction, flicking expert eyes over my panting, pathetic figure. Finally, far behind and to my left, someone called out, "*Osu,* Kaicho," and proceeded to rattle off four or five things I could have been doing better: deepen my stance, turn my front knee in further . . . quite a lot of advice from someone who was at least half a football field away from me.

Bootlicker, I thought bitterly to myself.

But Kaicho was not impressed with this extended critique. He shook his head and then turned to me and said simply, "Front hand goes inside."

The instant he said it, I snapped to my mistake: I had put the wrong hand on the inside when I prepared my knife-hand block—something I already knew I did habitually, especially on this particular movement, in this kata. I'd been warned about it back in Austin at least a dozen times; in fact, I'd worked on it to the point where I'd pretty much stopped doing it. Until I was sweating under Kaicho's watchful eye.

"*Osu,* Kaicho," I replied gratefully, and performed the block again, properly this time. Kaicho nodded. And that was that. The kata continued; the class ended. The sky didn't fall and the earth didn't open and swallow me up.

People told me later that I took this scrutiny very well, but what the hell else was I going to do? I hadn't come all the way from Texas to make excuses. So instead, I said, "*Osu,* Kaicho."

Having survived Kaicho's scrutiny, the rest of Gasshuku was a breeze. Under any other circumstances, it would have been a horrifying ordeal because the final evening of the retreat involved a traditional form of group sadism known as the "talent show," where teams of students were required to perform an original song extolling Kaicho, or Seido, or the Gasshuku experience generally.

Believe me when I say that this wasn't because Kaicho wanted to listen to us sing. The point of this public mortification, as I saw it, was to make us oblivious to embarrassment. It was an exercise in killing shame. And it worked, too. After standing up in front of 150 people, almost all of whom outrank you, and singing "I wanna go to Seido!" to the tune of the Ramones' "I Wanna Be Sedated," there is literally nothing else you can do that would cause you to feel shame. You could go home from Gasshuku and post naked pictures of yourself on the Internet for all the world and your grandmother to see, and it wouldn't cause you the least bit of discomfort. You've already been through the worst experience your ego can possibly suffer. You no longer care who looks at you, or what they see. You feel, in a way, untouchable. Which is a nice way to feel even if you have to go through hell to get there.

So much of what we read into other people's observation of us is entirely within our own heads. Looking isn't criticizing. Looking is just looking. I often make the point, in self-defense classes, that looking at someone isn't necessarily a hostile act. Looking someone in the eye is an act of assertiveness, not necessarily aggression. But so much of the scrutiny we receive in daily life is critical that we learn to shrink away.

Being observed can make you feel like everything you thought you knew has changed, like you have no frame of reference. And nothing blows your concentration like having your every movement scrutinized by the grandmaster who founded the system you're training in. I think I understand, now, why Kaicho has his students close their eyes during class. You really don't want to know if he's looking at you.

Still, I was glad that Kaicho noticed my error during the kata class and pointed it out. It was horrible at the time, and I wished I was anywhere else, back in Texas or waiting to be hit with a stick, or even in an ambulance stuck in traffic on the Long Island Expressway, somewhere in Queens. I didn't enjoy having a hundred-odd people observing my crappy form. I remembered, though—for once, I remembered—what Kaicho had told us at our meditation class: It's not about you and anyone else. It's about you and *inside* you.

If you look at yourself, really *look,* it doesn't matter who else looks at you, because you know what they're going to see. If they see faults, you've already acknowledged them. If they see something admirable, you know they're not imagining it. You don't have to worry that you'll be mistaken for something that you're not, or exposed as something you wish you weren't.

Developing the ability to look at yourself honestly can make you, incredibly, wonderfully, fearless, if what you fear is criticism. Once the scrutiny of others holds no terror for you, you can just be what you are, whether that's a first-degree black belt from Texas making her very first trip to Honbu at the age of forty-three, or a fourth-degree black belt from Brooklyn or New Zealand or Poland who can rip out Seienchin Kata perfectly in the middle of a cow pasture. And being what you are is the first step to becoming what you want to be.

A warrior cultivates the virtues of loyalty, courage, and discretion. Along with some light typing and filing.

ここには、立派な勤め方と、
現代のビジネスの世界についての雑多なメッセージが含まれている。
著者はここでも皮肉を用いている。

> One who is a samurai must keep constantly in mind, by day and by night, from the morning of New Year's Day through the night of New Year's Eve, the fact that he has to die.
>
> — DAIDOJI YUZAN

JUST WHAT WAS I becoming? After following the martial arts' way of *budo* for ten years, I was stronger, a better fighter, a more strategic thinker. Still, despite my dedication to the path of *budo,* I didn't feel like a warrior. I hadn't stopped any spears, nor did it look like I'd be called upon to do so. I thought of myself as an average middle-aged woman with an above-average knowledge of how to hurt people.

It was my professional life, of all things, that showed me what warriorship actually entails.

Daidoji Yuzan's seventeenth-century work *Budo Shoshinshu (The Code of the Samurai)* explores the paradox of warriorship during peacetime. Composed when Japan was one century into the Pax Tokugawa, a three-hundred-year period of relative military calm, Yuzan's treatise describes a world in which the average samurai—a professional soldier born into the hereditary military class—could hardly be blamed for feeling at loose ends. And since aimless, highly trained killers tend to make governments nervous (especially in large numbers), much of the apparatus of state power in Japan during the Edo period was deeply vested in domesticating the samurai, turning the steely warriors of Honshu into, essentially, a bunch of bureaucrats. The *Budo Shoshinshu* and similar works, like *The Book of Five Rings,* aimed to indoctrinate this new class of warrior-administrators with all the diverse virtues their era demanded of them.

Success was spotty. As you might expect, when you convert warriors into midlevel managers subservient to process and protocol but nonetheless admonish them to "keep death in mind at all times," you are bound to have misunderstandings, and these can range from the merely embarrassing to the breathtaking. The Forty-Seven Ronin were a legendary group of samurai who committed ritual mass suicide around 1701 after killing the man who caused *their* overlord to commit suicide (all because the overlord didn't pay a big enough bribe to someone or other). Not the most efficient way of resolving conflict in the workplace; that's forty-nine deaths altogether, and they occurred *during a time of peace.* A more obvious failure of human resources management is hard to imagine. Certainly it's difficult to think of any single person today who has the power to make forty-eight grown men commit suicide (apart, perhaps, from a few wedding planners). But more importantly, the fate of the Forty-Seven Ronin illustrates how tough it was to live up to the uncompromising code of the samurai.

In his *Budo Shoshinshu,* Daidoji Yuzan offers a wealth of helpful advice for those who want to try. For instance, if there is a disloyal knight in your overlord's house, he counsels, the logical thing for you, the loyal samurai, to do is *not* to report the offender to authorities—that could cause a public scandal—but instead to seize the malicious knight, cut off his head, and then disembowel yourself. "Then there will be no government inquiry," Yuzan explains comfortingly, "and the overlord's reputation will be preserved. The establishment will be secure, and the country will be peaceful." Excellent! Except that of course you, the loyal samurai, will be dead. Which shouldn't be a problem as long as you remember: as a samurai, *that's your job.*

Even as the samurai's professional arena shifted from the battlefield to the halls of government during the Pax Tokugawa, death remained the most important part of his job description. Beheading and disemboweling were everyday hazards, and in the highly ritualized world the samurai inhabited, accusations of impropriety could also be lethal weapons. This is no doubt why the *Budo Shoshinshu* sounds, to Western ears, a bit like *The Anarchist Cookbook* as written by Emily Post. Yet somewhere deep beneath the work's exoticism and ritual gut-spilling, the samurai's schizophrenic job description strikes a familiar chord. It is not, perhaps, all that different from the experience of many of today's soldiers, citizens, and corporate drones.

I've often thought that the contrast between the reality of

our daily lives and the way we're supposed to live them is, just as it was for a samurai in 1700, absurd. Like the samurai reading Yuzan's text, wondering whether its advice on teakettles is truly relevant to his life, I find myself looking askance at the elaborate codes I'm expected to master for rituals like parent-teacher conferences and Internet flame wars. The expectations we labor to live up to are ambiguous, and often contradictory —and nowhere is this more apparent than in the workplace. Just as with the samurai Daidoji Yuzan was addressing during the Pax Tokugawa, our twenty-first-century livelihoods depend on our willingness to do a lot of obnoxious and difficult things for no readily apparent reason: Wear pantyhose if you're female, a necktie if you're male. Return the blue form, keep the yellow one. Don't use Chrome; the IT department doesn't support it. Don't ask, don't tell.

And women have to confront particularly exasperating role conflicts tied to our gender. Everyone just naturally expects us to stay home when the kids are sick, but then again, we're often the only people in the office who know how to manage the boss's online calendar. How are we supposed to reconcile all these competing roles? How do you create a coherent picture, a code to follow?

It turns out that the advice Daidoji Yuzan gave to the samurai is still surprisingly relevant. Minus the bits about dying.

> It goes without saying that strength is paramount in the way of the warrior, but if you cultivate strength alone, you will seem more like a peasant than a samurai. You should study such things as poetry and the tea ceremony in your spare time.

When I fled Hawaii I sidestepped into a career in academic administration, which means I sit in a windowless box for nine hours a day and try to find out if college students are getting any smarter. I've been doing this for twelve years now, and while there are some things I don't especially like about my job, most of them involving deans, I still feel fortunate in that I'm not required to think about death all the time. Plus I work around smart people, next to a giant library full of poetry and, probably, books about tea, and on an average day the most dramatic threat I'll encounter is the guy who likes to stand outside the student union yelling about Jesus.

Another good thing about my job is that it provides health insurance for me and my family, which in this day and age, is almost more important than a salary. I feel this way in part because of my own mother, who was not only a nurse but worked for BlueCross for many years, and constantly reminded her children how screwed we would be if we ever went without health insurance. Mom was totally on board with Diadoji Yuzan here: she made sure we kept death constantly in mind, in the form of untreated infections, kidney failure, and blocked arteries. So even though my job means that I leave my house at seven o'clock every morning, and return after six in the evening (more like nine if I have karate), leaving me about an hour a day to see my children, I still consider my career an integral part of my role as a mother. Any parent who has stood at the emergency room admissions desk with a sick child knows what I mean: *the* most important thing in the world, at a time like that, is your ability to pull out your insurance card when you're asked for it.

So I've managed to reconcile the conflict between my mother-nurturer-provider responsibilities and my professional worker-bee role. It's not convenient, but it makes a certain kind of sense. On the other hand, anyone whose primary problem-solving method involves brute force is going to fit awkwardly at best in a bureaucracy, so my job isn't without its challenges. And here, too, Daidoji Yuzan has much to say that is helpful, or at least consolatory—particularly in his chapter on the duties of vassals.

> A samurai who receives a salary from an overlord should no longer regard his body or life as his own.

Three years after I'd started working as a university administrator, I acquired a new boss. It was a package deal: I also got a new office mate, a new neighbor, and a new source of stress. Joan came into my life in 2004 just as Sensei Suzanne was departing, essentially replacing one female mentor possessing strong opinions and a forceful personality with another.

Working with Joan gave me a sustained opportunity to employ what I had learned at Sun Dragon outside the standard context of self-defense, the framework of physical safety, sexual harassment, and relationship violence. My new boss forced me to transfer the skills I'd worked so hard on to a new arena—the professional world, instead of home or the dojo. I learned a tremendous amount from Joan—about research in our field, about teaching, about ways to coax and conjure professional necessities from an academic bureaucracy as complex as the imperial court at Kyoto. Working with Joan taught me things like the importance of good catering (including tea), and when to make a phone call instead of sending an e-mail (short answer: if you have to say anything even remotely unfavorable about anyone). But the main thing I learned was how to set and maintain professional boundaries.

The first clue that our work relationship might present some challenges came when Joan and I learned that the new office "suite" we were due to move into was, in fact, one very nice but smallish room. She was displeased, and I was appalled, but we arranged our desks as cheerfully as possible, back to back, chatting all the while about how best to avoid tripping over each other as we worked. At the last minute, caution prompted me not to unpack the box of photos and tchotchkes I'd brought over from my old office—the magnet that warned, I BITE; the pencil sharpener shaped like a miniature Bible; the Powerpuff Girl action figures. Maybe later, I told myself. Let's see how things go.

Then I watched as Joan set out her own photos and mementoes on her desk—the usual photos, a stuffed replica of the bacterium that causes stomach ulcers, and topping off the display, a five-foot-long black leather whip, which, she explained cheerfully, was a gift from her previous employees. She cracked it expertly a few times to make sure it hadn't been damaged in the move, causing a few heads to turn in the dean's waiting room outside. The implications were mildly unsettling, but I have a soft spot for anyone who handles weapons confidently. I decided the whip was, on the whole, a good omen. Maybe things would work out.

I remained cautiously optimistic until Joan purchased a house in South Austin, about three blocks away from mine.

"Oh, you live over by the elementary school?" she asked with great interest when I pointed out our new residential proximity. "We're just a few streets apart, then. That'll be convenient." I found her enthusiasm more sinister than the whip. Life at the office already required a good deal more tact than I was in the habit of exercising; if I didn't have the privacy of my own home and neighborhood as an escape valve, I wasn't sure what would happen to my sanity or my blood pressure. If the thought of walking out of your house and finding an alligator on your front porch alarms you, imagine waking up and seeing your boss there instead.

But what could I do? I didn't have a choice; I wasn't about to move and I certainly couldn't quit. My family depended on my salary, and given the stress I was now under every day, the health insurance was more important than ever.

If you accept the salary, Yuzan tells the samurai, you have to do what the job demands. That's vassalage, in a nutshell.

> The samurai's code requires bathing morning and night, washing your hands and feet and always keeping your body clean; shaving and binding up your hair every morning, dressing correctly according to the season; and always carrying your fan and your long and short swords.

Like the samurai, I have my own established morning ritual to help me present a civilized face in the world of academia. It involves a lot of coffee, a very long shower, and a "power wardrobe," heavy on black, gray, and red (which Scott says makes him feel like he shares a closet with an SS officer). I don't usually carry a fan, or swords, or any similar regalia, unless you count my Batman watch. I have often wished that I could carry a sword at work. I think this would dramatically improve my interactions with faculty, particularly the tenured ones. But even swordless, I feel like I'm girding myself for battle. While I'm not a night person by any means, morning and I regard each other warily, too—circling, measuring, looking for an advantage before we come to grips. I need some time by myself to process the audacity of what I'm about to do: go out in public and act like I know what I'm talking about.

Once Joan moved in across the street, the ritual had a new element. At eight o'clock sharp, her car pulled up in my driveway so she could give me a ride to work. This was a generous gesture. It meant I could leave home an hour later and not have to walk half a mile from the bus stop to the office. Still, the carpooling arrangement was no gift. Because everywhere Joan went, she worked. I mean the woman never, ever stopped working. And as soon as you were sucked into her orbit, you found yourself doing it, too. Joan and I mapped out workshops in her car, drafted budget reports at the coffee shop, and fine-tuned survey questions in airports. It was exhausting. And now the process followed me up to my very own doorstep every blessed day.

It felt unnatural, the extent to which our lives and activities merged. Being someone's vassal was a struggle for me, and I didn't enjoy it. I do have to say, though: as a means of getting shit done, it really works. I was more productive as Joan's assistant than I had ever been in my working life. Together, we launched a substantial cross-curricular program at our university, conducting surveys, leading workshops, writing reports, cajoling unwilling faculty, quelling resistance, and smiling steadfastly in the face of outright insults. And the skills that Daidoji Yuzan recommends to conscientious samurai helped at every step.

Over time, I learned what was likely to make Joan happy and what inevitably pissed her off, and I found ways to head off anything in the latter category before it reached her desk. ("Low-ranking warriors must learn to be sensitive to the moods of their superiors," Yuzan warns.) Because Joan attended academic conferences in Europe every year, I became adept at the solemn three-way brand of poker required to ensure that money from the dean or her department chair landed in the correct accounts to pay for airfare to Greece, or Istanbul, or wherever she was headed. ("A warrior charged with administering funds has a very difficult job.") I went to conferences with her and met all the outstanding scholars in our field who had been her friends for decades. ("A warrior should study the origins of the overlord's house, his blood relatives, and his distinguished colleagues.") Like a samurai adjusting to the brave new world of peace, I learned to do all manner of things I had never dreamed of attempting—a state of affairs that was admittedly somewhat familiar after all the times I'd been forced into it at Sun Dragon.

Working with Joan wasn't just a job, or even a career. My vassalage turned out to be a whole new way of life—a discipline, if you will. Because all of this high-intensity professional collaboration was just one facet of our relationship. I also fed Joan's cats and watered her plants when she was out of the country. I helped her choose colors when she painted her dining room. I drove her to and from various medical appointments that involved sedatives. Luckily, I liked Joan. She was smart and funny and had a lot of experience in our field, and she kept a five-foot-long whip on her desk. How could I not like someone like that? She was also one of the few people I could always count on to say something kind when I showed her pictures of my children.

"I don't see why you're so upset," she said, when I put a new photo of Lilly out on my desk. "She looks adorable in an eye patch. How long does she have to wear it?"

"Only six weeks," I said. "Thank God. She's even more dangerous without depth perception."

"You'll survive," she reassured me.

Still, our 24/7 relationship was exhausting, especially since I'm an antisocial lump at the best of times, whereas Joan has no OFF switch. Things would have become unbearable if I hadn't belatedly remembered that, vassal though I was, by golly I knew how to set and maintain personal boundaries. They may not have taught that sort of thing to the samurai back in 1700, but Sensei Suzanne, God bless her, had made it part of my basic training. Subtlety, I noticed, was often lost on Joan. I had to learn to be direct with her when we had a difference of opinion. And here, all that practice I'd had saying no began to pay real dividends. After all, I wasn't accosted in nightclubs very often, but I saw Joan every day, so I had plenty of opportunity to tell her no. I remember her surprise the first time I did this. She had been planning our schedule for the single day we had in the office between a three-day conference and a two-day retreat.

"I won't be in on Monday," I informed her. "I'm taking the day off."

She looked hurt, and then concerned. "Why do you need a day off?" she asked, puzzled. "Do you feel okay?"

"Joan, we just spent three days in the same hotel room," I reminded her gently. "Don't you think we've had enough together time lately?"

Clearly, she didn't think so, but she heard the message. I took the day off, and she didn't even call me. Though she did send me about a dozen e-mails regarding the catering order for the upcoming retreat.

Emboldened by this success, I plucked up my courage again to address our work space situation.

"I was thinking," I ventured one day after lunch in our office. (Joan worked through lunch, so, of course, I usually did, too.) "Since you're teaching two classes this semester, and you have appointments with your students during your office hours, you really should have more privacy. I mean, student-teacher communications are supposed to be confidential, aren't they?"

"It's true," Joan sighed. "But where could you go? Do you want to go sit in the library or something?"

By now I knew her too well to take offense at this suggestion. "What would you think about me working from home two days a week?" I countered. "Then you could have the office all to yourself, and your students could come in any time."

Somewhat to my surprise, she agreed, and that is how I obtained the Holy Grail of office work in the modern era: a telecommute schedule.

It may have helped just a little that I had brought a particularly unappealing frozen entree for lunch that day, and that the stench of microwaved cardboard still lingered in the office. I mean, sure, I was a vassal, but I wasn't above a little tactical maneuvering. As Daidoji Yuzan puts it, "There are traditional combat principles that involve various maneuvers and strategies. Victory depends upon knowing these secrets."

After three years of unbridled merriment with Joan, one of those ideological skirmishes so common to the academic world swept through our school, in the form of a "program reorganization." Initially I didn't grasp the extent of the change that was in the wind. As the youngest member of a large family, I developed the tendency in childhood—maybe it was a coping skill, maybe it was just laziness—to let a lot of things go on above my head. Apparently the same tendency to slide under all the chaos held true for me professionally, too. But gradually even I figured out that *something* was up. There were currents and crosscurrents, eddies and whirlpools of drama, or what passes for drama in the academic world. (People start quoting Foucault and Baudrillard.) I started hearing about odd goings-on in meetings. I fielded strange phone calls from people who had been grievously misinformed about our budget. Most ominously, our dean, who had hired Joan, departed for a job in another state. Joan grew uncharacteristically grim, and I felt like Richard Chamberlain's character in the first few episodes of *Shōgun,* watching nervously as the obscure intrigues of warlords unfolded around me.

It was surprising how little useful advice the human resources Web site offered for a situation like this, and even Daidoji Yuzan couldn't do much more than tell me to die well, which frankly seemed like a pretty unappealing option, not to mention a bad long-term career move. So I reverted to my default tactics: I went into the office each day as if it were another round of a *gamet.* Put your guard up, I would tell myself. Protect your head. Keep your feet underneath you and don't forget to breathe. It wasn't a perfect solution, but this strategy did allow me to retain some shreds of my sanity. (I won't say dignity; I think you give that up when you start working with people who quote Foucault.)

When the dust settled, Joan had packed up her whip and moved on to a job as department chair at a university in Illinois, and I found myself with a new boss (who worked in another building and lived across town from me), a new office that I didn't have to share with anyone, and plenty of peace and quiet in which to look back over my stint as a vassal.

God knows I hadn't made it look glamorous, but I had done the job, I thought, reasonably well. Taking on the role of the loyal second-in-command was one of the hardest things I'd ever done, and if I hadn't already assumed the roles of black belt and self-defense advocate, it would have been even harder. Luckily, I was able to leverage those two roles and force some adaptations in the new one—to change it, update it, and make it consistent with my own needs.

And that, I decided, was something Yuzan and the other authors of the Edo period were trying to tell the samurai: Roles that seem to conflict can just as easily inform and improve each other. They can evolve along with the people who fill them. If the situation demands it, you can be a warrior and still master the tea ceremony. You can be a lowly academic administrator and a black belt, and, in fact, being good at one role can make you better at the other.

Provided, of course, that you keep a firm grip on the underlying values that led you to take on each role in the first place. That's the key, and that's what is so hard to remember: if we're smart, we choose our roles—spouse, parent, employee, black belt—for a reason, because they are necessary to accomplish something we want, something we believe in. Those values are what make you one person, whole and integral. If you stay in touch with them, you can perform any role you take on, because you'll know how the role aligns with the magnetic north of your own beliefs. You'll know which parts of the role are consistent with your values, and you'll know which parts aren't. It will be clear which parts of the role need to be lived up to, and which need to be changed.

Fulfill your duties as a warrior, Daidoji Yuzan says, and you will be healthy and successful; "your character will improve, and heaven and earth will favor you." As tough as vassalage had been, I decided it had been a good experience. Certainly I was still better off than a samurai. At least my job wasn't hereditary. And no one expected me to commit hara-kiri when Joan left. Not even Joan. A couple of weeks after she reached Illinois, I received proof that she harbored no ill will over our parting, in the form of a two-gallon container of Beer Nuts from the factory located in her new hometown. I placed the huge red metal can on my desk between my Powerpuff Girl dolls and the plaque Joan had brought me from a trip to London (THE BEATINGS WILL CONTINUE UNTIL MORALE IMPROVES, it read), and stuck the I BITE magnet on top. It was like a little shrine to my departed overlord, acknowledging the debt I could never repay.

Self-criticism is easy. Self-improvement is hard. You're here for the hard stuff.

ここで著者は、自我によって駆り立てられる自己批判と、
謙虚さの産物である自己改善との違いを指摘している。
自己改善の方が良いのである。
なぜ著者がはっきりとそう言わないのかはわからない。

I STILL CAN'T QUITE believe the new dojo.

We've been here for five years now, and every time I step through the door I glance around in astonishment. The space itself is unremarkable. It's clean and airy but not large; it has run-of-the-mill shopping-center windows and generic bluish-white fluorescent lighting. But it's such a change from the old dojo that, especially in the beginning, it had an air of unreality about it.

After we moved in, new students appeared, which only heightened the feeling of make-believe. We weren't overwhelmed, by any means, but a steady trickle of white belts came into the new school, with its new plumbing, and air-conditioning, and changing rooms, and—wonder of wonders—many of these white belts *stayed.* This, too, seemed incredible.

High attrition rates are a fact of life in karate. This art is harder than it looks, and learning to do it can be frustrating and boring at times, even for the most passionate student. Modern schedules make it hard to find time to train, and modern bodies don't always adapt well to the demands of the training. It can be expensive, too, if your school doesn't have a scholarship program. So a majority of the people who start karate don't train for very long.

This doesn't mean they're undisciplined, or weak, or that, as some more macho dojos might put it, they "haven't got what it takes." It simply means that they caught a glimpse of something in karate they thought might benefit them and then found that it didn't, or that the benefits didn't outweigh the required sacrifices, or that they just didn't have the means to realize the benefits at that particular point in time.

I was a martial arts dropout for ten years myself before I even started at Sun Dragon, so I have a special sympathy for people who leave the discipline. I've always felt an obligation to make the early part of our students' training worthwhile, in part because the odds are good that it's all the training they'll ever have, but also because I feel I owe it to them. First-time students risk an awful lot when they get up off their couches and venture into the dojo. Our school—like all schools—depended on people being willing to take that risk.

Noble sentiments, for sure; they placed a considerable burden on me when the new teaching schedule came out after the move, and I discovered I had been assigned to teach Sun Dragon's new all-white-belt class. I'd been an assistant instructor, or *senpai,* ever since I earned my first black belt. Now I'd be adding yet another layer to my identity as a *karateka*—lead instructor. I would be in sole charge of the entire class, from beginning to end.

I digested the news in the interval between sparring class

and meditation, as the other black belts discussed Amy's toenails.

"*Three* of us are bleeding tonight, Amy. Three!" KJ said, waving a bloody forearm in the air. Overgrown toenails are a common grievance during sparring; they can leave nasty cuts, especially on the arms. Not to mention that, toenails not being the cleanest part of the body, such wounds can be slow to heal. Disgusting? Yes. Such are the realities of contact sport.

"I do need to trim them," Amy admitted, inspecting her offending digits. "I meant to do it before class, honestly."

"Well, what's it gonna take?" Denise asked her. "Come on, Amy; how many people have to *die*?"

Denise and Amy would be teaching in the kids' program, according to the new schedule. When not squabbling over podiatry, they were both wonderful with children—Denise, in fact, being a highly trained professional. She could even keep KJ under control, something the rest of us, including Sensei Joy, had trouble doing. Denise would listen patiently to one of KJ's long, discursive rhapsodies about breaking someone's elbow, and then say, "OK, I need you to focus on me for a minute."

KJ had been tapped to lead a sparring class and an advanced session for blue belts and up. This was also a natural choice. KJ is basically a walking sparring class, and while she's great with all levels of students, she can be slightly alarming until you get to know her. I remember watching her drill some yellow belts on their guard position for sparring one night, and hearing her ask, "Janice, you're going to tuck that thumb in under your fist before I start chewing on it, right?" It was a rhetorical question, presumably, but she followed it up by gnashing her teeth in a way that really made you take the sentiment to heart.

The rest of us were more laid-back. "Darlene, honey, cover your groin," Denise would drawl as she put a bunch of teenagers through the basic stances. "Alex, put your left foot in front. No, your *left.* Your other left, sweetie. That's it."

I am neither high-energy nor sweet, so I surmised that I had drawn the white belt class by default. My work schedule allowed me to teach at the dojo only one night a week, and the white belt class was the only open spot on the schedule.

It'll be fun, I told myself nervously. After all, they're only white belts. They can't eat me.

I didn't get eaten, but I felt pretty well chewed and digested after a few weeks of teaching the white belts. It was different from teaching self-defense; it demanded more precision and more attention to detail. In self-defense workshops, I was teaching skills that pretty much anyone could master with a little explanation and practice. In karate, I was teaching skills that no one ever perfected, even after a lifetime of training. Talk about pressure.

Not that it wasn't fun. The first months of karate can be tough for the student, but they are undeniably exciting. Most beginners make the kind of rapid, visible progress that old-timers can only remember wistfully. The way you stand and move and even think about yourself changes dramatically in a very short time. Your body starts to get the hang of new gross-motor movements, and reflects the benefits of regular, intensive exercise. Plus you're learning the most basic and effective techniques—punches, front and roundhouse kicks, and simple blocks—which showcase any strength and athletic ability you already possess. Instructing students at this level is like teaching a bunch of awkward, knock-kneed little fawns how to wield a sledgehammer. It's hard to imagine anything more rewarding, or entertaining.

The downside is that these sweet little fawns are wandering into your class from all different parts of the forest. People bring their own challenges with them to karate, and you never know exactly what will walk through your door next. Sun Dragon subscribed to the Seido philosophy of "karate for everyone," and we had our own long tradition, from our days as an independent dojo, of making karate accessible to as many people as possible. This was one of the things I had always loved about the school. As the instructor of the white belt class, however, I had to translate that ideal into actual instruction.

There's no good way to plan for this, but I tried. I wrote carefully sequenced exercises on index cards, cross-referencing every activity to the white belt section of the Seido study guide, and sometimes made it as far as ten or fifteen minutes into a class before tearing the card up into tiny pieces.

The problem is that while white belts are all learning the same material, they are very different people, and their idiosyncrasies rarely fit on one index card. On any given night I might have to adapt my painfully crafted lesson plan to accommodate a student who spoke no English, another with arthritic knees, and another who was legally blind. Lots of our new students weren't in peak physical condition, either, but that was to be expected. Since we had started as a women's school and still attracted more female students than male, we had plenty of timid beginners. Those, too, I could handle—I'd seen Sensei Suzanne do it for years. But there were special cases as well, such as students who were survivors of violence. Some aspects of karate training, like the yelling and physical contact, can trigger reactions in people who have undergone trauma.

Someone teaching such a diverse population really needs

the ability to adapt on the fly, under pressure. Unfortunately, improvisation is not my strong suit. I tend to have my best ideas just after the caffeine hits my bloodstream, or just before I notice I've been running downhill. I don't process language particularly well when I'm doing physical stuff, either, and the mix of Japanese and English was a constant tripping-up point. And I've given up entirely on trying to use my limited Spanish with Spanish-speaking students. Under normal circumstances I'm perfectly capable of remembering *alto* and *bajo, rápido* and *lento.* When I search my brain for them in the middle of class, all I can come up with is a handful of irregular French verbs and the rule for the ablative absolute in Latin.

One night I was showing students how to perform rear breakfalls—a simple falling technique we teach from a seated position to build the core muscles and help students become comfortable on the mat. "Tuck your chin down to your chest," I kept telling the class, as the students rolled backward and slapped the mat with their arms. "You need to protect the back of your head."

One student seemed to be ignoring this admonition, and I went over to check on her.

"Wendy, you're not tucking your chin," I pointed out.

"*Osu,* Senpai," she replied nervously. "I can't, I'm sorry."

"Don't apologize," I told her. "Do you have a neck injury?" I couldn't remember if she'd listed anything unusual on her medical disclaimer.

"No, I have bolts in it," she explained.

This was a new one. I tried to think fast—an activity which I'm always certain exposes the people around me to loud clanking noises and the smell of smoke.

"OK . . . can you slap the mat?" I asked her.

"Oh, sure," she said. "I mean, *Osu,* Senpai."

"All right, then, instead of rolling back," I told her, "just lie on the mat and slap when everyone else does." Then I thought of something else.

"Can you tuck your knees to your chest?"

"*Osu,* Senpai."

"All right, so try bringing your knees up to your chest when everyone else rolls backward, and extend your legs when everyone else rolls forward." The net effect would be something like a rear breakfall without the backward motion, I figured, and would at least train a lot of the same muscles without involving her neck. I watched her do this a few times while I made a mental note to myself: *Don't just ask about injuries. Ask about hardware.*

Dealing with student limitations is hard enough all by itself. That difficulty is compounded when students start apologizing.

"Sorry, Senpai," my students would mutter as I explained yet again the correct way to line up, or make a fist, or point their toes. We wasted more time on apologies in the white belt class than almost anything else.

"There is no 'sorry' in karate!" I would tell them, over and over again. "If you have to say something, say *osu!*"

"Osu," they would correct themselves. Still, the stubborn habits of apology and self-criticism persisted. There was the new student who shook her head in irritation every time she punched with the wrong hand. The blue belt candidate who giggled apologetically whenever she turned the wrong way in a kata.

Finally I remembered what Sensei Suzanne had told me when I was a white belt. I had been one of those students who reacted to every mistake with a grimace, a flinch, an exasperated laugh.

"Stop that," she told me bluntly one day. "You're criticizing yourself when you do that, and that's not appropriate or respectful behavior in the dojo."

"Osu," I said, mildly horrified at the thought of being disrespectful in Sensei's dojo.

She took pity on me and explained more kindly: "Look, I don't allow people to criticize my friends. You're one of my friends, so I can't let you treat yourself that way."

I nodded.

"And you've got to remember, too," she went on, "when you criticize yourself, that's your ego talking. You're displeased because you're not perfect. Well, no one's perfect. Get over yourself."

"Osu," I said again, feeling strangely liberated.

I didn't tell my white belts to get over themselves, but I did lecture them a little.

"One of the rules in this dojo is that we don't criticize our fellow students," I told them. "You're a student. That means you can't criticize yourself, either.

"Furthermore," I went on, warming to the subject, "there isn't a single instructor here who is going to look at your form and say, 'That's terrible.' And we know more about karate than you do." By now I was striding up and down in front of the class like Mister Rogers addressing Patton's Third Army. "So if *we're* not criticizing you, *you* certainly have no grounds for doing so. Understand?"

"Osu," they responded dutifully, looking serious and relieved at the same time.

• • •

What with the curriculum, the adjustments for individual students, and the periodic harangues about egos and apologies, there was a lot to keep track of in white belt class. Most nights I counted myself lucky if I had everyone lined up facing the same direction at the beginning and end of our allotted hour.

What I wanted more than anything were mirrors—a solid wall of mirrors like they had at the well-funded *dojang* I'd trained in years and years ago.

Mirrors are helpful in the dojo because they provide constant visual feedback for students and instructors. You can direct students to look at them, or they can refer to them on their own, or they can ignore them if they find the feedback overwhelming. Mirrors give everyone a 360-degree view of the class.

We'd never had a mirror wall at the old dojo. We couldn't afford it, and anyway the walls around the beer garden had been split horizontally by chest-high windows. At the new location, we still couldn't afford mirrors, but we had a lovely blank wall where we intended to put them, someday. In the meantime, I dashed around in class every week, trying to keep an eye on the students at the other end of the training floor, the ones in the back row; trying to keep track of what was going on wherever I wasn't. I got twice as much exercise as anyone else in the class.

I whined about the lack of mirrors for months, and then lo and behold, the morning of the celebration marking our first full year in the new location, when I walked into the dojo—there were mirrors on the wall. Huge, sparkling slabs of glass in a silver frame; they made the space look twice as big.

"How did we manage this?" I asked Sensei Joy, goggling at the pristine reflection of the training floor, the calligraphy on the opposite wall, and the *shinzin,* the wooden structure indicating the spiritual heart of the dojo.

"Bart," she simply.

Bart was one of the rare fathers who had followed his kids into the karate program at Sun Dragon. His wife, Senpai Doris Ann, was already a black belt, and Bart was about to test for his brown belt. So we'd known Bart's whole family for what seemed like forever, yet he still retained an air of mystery. He was not a small man, for one thing, and he was a tattoo artist by trade, with his own shop. Furthermore, he had a way of taking off his jacket that made you think, Uh-oh; whatever I just said to this guy was a *big* mistake.

The impression I gleaned from Sensei Joy was that Bart had arranged, on remarkably short notice, for some unnamed friends of his to donate the mirrors, as well as the labor required to deliver and install them (in the dead of night apparently). I was hesitant to ask for more details, even though I was on the board of directors and could presumably claim a need to know how much the mirrors were worth and where they had come from. I didn't want to ask. If someone had told me they'd fallen off a truck, I would have accepted this explanation without a murmur. All that mattered to me was that now I could see all my students, from both sides.

This meant they could also see me.

"Look at yourself," I'd been told at Honbu, and I was prepared to take this admonition literally as well as figuratively. Seeing myself teach karate to all these people helped convince me I really was doing it. It also, somehow, made me infinitely more sensitive to the fact that others were looking at me for information, direction—as an example. Now *I* was the role model.

Some years before, at an instructor-training class, several of us senior students had asked Sensei Suzanne how to interact with a new student—a young woman who was taking classes because her mother wanted her to be able to protect herself. She was fiercely, obdurately shy. She wasn't resistant to training. She would comply with all our directions. She just wouldn't respond verbally or make eye contact. Sensei Suzanne counseled patience, and she also told us this, based on her decades of experience: "Here's what you need to remember about shy people: They are *watching.* They are *listening.* They are scrutinizing you, the leader, out of the corner of their eye, nonstop. They're noticing everything you do—every interaction with other students. They're watching to see how you treat other people. That's how they judge whether you're fair, if you're kind—if you're someone they can trust. So even when you aren't directly interacting with them, you're building a relationship with every word and every action. Don't forget that."

I haven't. And once I was put in charge of what felt like a small army of white belts, all of them *watching me,* I was profoundly aware of it.

As the dojo settled in at the new location and started to thrive, our schedule of self-defense workshops also began to pick up, and I was asked to teach some of these classes. Now I had to learn to shift gears between quite different teaching philosophies. In self-defense instruction (at least, the way we do it at Sun Dragon), you can't order your students around, or you defeat the whole purpose of the class.

When you take an empowerment approach to self-defense, you begin with the assumption that students have to integrate the concepts into their own experience, their own understanding of the world. You hope to show them a new perspective on violence, and to heighten their sense of agency, but those aren't things you can "give" to someone else. You can't empower someone by telling her what to think; empowerment has to come from within, from a recognition of one's own inherent power.

It's a delicate dance, very different from showing someone how to make a fist. There's a right way and a wrong way to make a fist, and I'm confident in my ability to do it the right way. I've done it thousands of times, and it works more or less the same way, no matter how different my students are. But there are as many ways to defend oneself as there are people.

Some of the methods I use to teach karate do come into play in a self-defense workshop: direct instruction (*Strike the chin from underneath; use your voice*); redirection (useful when working with students like Anna, the *Obergruppenführerin* of Girl Scout Council 57); and even a little bit of manipulation —though we try to be transparent about that.

For example, I'll often open a self-defense class with something called a "clothesline activity." Sometimes it's done with a real clothesline and a bunch of clothespins; sometimes we use a stretch of wall. At the new dojo, I use our mirror wall, which has the advantage of letting us see one another as we conduct the exercise. I map out a spectrum, or scale, on the mirrors, labeling the left side "Irritating Behaviors," the center part "Dangerous," and the right end "Life-threatening." Then I give my students a number of cards describing different personal safety scenarios: "Someone follows me to my car or the bus stop." "My partner insults me in front of my friends." "Someone grabs me or holds me so I can't leave." "A stranger threatens me with a gun or other weapon." And then I ask students to place these statements somewhere along the scale, according to how dangerous they think the scenarios are.

What happens initially is that people walk to one area of the scale, then think about it a little more, and move their scenario up or down the scale of danger. At the same time, they observe the other participants moving *their* cards around, and as they do, they also perceive—without my ever having said or done *anything*—that threat and risk are somewhat subjective terms.

If people can hold different opinions about threat levels, then we should also be able to analyze threats by discussing those opinions. Which is precisely what we do next: when all the cards are up, we talk about their placement, and everyone has a chance to think about the reasons we judge a scenario to be dangerous. This is where we usually start to talk about probability, and how risky each of the scenarios is known to be statistically. Comparing those risk levels to the kinds of scenarios that women *fear* most, or worry about most often, is a key moment in this activity. It becomes obvious pretty quickly that the more dramatic scenarios are uncommon, but disproportionately represented in the media and people's minds, whereas the less spectacular scenarios are the ones most of us need to be prepared to deal with.

Looking at the range of scenarios—at all the evidence laid out there on the mirror—also helps people recognize that truly life-threatening behavior rarely occurs out of the blue. Instead, it's much more likely to start as something on the "irritating" end of the scale, and escalate into something dangerous. This discovery opens the door to a discussion of early intervention to reduce violence—the importance of saying "leave me alone" early on, of recognizing danger signs in an intimate partner, of sharing concerns about behavior with others, and otherwise taking steps to prevent escalation.

This approach is quite different from what people tend to think of as "safety," which instead involves someone bigger, stronger, smarter, or more powerful than they are telling them what to believe and what to do—in other words, the "9 Safety Tips for Women" approach.

You don't make people safer if you just replace one set of safety rules with another. You make them safer when you teach them to analyze the rules. This is not an easy thing to teach, and I never know, from one workshop to the next, if I'll be able to pull it off.

Sensei Suzanne had made it look easy. She embodied multiple roles in the dojo; she taught everything and everyone with complete conviction. Sensei Joy had been able to move into that role with aplomb. I, as usual, was plagued by doubts. I'd look at myself in the mirror and think, I can't possibly do what Sensei Suzanne did.

Well, of course not, the mirror would say back to me. No one could. That wasn't what I was there to do. I was there to learn, and to look inside myself, and share what I discovered. As a teacher, all I really had to do was to make sure that the students looking at me were seeing the same person I saw.

Survival is the bravest fight, and the most beautiful victory.

生き残ることは、最も勇敢な戦いであり
そして最も美しい勝利である。

BY 2009, WHEN I entered my second decade at Sun Dragon, I was applying the school's philosophy to nearly every facet of my life and still finding new ways that training could move me forward past anxiety, anger, and fear. And yet as I grew ever more convinced that karate was the right path for me, I was increasingly seeing that my path to fearlessness wasn't the only one. Teaching self-defense, for example, introduced me to many women who *didn't* have karate in their daily lives. I was astounded, time and again, by the trauma my students had survived, and by the courage and ingenuity with which they had striven to free themselves from its influence.

Around this time I also became aware of the extraordinary journeys away from fear that two of my close friends had undertaken. The first was Laura, whose mother's death had become a touchstone for me in adolescence and beyond. In the years after high school, Laura had bounced from one exotic place to the next—she went to college in Europe, lived in a poverty-stricken New Orleans neighborhood, and then moved to a ramshackle old Texas farmhouse miles away from any neighbors. She hitchhiked and sang in nightclubs and went to the kind of parties I never got invited to—the kind that attendees either remember forever or can't recollect at all.

Laura had lived fearlessly during those years. And while in some ways it was a curious approach to life for a woman whose mother had been murdered, I thought I understood why she chose it. When something truly devastating and terrifying happens to you, I reasoned, you essentially have two choices. You can live under a rock for the rest of your life, and be afraid of everything, and never go out into the world again. Or you can simply say, "I refuse to acknowledge fear." Laura had chosen the latter.

I sympathized with that choice—her decision to go into the darkness and claim it as her own. I always regarded Laura as an extremely brave person for confronting her fear—though she didn't, perhaps, go about it in the healthiest way possible. G. Gordon Liddy conquered his fear of lightning by chaining himself to the top of a tree during a thunderstorm, but few therapists would recommend his approach. I worried about Laura during her nomad years, not just because she lived dangerously, but because I felt that if a person's *only* choices are life under a rock or no fear whatsoever—well, that isn't really much of a choice, is it?

Laura eventually settled down in Austin. We got back in touch after our twentieth high school reunion in 2005, and over the next few years we saw each other quite often. The memory of her mother had stayed with me, and I finally asked Laura about her loss one evening as we sat in a tiny, dim bar in one of the funkier neighborhoods of East Austin. We had both recently turned forty. Laura looked great; she seemed happy. But I wondered about all the choices she had made over the past twenty-five years, and about the choices she had been denied. It was hard to put my concern into words; hard not to feel like I was prying or indulging in morbid curiosity. We had been discussing high school, and our parents, and inevitably her mother's death came up. In the awkward pause that followed, I blurted out, "How did you work through the loss of your mother?"

Laura grimaced, and then she smiled, a little wistfully. "Do you know," she said, "that neither me nor my brother got any counseling after Mama died?"

"None?" I asked in disbelief.

She shook her head, her eyes distant. "There were these two girls who lived next door to us," she said. "They started having nightmares after the murder, and their parents took them to a counselor. Those kids got more therapy than I did."

We regarded each other, me in blank dismay, Laura smiling in pained amusement. It struck me as an appalling failure, that two children could lose their mother to violence and never be given the opportunity to explore their grief with a professional counselor. I could only assume that shock and fear made the adults around Laura rush to reassert normality too quickly. Everyone was concerned for her safety and survival, but they failed to consider how she would make sense of her loss.

I told Laura my impression of the life she had led after college, how she had appeared to be responding to the tragedy by denying it, and she agreed with me.

"Really," she said, referring to her residence in the old farmhouse, "what I was doing was terrorizing my father. Poor Daddy had to *beg* me to move off that farm." I couldn't imagine the agony her father must have suffered, seeing his daughter live in exactly the kind of lonely, isolated place where his wife had died. No, it hadn't been a healthy way to confront fear.

It was only as she had grown older, Laura confided, that she'd been able to admit that she *was* afraid. Especially since she had stopped moving around, bought a house, and given herself time and space to reflect.

"Once I acknowledged my fears," she went on, "I realized that I'm afraid of everything, all the time. I mean, you have kids. I could never have kids, because I'm afraid I'll die. You're married. I could never get married, because the person I married might die. All I have are my dogs, and I have at least one moment every single day when I picture myself coming home and finding *them* dead."

Denying her fear, evidently, had been only a temporary solution. The fear had been there all along, and while Laura hadn't succumbed to it, it had nonetheless colored her existence. Still, we agreed, it was a step forward to finally acknowledge her fear, to come to grips with it. That change of direction had started in the mid-1990s, Laura said, when she ended a long-term relationship and moved to Austin. "I was living alone again, and decided I should learn to protect myself," she told me. "So I took a self-defense class from this woman named Suzanne."

Of course, that could mean only one person. "Suzanne Pinette?" I asked Laura. "At Sun Dragon?"

"Right," she replied. "I forgot, that's where you took karate, wasn't it? Isn't the school closed now?"

"Suzanne retired, and we moved the school," I explained.

"She was amazing," Laura said, and I laughed, and agreed.

"When did you take her class?" I asked.

It turned out that Laura had met Sensei Suzanne about a year before I had. And even though she'd had only one class with her, she remembered my instructor almost as vividly as I did.

"She started the workshop by talking about the different kinds of violence and abuse," Laura recalled, "and to demonstrate that an abusive relationship didn't have to involve physical force, she yelled at us, '*I can't believe you forgot to buy spaghetti sauce at the grocery store!*'"

I recalled this portion of Suzanne's curriculum.

"And I burst into tears," Laura went on. "That's when I finally recognized that the relationship I had just ended was an abusive one. That was really an eye-opening moment for me. It showed me I should take better care of myself.

"And after that I did," she went on. "I got some therapy. I reconnected with my old friends, and I found new ones who were healthier to be around."

"And how are you doing these days?" I asked tentatively. It was a vague, silly question; a weak attempt to communicate what I wanted to say but couldn't: *Are you OK? Are things getting better? Is there anything I can do?*

"Oh, I'm fine," Laura said, signaling the bartender. "I'm living my life, and it's not quite the same as most people's, but I'm happy. You don't have to worry about me."

I wasn't *worried,* exactly. Instead, I was *angry,* still so angry, on her behalf. Because sorrow and loss come to everyone, even people whose lives aren't marred by violence. But someone had *done this* to Laura, left her with these images in her mind and this ache in her heart, and the injustice of such a vicious theft made me wish more than anything that I could find that person, and crush his windpipe, the way Sensei Suzanne had taught me.

All I could do instead was talk to Laura about her path, and follow my own. It didn't seem like enough, and yet it had to be. Laura was on a longer, slower journey than mine, but she was making progress. And as Sensei Suzanne used to say, anytime someone survives violence, it's a victory and deserves to be celebrated.

I have another friend from high school, Jennifer, whose adolescence was more like mine, free of the kind of violence Laura had known. Jennifer was an adult with two children of her own when fear entered her life. For Jennifer, fear wasn't an unseen force that struck in an isolated place. It was a convicted felon who, in 2005, crashed through the ceiling of her apartment in the middle of the night and attempted to rape her.

Yes, through the ceiling.

"He was a stranger that literally fell from the ceiling and tried to commit a brutal crime!" was the way the local NBC affiliate described Jennifer's attacker.

"That was my favorite news story about the attack," she reminisced when we met at a restaurant in College Station. In the assault's aftermath, she and her children had moved back to Texas from Virginia, and when she opened up to me about her ordeal, I asked if she'd be willing to discuss it someday, since I was trying to learn more about how people survive violence. Sure, Jennifer said. By the time we met for dinner, the crime was four years behind her, but she still remembered every detail.

"It was reported on three TV stations and in the newspaper," she said, "but NBC sensationalized it the most. They even created an animated computer graphic of the apartment building I lived in with a dotted line showing the guy's route through the crawl space. And they got it wrong. I thought that was hilarious."

What the man had actually done was break into another unit in Jennifer's complex, cut a hole in the ceiling, and crawl over several empty rooms to reach her apartment.

"I woke up because I felt someone covering my face with a blanket," she said. "I had been alone in the apartment; my divorce wasn't final yet, and my kids were with their dad. I fell asleep on the sofa with the TV on, and TCM was showing gangster movies that night. I must have heard the noise when he broke through the kitchen ceiling, but I just assumed it was gunshots or car crashes."

Her attacker held down her arms and asked if she was going to fight him. Jennifer, thinking he had asked, "Are you *frightened*?" answered, honestly, "Yes."

That confused the man. Like a lot of attackers, Jennifer's assailant ("my gentleman caller," as she now refers to him) had a script he expected his victim to follow. He asked Jennifer again if she planned to fight. This time she understood him, and answered "no."

She explained this decision to me: She couldn't see anything. She didn't know how strong the man was, whether he was armed, or anything else about him, but she did know that he wasn't hurting her at the moment and that he was talking. So she decided to try to keep him talking.

It bears emphasizing here that, of all my friends, Jennifer is by far the savviest, most quick-witted, and sharpest-tongued (and I'm an avid collector of sharp-tongued friends). She also has very deeply held religious beliefs, a fact that somehow never fails to surprise me. This combination of traits helped her excel at the job she had when she lived in Virginia: answering calls to a toll-free prayer line. Jennifer's specialty was handling the prank callers.

There are many situations in life you can't possibly prepare for, but Jennifer's personality and job training gave her a unique set of skills that turned out to be very well suited for handling a talkative rapist. She kept him talking. She also told her attacker to leave the blanket over her head, and managed to maintain her composure even in that ridiculous costume.

"I must have looked like a ghost." She shrugged. "But I figured he'd be calmer if he knew I couldn't identify him. I didn't want to increase the tension beyond what we were already dealing with." So he left her covered up, and subsequently, due to what Jennifer demurely describes as "equipment failure," he did not commit the rape he had taken so much trouble to plan. At that point the attacker noticed the pictures of Jennifer's children on her living room wall, and what remained of his script evaporated.

"He started apologizing," Jennifer recalled, "saying he knew I could never forgive him. He said he was a Christian and couldn't believe what he had done. I told him I could forgive him, and so could God. I told him everything I could think of to help him calm himself."

Jennifer was sincere when she talked to her assailant about forgiveness. But, she told me, she was aware the entire time of the danger she was in. She continued to think and act with extraordinary focus and strategic awareness. She asked her attacker if she could have a drink of water, and had him lead her (still covered with the blanket) into the kitchen. She asked him to take the glass out of the cupboard for her, hoping to obtain some of his fingerprints, but they ended up being too smudged for the police to use.

When he finally left, he was crying. Jennifer attributes his tears to shame or perhaps a response to the compassion she showed him. At the door, Jennifer asked if she could give him a hug to show that she really meant what she'd said about forgiveness. He said yes.

"So I hugged him," Jennifer explained, "and when I did, I was able to gauge his height and build. I could also see beneath the edge of the blanket. And that," she continued matter-of-factly, "was how I got a look at his pants, shoes, and belt buckle, all of which helped the police identify him later."

I was dumbstruck by the brilliance of this stratagem. I was awed by the whole story, in fact, but especially by the way Jennifer had navigated the dangers using the strengths she knew she possessed. And yet, knowing Jennifer as I do, her survival seemed in some ways the only possible outcome for such a bizarre scenario. Jennifer thwarted her attacker using skills that were completely intuitive for her—skills that most people don't think of as components of self-defense: communication, quick thinking, compassion. No chain e-mail ever hyperventilates about the importance of those skills.

What my training had taught me to see in Jennifer's story was the evidence that we are endlessly creative about surviving, even if we have no training at all. It renewed my conviction that the most important safety skills to cultivate are those of assessing a situation, connecting with people, and believing in your own ability to survive.

If someone like Anna, my rebellious self-defense student, were to draw lessons from Jennifer's story, they'd probably sound more like "Never watch gangster movies," or "Always wear a blanket over your head"—pointless reductions of the facts that would not only be useless to others, but also fail utterly to give Jennifer credit for her heroism.

Jennifer's attacker is now back in federal prison. (He was on parole at the time of the assault.) I asked her how she had coped in the years since the assault, and, like Laura, she assured me she was fine now. For a couple of years, she said, she had issues with being alone at night. She adopted a dog so she'd have an extra set of ears to alert her to any unusual noises around the house, and that helped. And she invented a game she played with her kids, to make them more aware of their surroundings. "OK, close your eyes," she would tell them when they were going somewhere in the car. "That man who just walked past—what color shirt was he wearing?" She moved back to our hometown, where she knew people. She found her way past the crime, and past the fear.

Two statistical anomalies—the unknown murderer who changed Laura's life, and Jennifer's gentleman caller. These are rare specimens among the rest of humanity, and most of us will never encounter anything like them. My friends hit the jackpot in the lottery of violence we're all born playing. So when I reflected on Laura and Jennifer's stories, trying to put them into context with what I teach others, I felt a vague sense of inadequacy. Here I was, ripping the balls off of imaginary bad guys two or three times a week, and I had to wonder—was this helping anyone at all?

The dangers I've faced have been nothing compared to what many women struggle daily to overcome. If I'm lucky, I'll never have to fight like they have. But I train anyway, just in case. I train in darkness, so I don't waste my life worrying about what might come out of the dark. I train to make sure I know my own strengths, so I can use them to their fullest if I ever need to. And I talk to survivors, and ignore the chain e-mails that land in my inbox, because I want to know about the reality of violence, the truth about how it happens, and how we survive it. I want to demystify it, and take away the power we ascribe to it when we fear it. Not just the anticipatory fear that we might become victims, but also the fear of what comes after—the fear that we may be unhealable, that our world will be irrevocably broken.

Training at Sun Dragon taught me to recognize the incredible courage and resourcefulness of people like Laura and Jennifer. Now I can do what fear and anger alone wouldn't allow. I can celebrate their survival for the victory it is, and for the hope it gives all of us.

Believe it or not, you are more than equal to the challenges you face.

信じられないかもしれないが、あなたは自分が直面する試練以上の存在なのだ。

THE DAY AFTER our 2011 New Year's celebration at the dojo, Sensei Joy pulled me aside and said, "Congratulations! Honbu has invited you to test for *nidan* this July, during Gasshuku."

Nidan (literally, "second *dan*"; *dan* meaning "level" or "degree") is a Big Deal. One in a hundred students, the saying goes, makes it to the rank of black belt. Only one in a thousand black belts makes it to the next level. In Kyokushin and Seido, as in many martial arts, attaining the rank of *shodan,* first-degree black belt, means that you've learned the basics. You're a serious student. After you receive your black belt, you're expected to do more than just learn new techniques and polish old ones. Moving up the *dan* ranks, to second-, third-, fourth-degree black belt, and higher, requires a demonstration of teaching ability, service to the school, and all-around personal self-improvement.

Well, I was teaching, for better or worse, and I'd been on

the dojo's board of directors for a couple of years. What about the self-improvement?

I'd been trying; for years I'd been working to make myself someone I and the people around me could live with. I was pretty sure I'd made some progress, because I wasn't in jail or divorced, but then again, I still got on my own nerves pretty regularly.

But preparing to test for *nidan* would require a huge time commitment over the six months leading up to the test. Was I up for it? Was my family? Was this the right thing to do?

I belatedly realized I should have asked myself that question at some point during the three years since I'd been awarded my first-*dan* Seido black belt. Somehow, even with all the doubts and distractions in my life, I'd kept coming to class, and now I had managed, through nothing more than sheer inertia, to rack up the three hundred–plus classes required for *nidan* candidacy. The only thing remaining was to actually learn the *nidan* curriculum, which, unfortunately, those three hundred classes had not quite cemented in my brain yet.

Here, no doubt about it, was a challenge. All of the *shodan* material I had crammed in over a very short period for our Seido black belt test now had to be really *learned,* backward and forward, and inside out. I mean that literally: prearranged sparring and self-defense sequences we had learned on the right lead now had to be learned on the left. Kata had to be relearned *migi hajime* (starting to the right instead of the left), and *ura* (with 360-degree turns added at each step). There were several new, longer kata in the *nidan* curriculum, and new sets of partnered sequences. It was a lot to be tested on.

At least, though, I wouldn't be distracted by the thought

of who was looking at me during the test. For a large portion of the ordeal, we would be blindfolded.

With a familiar mixture of panic and resignation, I sat down to draw up a list of what I needed to learn, and a time line of how long I had to learn it. It was a long list and a short time line, and I used every learning method known to man in an attempt to pack everything into my brain.

I made flash cards for the Japanese vocabulary, carried them around with me, and reviewed them on coffee breaks. I wrote out self-defense sequences on slips of paper and kept them in a pencil holder on my desk at work, pulling them out randomly between meetings and phone calls to see how quickly I could execute them.

I enlisted Lilly (now seven years old and recently promoted to blue belt) to roll dice and call out numbers so I could randomly practice advanced knife defenses. I went to Saturday afternoon sparring classes and crammed my skull into the foam helmet Seido sparring required. (KJ and I shook our heads mutely at each other every time we put these on, mutually pining for the good old days before head protection.) I got the snot kicked out of me by all the young green and brown belts, who were eager to test their fledgling sparring skills against a black belt. I practiced kata in our bedroom every night, working around the bed and the dresser and the dogs and Scott. He would edge past me on his way to the shower as I wielded my *bo* staff or practiced another one hundred *ura* turns, grimly determined to not fall over on half of them this time. And he rearranged his teaching schedule so I could go to the dojo three or four times a week.

Fourteen-year-old Dave was less involved in my training,

for the simple reason that he was preparing for his own junior black belt test, which would take place at his school the month before I tested in New York. The two of us walked around the house muttering, shadowboxing, and littering the halls with invisible opponents. It was a tense time at our house.

This made me more appreciative than ever of my practice time at the dojo. I was especially grateful that Graham would also be testing for *nidan* at Gasshuku, even though he would make me look awful by comparison.

Graham was perfectly happy doing what, to me, is the most comforting and least frustrating bit of my karate practice, which is simply: practicing. The plain vanilla, over-and-over repetitions that provide the base for any accomplishment in the martial arts. We must have done Bo Kihon Kumite, a ten-strike/ten-block partner sequence for the long staff, or *bo,* about a hundred times one night. Up and back one long side of the dojo in a straight line: thrust, thrust, overhead strike; thrust, rib strike, reverse rib strike; spinning knee strike, overhead, thrust. To defend: parry, parry, high block; parry, vertical block, vertical block; reverse vertical block (lift the front foot), high block, parry, counter.

Clack, clack, clack, went the staves, with occasional muttered corrections to ourselves but very little conversation. The weapons were the primary means of communication. It was soothing, in part because of the repetition, but also because I knew, intellectually and viscerally, that this was what I really needed—endless reiteration of the pattern, driving the motions into my musculature and nervous system. The body is a slow learner, but it will often remember when the brain cannot. Physical memorization, I find, is equivalent to backing up your hard drive. When your memory fails you, the well-trained body can usually tell you what to do next: That hand drops. The rear foot moves. We're about to turn *this* way.

Over and over again, Graham and I stabbed at each other with fake knives, threw each other into forward rolls or front breakfalls, blocked and kicked and forgot things; swore, started over, did it again. All that spring and into the summer, until there was almost nothing left in our brains and nervous systems but sequences of technique.

In April, when Austin's weather was hot enough to approximate July in New York, the three of us testing at Gasshuku met at a nearby park for field practice. "To perform well on a test, you have to practice under conditions that mimic the actual testing conditions as closely as possible," I explained to Graham and Max, one of our students who would be testing for *shodan*. This was a maxim I'd learned as a professional in higher education, and while I wasn't entirely convinced of its truth, I had started giving in to a lot of superstitions by this point.

KJ came to help us out, since she had spent a lot of time on football fields, yelling and being yelled at. She had also been through her *nidan* test at Gasshuku the year before and therefore would be able to re-create testing conditions for us with near-total accuracy.

The park was already steaming in the heat when we arrived. Standing in the shade of the lone clump of trees, we solemnly applied sunblock and put on the shoes we'd chosen for the novel exercise of doing karate in something other than our bare feet. I preferred to train barefoot even outdoors, but everyone I'd seen at the black belt test at Gasshuku the previous year had worn shoes of some kind, except during sparring. We had puzzled over our footwear; I chose ultralight sneakers;

Graham had Vibrams, and Max had running shoes. In our *gis*, I thought shoes made us look ridiculous; they made all of us feel awkward. We tied on our belts—white belts today, since we were black belt candidates. Max looked nervous; Graham, resigned. KJ was psyched.

"This'll be great!" she told us. "This is almost exactly how hot I remember it being last year. You'll work up a good sweat."

"I'm already sweating," I pointed out.

"You think this is bad?" KJ scoffed. "Try doing two-a-days in full pads and helmet."

We filed out onto the scraggly grass, our feet shifting nervously in our unfamiliar shoes, donned our blindfolds, and awaited instructions.

"Intermediate Self-Defense Number Six, left punch!" KJ hollered, and the dress rehearsal began.

Being tested with a blindfold on was different from learning Gekisai Dai in the dark. Now I wasn't learning a new kata with Sensei Suzanne in the blacked-out dojo, but struggling to remember what I should have learned already. Instead of exploring the darkness, I was defending against my own blindness and faulty memory. When I learned Gekisai Dai, the darkness made me feel invisible and oddly omnipotent. Conversely, the darkness imposed by my blindfold exposed me dreadfully, stripping my abilities to their pathetic bones.

In practical terms, what I always notice about doing karate without eyesight is that it requires a conscious effort to make each movement bigger, because your instincts tell you to draw in and move conservatively. The space around you feels different when you can't see it; there's more of it, somehow. Without a visible horizon, the ground shrinks until it's nothing more than the spot precisely under your feet, and everything else solid withdraws to an unknown distance. Each step you take surprises you with the revelation that the earth, in fact, extends over there, too.

The only heartening thing was that the other candidates were, from the sound of it, having almost as much trouble as I was.

"Max, that's a lower block," KJ would yell, or "Graham, I said Advanced Self-Defense Number *Ten.* You're doing Number Eight."

And even KJ, who wasn't blindfolded, got distracted enough to run me and Max into each other during one kata.

"Oops—sorry about that, Senpai," she called out as I narrowly avoided pitching headfirst into the dead grass. "Max, take a couple of steps back, would you?"

We stumbled around for an hour or so, until everyone was streaming with sweat and coated with dust, then took off our blindfolds and consulted KJ's notes on our performance.

"Advanced Self-Defense Number Four, don't forget the takedown at the end," I read. "*Ura* turns are shaky. Seido Kata Number Five: Shift guard on the back kick." More things to add to the list at home. I had thought I'd be able to check some things off it by now. Instead, it kept growing longer.

The last thing we did at the park was practice our essay presentations. One requirement for all black belt candidates is to write an essay on a topic of Kaicho's choosing (ours was "balance").

"God, I hated the essays," KJ recalled. "I stood up, made my two points, and sat down. Thirty seconds, boom. I just wanted it over."

Writing and talking come as naturally as breathing to me, and I could already recite my essay, practically word for word.

I was relieved that there was at least one portion of the test I didn't have to put on my to-do list.

We arrived in New York City two days early, to settle in and take a few classes at Honbu before the test. Sensei Joy and I shared a room at Leo House, a Catholic guesthouse in Chelsea run by the Sisters of St. Agnes. Because we were headed for the Mount St. Alphonsus seminary retreat center in a few days, the Leo House's austere fixtures and the crucifix hanging across from our beds made it feel like we'd started Gasshuku early.

Every time I phoned home during the five days of our trip, a different member of the family was throwing up. Someone had brought home a stomach bug, which I had, by some miracle, escaped. "Uh, well . . . I love you, hon," I would tell Scott rather helplessly at the close of these conversations. "I'm sorry I'm not there to help out."

That last part was a lie. And Scott probably knew it. But I felt obliged to say it, given the circumstances.

On our second day, to while away the time before class at Honbu, I made a pilgrimage up through Central Park to see the Dakota, the apartment building where John Lennon died. His murder, which occurred the year before Laura's mother's death, was another formative event in my adolescence. The July heat was oppressive even in the oasis of the park, and as I trudged along the path, I found myself once again battling my fears. What business did I have testing for *nidan*? What did I really know about karate, or self-defense, for that matter? What was I doing here in New York, while my family was halfway across the country taking turns being violently ill?

I emerged onto Seventy-Second Street from the shade of the trees, temporarily blinded by a blast of midday summer light that laid the pavement out flat in front of me. The Dakota loomed across Central Park West, its ornate gables and balustrades appearing hot, dark, and sinister in the sun's glare. I felt an odd, ominous reluctance as I approached the building; fear and anger seeping up from my thirteen-year-old self. I was struck by the size of the arched doorway, an iron-gated porte cochere that looked as if a black coach-and-four might erupt from it any instant, the coachman's cloak whipping out behind him and peasants scattering before the horses' hooves. Next to the archway, a sort of brass pod for the doorman squatted on the sidewalk, like something out of a Jules Verne story. Neptune heads and dragons twined along the black iron railings, and the net effect was creepy as hell, which I supposed was part of the building's appeal. But I looked up at the gas flames guttering in the Gothic iron lamps above the entrance and thought, Jeez, can't you people lighten up a little? A man died here.

I walked along the sidewalk, checking lines of sight and imagining how the attack must have happened. Did the doorman's brass pod have a phone line? I wondered. How far away was the nearest hospital? How much light did the grim iron lanterns cast at night? If the light had been brighter, might someone have seen Mark David Chapman's gun sooner? I was assessing the scene rather differently from how I might have as a thirteen-year-old, I noticed. If nothing else, the past thirty years had made me more methodical about analyzing violence.

I didn't stay long at the Dakota. I returned to Central Park and sat on a bench by the IMAGINE mosaic in Strawberry Fields. A pigeon waddled up and looked at me, then pecked at the sidewalk by way of a hint. I wondered how many handguns had been bought and sold in the United States since

1980. A male pigeon wandered onto the scene and, perceiving that the first pigeon was female, began chatting her up by cooing and strutting around in tiny figure eights. The lady, unimpressed, turned away. The male pursued her, still walking mindlessly in loops, as if he were trying to invent figure skating without the benefit of ice or skates or enough brainpower to run a digital watch.

"You need to tell him 'no,' sister," I muttered to the female pigeon. She finally flew away, and the male slowly came to a halt like a windup toy running out its springs.

"Did you learn anything from that?" I asked him, and he looked at me with uncommonly stupid eyes, even for a pigeon.

I sighed. Some of them never get it.

A steady stream of tourists snapped photos of the mosaic. They were all, in some small way, affected by Lennon's violent death. What had *they* done in response, I wondered? Did any of them grow up to become black belts? Probably not. It wouldn't seem like an obvious response to most people. Even in my own case, I wasn't completely sure it made sense.

My *nidan* test commenced at one o'clock the next afternoon, in punishing heat and humidity. Rain had threatened throughout the bus trip up from the city, but though the grass at Mount St. Alphonsus was wet, the sun now shone unrelentingly. We formed up in lines for basics, with the testing candidates in front and the rest of the retreat attendees spread out behind us. We punched, we kicked, we did push-ups, and I failed miserably at counting backward from ten in Japanese, even though I had practiced this conscientiously back in Austin.

I can't blame myself too much for this. "To perform well

on a test, you have to practice under conditions that mimic the actual testing conditions as closely as possible," as any good SAT coach will tell you, and there was no way I could have re-created, or indeed anticipated, the actual conditions under which this element of the test would be administered: with Kaicho walking down the line of testers as we held a plank position on the turf, flogging those of us who lost count with the cord of his whistle.

Sweat quickly flooded my eyes, making our impending blindfolding something to look forward to. To my chagrin, however, when we split off from the nontesters and were lined up for kata and self-defense, the command was given: *"Mokuso!"*—Close your eyes. We all had our bandannas tucked into our *gi* tops, as we'd been instructed, but we never used them. *Dang,* I thought as I screwed my eyes shut. *Blindfolds would have been so much more badass.*

Graham and Max were somewhere off to my left, I knew, but I had no idea how they were doing as the test proceeded. I only knew that I didn't hear them corrected for anything. I wasn't called down for anything, either, not even for blowing the ending of Seido Five. Trying to remember the correct position for the arms before the next-to-last back kick (and dealing with a sudden, alarming downward shift in my *gi* pants, which I must not have tied as tightly as I should have), I suddenly lost track of which direction I was facing. And the important thing about the ending of Seido Five, I had discovered soon after I learned it, is that if you confuse right and left during the last two kicks, you will finish the kata facing backward. That I simply could not do. No matter what it cost me, I was not going to end Seido Five with my back turned toward the man who had created the kata. So I threw one back kick and cut directly to the finishing move: a downblock and cross-body punch. This did not go unnoticed, but no one said anything at the time. (Jun Shihan Nancy took me to task for it later.) For once, at that particular moment, luck was with me, and Kaicho was looking elsewhere.

The essay presentations, nerve-racking for a lot of people, were a piece of cake for me. Some people grew emotional and choked up, and this was quite touching, but I wasn't there to be touching. I might fail to perform at my personal best on every other element of the test, but, by God, I was going to nail the damned essay. And I did, bringing my presentation in around two and a half minutes and even working in a somewhat sycophantic reference to one of Kaicho's books on karate. "In the past I've made the mistake of thinking that I should balance a large commitment of time or energy in one part of my life by making a similarly large commitment in another area," I recited glibly. "Over time I've come to see that you can't balance a scale by continually adding more and more weight to one side and then the other. If all you ever do is add weight, or obligations, you may achieve some form of equilibrium, but you'll eventually crush the scale." I thought back, as I spoke, to all the nights I'd trained instead of being home with my family; my struggle to adjust after Sensei Suzanne left; the juggling act I'd had to perform with my job, my family, and my training. And I thought about Scott, and his encouragement; about Dave and Lilly; about Sensei Joy and KJ, Amy, Graham—everyone who had made it possible for me to accomplish what I was doing now.

"When you stop trying to do everything yourself," I said in my wrap-up, "you learn how much help people can give each other. The people around us are critical to our own balance. We have to rely on them just as much as they rely on us." I didn't have any trouble remembering what I knew about balance; I had inscribed the lesson in my body, over the last ten years. I knew I wasn't going to forget it, ever.

The light grew less brutal as we sat through the essays, and by the time we lined up for sparring, the final portion of the examination, the pulsing summer sky had grown overcast, and a welcome breeze rippled up from the river. I was jittery with anticipation, not so much for the sparring, but for the end of the test. The low mutters of thunder that drifted up the hill, increasing in volume and frequency, matched my mood.

Graham and Max and I had worried and discussed and strategized about the sparring, since we would be fighting a lot of people we didn't know well, or at all. Sparring at Gasshuku could be intense, we'd been told. But we were also told that there would be no shots to the head, so in the end I figured, What the hell; I'll just fight the way I always do. I'd been hit hard plenty of times before. I'd survived three Kyokushin gamets, and I hadn't even worn a helmet for any of those. And while it would have been nice to demonstrate some actual sparring strategy at my *nidan* test, I had too many other things to memorize and polish, and my Kyokushin training was more than I could overcome in just a few years. Everyone said spirit was the most important part of your sparring technique, and I had enough of that to survive. If I fell down, I'd get back up.

Counting back afterward, I arrived at something like thirteen rounds that we fought, not including some warm-up bouts with the other candidates. I fought Amy twice and several students from Thousand Waves. As it turned out, the fighters from Honbu gave me my easiest rounds; I suppose they didn't want to take any chances with those of us from out of town. Some people hit hard, others didn't. Things moved fast in the warm-up rounds, and then people settled into their pace. This meant that the noncandidates, who rotated out to rest, were moving approximately twice as fast as us test takers. It was not unlike a gamet, except that we were in a field, wearing helmets, and there were a lot more of us. The energy level was the same, the intensity was the same, and the challenge—of breathing, staying focused, thinking tactically, not freaking out and running away—was the same.

We had a brief respite before our last round, while the candidates chose their final opponents (I chose KJ). The thunder was close and insistent now, and I noted uneasily the lone pine tree standing sentinel over us. Kaicho showed no sign of stopping the test, so I mentally crossed my fingers and hoped that my foam-rubber sparring gear might provide some sort of insulation from electrical conductivity.

For that final round, the *sandan* (third-degree black belt) candidates stood off to the side while the *shodan* and *nidan* testers took the field. It was a long round, and I was every bit as tired as I'd been at my Kyokushin black belt gamet. There didn't seem to be enough oxygen in the vicinity to fill up my lungs, and my arms barely responded when I tried to block or punch. I was also out of ideas. After that much sparring, you can't think of any fresh combinations or interesting ways to control the *mai-ai*. Every move is a rerun of something you did just a little while ago.

I would have been happy to just stand still and let KJ beat on me for a while, but I knew Kaicho was watching to see that we stayed engaged, and the best way to show that you still had energy was to kick. So I kicked, slowly, and without much power, but I did it, and I didn't fall down.

"Kick higher!" KJ kept telling me. I ignored her since (1) I was tired as hell; and (2) KJ only ever walks forward when she spars, and as I've told her many times, when you do that, you're going to get kicked low now and then. If you don't like it, try going around to the side once in a while.

Just as the final call of *"Yame!"* came, the rain broke in earnest. We bowed to our partners, and backed off the field through the downpour, ceding the space to the *sandan* candidates. We were done.

"Shodan, nidan, seiza!" we were told, and we promptly knelt down in a line on the wet grass.

"Helmets off!" Kaicho called. *"Mokuso!"* We closed our eyes.

The rain streamed over us as the *sandan* candidates fought their last round. Rain, which I had almost forgotten the feel of in drought-stricken Texas, spattered on our sweat-filmed eyelids, our grass-stained *gis*, our steaming shoulders.

I love my life, I thought.

I was grinning like an idiot, my eyes closed, in the rain. This is insane, I told myself. I've just been beaten up by thirteen people in a cow pasture in a thunderstorm, and it's the most awesome thing I've ever done. I should have been a basket case—half a continent away from home, surrounded by chaos, at the mercy of the elements. Instead, I felt only stillness. I felt like I belonged right there.

The rain fell on us like tears and holy water and the shower we all so desperately needed. It muddied the field and roared in our ears and washed away months and months of frustration and anxiety and confusion. All I felt, at that moment, was lucky to be there.

I listened to the *sandan* candidates fighting and the audience cheering them on. All of these people, I thought, most of whom I barely know. All of them are smarter and more talented than I am, and all of them have almost certainly put even more time and effort into their training than I have. All of them are seeking the same things I'm seeking—power, control, answers, peace. If they're searching out here in this field, in the mud, while they fight one another in the middle of an electrical storm, then I must be in the right place, too. And any doubts I had melted away in the rain and ran down the hill to the Hudson.

Behind each triumph are new peaks to be conquered. — Mas Oyama

一つ一つの勝利の背後には、常に新しく征服されるべき頂点がある一マス大山

AFTER FORTY, NEW challenges are harder to find. You've already passed a lot of the traditional "growing up" milestones—getting, and staying, married; having kids; achieving professional goals; maybe going back to school (if, unlike me, you ever left). Halfway through my fourth decade, I've checked off the boxes for the marriage, kids, and job. I have four college degrees (three in English, one in fine arts; none of them paid for). And in addition to those accomplishments, I've survived three black belt tests. Apart from being tired all the time, I have nothing on earth to complain about.

Except boredom. Because now the biggest challenge in my daily life is simply scheduling all the challenges I've already taken on. So I look for new peaks to conquer. Some of these are small ones, like running, which I started doing because it's a nice change from karate, requiring a very different form of discipline. No one is watching you, directing you, or instructing you when you run. There is no hallowed tradition to follow or live up to; no bowing, no foreign languages to learn. There's just a lot of suffering and pain and wanting to throw up, which, now that I think about it, isn't actually very appealing, but at least it's different.

Last year I even persuaded some of my fellow Sun Dragon students to sign up for one of those ridiculous "extreme" obstacle courses that are suddenly skyrocketing in popularity; basically it was a 5K race run in a horse pasture. Six of us ran along dusty trails, slogged down a creek, climbed through fences, over hay bales, up mud-slick gullies—in other words, we did pretty much exactly what I spent every weekend doing when I was a kid. The main difference was that, since I'm grown up and buy my own clothes now, no one yelled at me for trashing my shoes. Plus we got free beer afterward.

But even extreme racing can't satisfy me completely. The Sun Dragon running team passed on another obstacle race that featured (according to its website) a "live KISS tribute band!" as one of the obstacles. It turned out that they didn't let you fight the band. You just listened to them play as you ran past. This, in my opinion, was patently false advertising. I wasn't expecting a fight to the death or anything. But I felt like we should at least have been able to make them cry.

Like I said, it isn't easy to find a good challenge when you're over forty, and female, and—well, when you're me.

If I couldn't humiliate a KISS tribute band, I figured, maybe the best option was to beat them at their own game. Although I don't really "play" the guitar or bass in any meaningful way, I can fake it well enough to live in Austin, a town where it's considered ill-mannered to show up at a house party without a musical instrument. So it was only a matter of time before I found myself onstage with Denise, who had taken some time off from karate and learned to play drums. She liked hitting things, she explained, and drums don't hit back.

Being in a band with Denise gives me a chance to once again do something I'm terrible at, and to make no apologies for my terribleness. Then, too, poverty is a hallowed tradition of the rock-and-roll lifestyle, and most of the venues we've played have reminded me forcefully of the old dojo (which was, after all, a beer garden). Tuning up earlier this year for a show at a nonprofit girls' rock camp, I looked around almost nostalgically: the stage consisted of uneven planking laid over concrete blocks, the microphone gave me a mild shock every time I touched it, and one of the PA monitors appeared to have been urinated on by what I sincerely hoped was a dog.

We sounded awful that night, even for us, and Denise actually fell off the stage during our opening number. Keith Moon couldn't have done it any better, and Denise, I am proud to report, did it sober.

It felt like old times.

Lately Jan has been threatening to join us. She is mostly retired from martial arts these days, and does her fighting in heavy-weapons competition in the Society for Creative Anachronism—a fitting arena, given that Jan does everything as if she were encased in armor. She's particularly fond of a sport called "fighting at the barrier," which she has explained to me as two fully armored participants standing on opposite sides of a low fence, holding on to the fence with one hand, and smashing each other repeatedly with whatever weapon they're holding in the other hand. It sounds like a sport created expressly for Jan.

She's also teaching herself to play the guitar and trying to talk me and Denise into forming a trio to be called Jeezloowheeze and the Goddammits. Though if we ever do this, our set list will be somewhat limited, because Jan's hands are so mangled from fighting at the barrier that she can't play anything but power chords.

OK, it's a stupid dream. But becoming a black belt seemed like a pretty impossible project, too, when I started up that slope. Ending violence looks like an insurmountable climb, but you never know. You can go pretty far, I've found, if you have the right people climbing with you.

I'm still in touch with Sensei Suzanne, who now lives in Colorado. Sensei Joy was promoted to *sandan,* third-degree black belt, last year. Amy's illness is unpredictable but manageable, and she has kept her promise to continue training, though she sometimes feels compelled to explain to new students that she's not drunk, she just has MS. KJ, Graham, and Doris Ann are all still training. We have overcome so many obstacles together, it's hard to imagine any of us stopping now.

There are the peaks to be climbed with my family as well, those long-suffering souls who have watched my slow and laborious ascents for years. Scott and I are closing in on twenty-five years of wedded bliss, and while the air sometimes gets a little thin when a marriage reaches that altitude, the view is spectacular.

Parenthood presents an entire mountain range full of peaks I could never summit alone. Dave has learned to drive in the past year, a rite of passage that would make most parents blanch, but since this is Dave, we're pretty sanguine about it. In fact, Scott is planning to turn his car over to the boy entirely soon and ride his bike everywhere. I expect our insurance premiums to drop precipitously as a result.

Lilly will doubtless find ways to make up the difference.

I'm unwilling to think as far ahead as her driver's license. Her current plan is to become a supermodel, a scientist who studies stars *and* germs, and an angel ("*after* I die, of *old age,* because I ain't never gonna smoke cigarettes"). Who knows what she'll accomplish? I felt pretty awesome when I came home after my *nidan* test, until I took her to the pool and was instantly humbled by her demonstration of the butterfly stroke. I'm forty-five years old and I still can't swim fly. She was seven.

She'll tackle all manner of peaks, I'm sure, and even if we havc to pick her up every time she comes tumbling down from them—well, life is never dull with Lilly around.

I have at least a year and a half to go before I can test for *sandan.* That's a lot of time to fill up; a lot of new peaks I could be climbing. And then there are classes to plan, and students to teach; boards to break and people to learn from—people I've known my whole life, and people I haven't even met yet.

And somewhere out there, I imagine there's an alligator with my name on it—or a cave bear, or a bully, or a hurricane, or a minotaur—who knows what form it will take? It really doesn't matter. I'm planning to kick its ass regardless.

Japanese Terms

bo—long staff

bokken—wooden training sword

budo—"the way to stop the spear," philosophy underlying martial arts practice

Budo Shoshinshu—*The Code of the Samurai*

chudan tsuki—midlevel punch

dachi—stance

dan—rank, black belt and higher

dojo—training hall

Gasshuku—training camp or retreat

gi—karate uniform

hajime—begin

heiko dachi—ready stance

hiza geri—knee kick, usually to the groin

Honbu—central Seido dojo, in New York City

ibuki—breathing with abdominal tension

ichigeki hissatsu—"one blow, certain death"

jodan hiji uke—rising elbow block

juji uke—X block

Jun Shihan—master teacher, sixth-*dan* black belt

karateka—student of karate

kata—form or formal exercise

ki—spirit, energy

kiai—shout

kiba dachi—horse-riding stance

kihon—basic

kotegaeshi—basic wristlock

kowa—a proverb or moral for contemplation during meditation (similar to a koan)

kumite—fight or sparring

Kyokushinkai—student(s) of Kyokushin karate

kyosaku—light stick used to strike students during meditation

Kyoshi—fifth-*dan* black belt

mai-ai—interval between two sparring opponents

mawashi geri—roundhouse kick

migi hajime—beginning to the right

mokuso—eyes closed

naore—return to stance

nidan—second-*dan* black belt

Niju Kun—twenty rules; Gichin Funakoshi's guiding principles for martial artists

ni rei—bow

nunchaku—weapon consisting of two short staff sections joined by a chain

oshi shinobu—striving with patience

osu—contraction of *oshi shinobu*; used as a general affirmation

otogai—fellow students

Pax Tokugawa—period of (relative) peace in Japan, roughly 1600–1868

rei—bow, courtesy

sanchin—three-point stance

sandan—third-*dan* black belt

seiza—kneeling position

senpai—senior student; in Seido, a first- through third-*dan* black belt

sensei—senior teacher; in Seido, a fourth-*dan* black belt

shinzen—spiritual center of the dojo

shodan—first-*dan* black belt

shotei—palm-heel strike

tameshiwari—the practice of breaking boards and other objects, for testing or demonstration purposes

tanden—spiritual and physical center of the body

tenkan—180-degree pivot on the lead foot

ura—spinning turn

ushiro mawashi ashi barai—rear-spinning leg sweep

yame—stop

yoi—get ready

yoko geri—side kick

yumi uke—archer's block

zazen—seated meditation

zen or **zenkutsu dachi**—front-weighted stance

Martial Arts Styles Mentioned

JAPANESE

Aikido—"Way of Unifying Energy"

Judo—"Gentle Way"

Kyokushin—"Way of Ultimate Truth"

Seido—"Sincere Way"

OKINAWAN

Goju-ryu—"Hard-Soft Style"

Naha-te—style from the region of Naha in Okinawa

Shotokan—"Hall of the Pine Waves" (named for Gichin Funakoshi's first dojo)

CHINESE

Shaolin Do Kung Fu—"Way of the Little Forest" (named for the Shaolin temple at Song Shan, China)

FILIPINO

Arnis—derived from the Spanish term for "arms" or "armor"

ISRAELI

Krav Maga—"Full-Contact Combat"

KOREAN

Tae Kwon Do—"Way of the Foot and Fist"

Tang Soo Do—"Way of the Chinese Hand"

KATA AND DRILL TITLES MENTIONED

Kihon Kumite—prearranged sparring drill

Gekisai Dai—"attack the large fortress"

Gekisai Sho—"attack the small fortress"

Pinan—"peaceful and calm"

Sanchin—"three battles"

Seido Kata—kata series unique to Seido karate

Seienchin—"conquer the rebellious outpost"

Tsuki No—"punching kata"

JAPANESE PROPER NAMES

Miyagi Chojun—founder of Goju-ryu karate

Gichin Funakoshi—founder of Shotokan karate

Tadashi Nakamura—founder of Seido karate

Masutatsu (Mas) Oyama—founder of Kyokushin karate

Daidoji Yuzan—author of *Budo Shoshinshu*

Acknowledgments

Thanks first and foremost to my family, who have now lived through all of this twice: as it happened, and again while I wrote it all down. It wasn't fair, guys; I know that, and I owe everyone a pony.

Any self-defense information in this book that sounds even remotely intelligent probably originated with one of the amazing women in the National Women's Martial Arts Federation (NWMAF). These phenomenal martial artists and self-defense instructors have, for forty years, been teaching, advocating, and agitating to make the world a safer place for everyone, regardless of age, gender, income, or ethnicity. If you're interested in learning more about the feminist empowerment approach to women's safety (and trust me—you are), visit the NWMAF online at http://www.nwmaf.org/.

All the stupid and dangerous ideas in the book are mine.

This book would not exist without the staggering tenacity of my agent, Brettne Bloom, and my editors, Jenna Johnson and Johnathan Wilber. Between them, they basically created the book out of six white mice and a pumpkin (so read it fast, because there's no telling what will happen at midnight). My eternal gratitude also goes out to Randall Klein, who sent me the e-mail every writer dreams of but is never prepared for; George Hodgman, who saw the book inside the proposal; and my McSweeney's editors John Warner and Christopher Monks, who have been endlessly supportive. Joe Loya gave me the pep talk I needed at just the right moment. Many friends, family, and training partners read drafts, offered advice, and talked me down off various ledges throughout the process—Graham, Jeremy, Amy, Joy, Doris Ann, KJ, Laura, Max, Paige, Cathy, Ellen, and Joel among them. Akiko Oba and Atsuko McCulley graciously provided the kowa translations and tolerated all my jokes.

Grateful thanks also are due to the readers of "Bitchslap," who have been reading, encouraging, and arguing with me for much longer than I expected or deserved. To all of you: *Osu.*